Africa Today

Culture, economics, religion, security

Heather Deegan

Routledge
Taylor & Francis Group

LONDON AND NEW YORK

First published 2009
by Routledge
2 Park Square, Milton Park, Abingdon, Oxon, OX14 4RN

Simultaneously published in the USA and Canada
by Routledge
270 Madison Avenue, New York, NY 10016

Reprinted 2010

Routledge is an imprint of the Taylor & Francis Group, an informa business

© 2009 Heather Deegan

Typeset in Times New Roman by Prepress Projects Ltd, Perth, UK
Printed and bound in Great Britain by CPI Anthony Rowe, Chippenham,
Wiltshire

British Library Cataloguing in Publication Data
A catalogue record for this book is available from the British Library

Library of Congress Cataloging in Publication Data
Deegan, Heather.
Africa today: culture, economics, religion, security / Heather Deegan.
p. cm.
Includes bibliographical references and index.
1. Africa – Social conditions – 21st century. 2. Africa – Politics and
government – 21st century. 3. Africa – Religion. 4. National security –
Africa. I. Title.
HN773.5.D384 2008
306.0967 – dc22
2008023511

ISBN10: 0–415–41883–6 (hbk)
ISBN10: 0–415–41884–4 (pbk)
ISBN10: 0–203–88654–2 (ebk)

ISBN13: 978–0–415–41883–6 (hbk)
ISBN13: 978–0–415–41884–3 (pbk)
ISBN13: 978–0–203–88654–0 (ebk)

For my son

Jack A. M. Deegan

Contents

Figures

Maps

Tables

Boxes

General map of Africa

Preface

Why write a book about Africa today? Many scholarly and eminent works have analysed the anthropology, history, development, socio-political environment and international dimensions of the continent to much acclaim. What is important, then, about Africa now and why is it essential that contemporary issues are acknowledged and understood? Well, in the post 9/11 global environment Africa is standing at a crossroads in international affairs as the combined issues of politics, religion and security attract increasing interest. African perspectives on peace and security have received attention at UN level and the US Millennium Development Goals highlight conflict resolution and good governance along with higher levels of accountability and transparency. Yet the continent is asymmetrical in that, while some countries may seem to have greater levels of confidence and stability, others are mired in conflict and religious or ethnic division. Islam has spread rapidly over recent years, terrorist attacks have occurred and links have been established between al-Qaeda groups/sympathizers and certain countries and political elites. It is clear, then, that many African states face profound challenges now and in the decade ahead and those difficulties will be of considerable concern to the wider international community.

Africa Today presents an analysis of the pressing contemporary issues that confront the continent now. The chapter topics form a cohesive and interlinking structure and analyse the critical areas of concern. Although the work draws on the author's empirical research it also seeks to situate discussion within the context of wider debate. Consequently, although the chapters concentrate on specific themes, certain areas have been chosen for special analysis. Equally, particular case studies are presented which provide the reader with an in-depth focus on an especially relevant issue. The case studies are used to both highlight and inform. Chapter 1 considers the past and the present in a brief appraisal that sets out the themes which continue to connect the historical and contemporary world. Chapter 2 looks at how religion affects the continent and provides a specific case study on the clashes between Muslims and Christians in Kano, northern Nigeria. As Islam is such a powerful force within Africa, the chapter's Analysis focuses on discourses about Islam, law and society.

Chapter 3's issue is development, which continues to be a crucial factor in the lives and life chances of Africans. The continent's democratic environment is the subject of Chapter 4, and Chapter 5 examines gender, an important aspect of contemporary Africa in that it is acknowledged that women are unfairly disadvantaged. Also, the charge has been made that 'poverty wears a female face'. Chapter 6 deals with corruption, a topic that seems never to disappear from elites and societies. The combined concerns of disease and human security are the subjects of Chapter 7, as these two problems have become increasingly pressing.

It would be impossible to write about Africa today and not include a study of conflict, arms and reconstruction. Consequently, Chapter 8 focuses on the impact of wars and violence. It also includes a case study of Sierra Leone, a country that suffered an 11-year war and is seeking to move forward. Chapter 8's Analysis looks at Darfur, Sudan and the trajectory of that conflict. Chapter 9 deals with terrorism and the extent to which it concerns both Africa and the international community. Although the chapters engage with particular and discrete topics they are, of course, interconnected, which the concluding Chapter 10 addresses.

Africa Today could not have been written without the research the author has conducted in the continent since the early 1990s and she would like to thank all those who have given of their time to help provide information, interviews and data. However, the views expressed in the book are those of the author alone.

Heather Deegan
London, UK

1   Past and present

Looking back in time

A decade ago an eloquent Namibian intellectual called for more 'Africanness' to be put back into Africa, with whatever consequence (Diescho 1995). But what is 'Africanness'? Is there an African identity that transcends the differences which distinguish one African culture from another? Or are there no commonalities over and above those that have been imposed by one form of domination or another? In short, is there more that divides Africa than unites it? These are difficult questions and the possible answers rest upon particular perspectives and time-frames. Africa's history as a whole is varied and stretches back through millennia. North Africa is awash with antiquity from ancient history and buildings and artefacts of that period appear in other countries. Pyramids and archaeological evidence are present in Sudan and would be sought out by tourists and travellers if the country were at peace with itself. Strong links existed between pre-colonial Africa and the Middle East, especially after the Arab empire extended its conquests in AD 656. Trade, intermarriage and conversion spread Islam across sub-Saharan Africa,[1] and according to Jean-Francois Bayart, as a trans-regional religious movement, was a 'powerful means of social rapprochement.' In essence, a 'process of assimilation between communities occurred' (Bayart 1992: 177).

European expansion began with the explorations of the Portuguese in the fifteenth century but was to reach its zenith in the nineteenth and early to mid-twentieth centuries. D. K. Fieldhouse (1973: 147) viewed the motivation for nineteenth-century colonial expansion as fiscal or political: 'The desire of existing colonies or trading bases to extend the limits of their customs collection to raise more revenues; . . . and in the special case of Senegal, fear of Islamic power inland,' together with a desire to increase colonial revenues. When the imperial powers agreed at the Berlin Conference of 1884 that no new annexations on the African coast were to be recognized as valid unless they were accompanied by effective occupation, it is generally acknowledged that the African continent was, as the phrase goes, 'carved up' indiscriminately 'with casual disregard for the people whom they thus allocated into one or another colony' (Clapham 1985: 17). As Maps 1.1a, b and c indicate, the European colonial penetration of Africa was

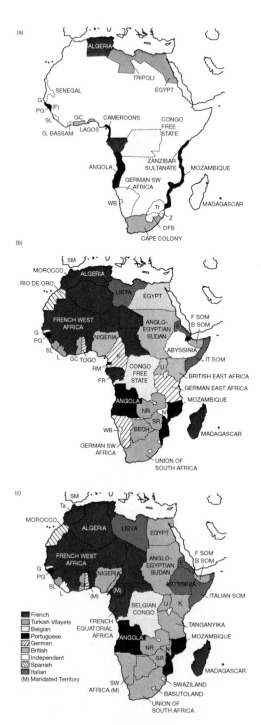

Map 1.1 Historical maps of Africa. (a) 1885; (b) 1914; (c) 1939.

immense and arbitrary. It was both the scale and the territorial rearranging of the continent that separated tribal groupings. East Africa, for example, was partitioned into two areas, one initially under German control, Tanganyika, and the other land, which included part of Somalia and was later to become known as Kenya, under the British. However, colonial administrations, particularly the French and British, were aware of the powerful Islamic communities and cooperated with established leaders, for example the Fulani Emirs in the northern provinces of the Cameroons and Nigeria, and the Muslim brotherhoods of Senegal. Arabs and their African offspring occupied high government offices in Tanganyika and Kenya and it is alleged that in some cases Arab commercial activities were facilitated by the improved infrastructure and transport systems established under colonial rule (Haseeb 1985: 132).

The cultural inheritance of Africans is important in assessing whether or not peoples have any commonalities. One analyst asserted 'Whatever Africans share, we do not have a common traditional culture, common languages, a common religious or conceptual vocabulary . . . and we do not even belong to a common race' (Appiah 1992: 26). Religion has, of course, served to separate groups: 'the role of religion as a symbolic medium of contact and conflict is striking in the colonial history of Africa' (Bayart 1993: 177). Bayart (1993: 190) maintains that the two monotheistic religions, that is Christianity and Islam, have both had 'long experience of accommodation with the State,' colonial and other. Certainly, privilege, power and status were accorded to some ethnic groups and this has led to discussion of how the 'carve-up' of Africa affected relations between Africans and Arabs. Did, for example, Arabs, Africans of Arab descent and Africans of different tribal inheritances share common objectives or were their interests separate and possibly contradictory? One view supporting the first proposition suggests that 'At no point in the long history of Islamic power did a non-African Islamic ruler succeed in controlling African Muslims.' As such, Islam presented no threat to the interests of Africans as it 'allowed for compromise and harmonious relations with the African way of life, traditions and customs' (Yousuf 1986: 28). From such a perspective there can be no distinction between Muslim and non-Muslim Africans. If some powerful Muslim African leaders cooperated with colonial powers in the administration of truncated territories, it should not imply a betrayal of the interests of other non-Muslim Africans but should be viewed as the only available option open to subjugated peoples. Colonial rule would be in the interests of neither native Africans nor those of Arab descent as it demarcated territory, imposed administrative structures and introduced a colonial economy which advantaged European powers through fiscal and trading procedures at the cost of the colony itself. For some, when the foundations of colonialism were laid down in East Africa, 'Arab political control was ended once and for all' (Salim 1985: 130).

However, if it is possible to consider the interests of African Muslims as differing from those of other indigenous Africans an alternative picture emerges: one of complicity with the colonial power to the detriment of the native non-Muslim African population. The old colonial strategy of 'divide and rule', that is the privileging of one community over another, would have little meaning in a society where interests were one and the same. Difference between sections of society were both perceived and acted upon by colonial authorities, who identified certain groups as tribes and were actually instrumental themselves in creating distinctions between peoples (Chazan *et al.* 1988: 103). Anthropologists have viewed African societies as consisting of 'descent groups' which define the norms and limits of behaviour and establish lines of authority. Sometimes these groups would be in competition and would fight each other but, interestingly, if attacked by a third party, would unite: 'Brothers could be naturally opposed to one another, but if a more distantly related third party fought with one of the brothers, the two brothers would unite to form a single segment and fight' (E. E. Evans-Pritchard cited in Grinker and Steiner 1997: 5. See also Falk Moore 1994). So, to put it another way, artificial unity could be achieved at intervals depending on the nature of the perceived threat, be it European colonisation, neo-imperialism or Western economic dominance.

Ali Mazrui acknowledges that the 'interplay of Africa's indigenous cultures with Islam on the one side and Western civilisation' on the other has had not only political/economic effects, but also 'cultural and civilisational' influences. Culture he defines as a 'system of inter-related values, active enough to influence and condition perception, judgement, communication and behaviour in a given society', whereas civilization embraces a 'culture which has endured, expanded, innovated and been elevated to new moral sensibilities' (Mazrui 1986: 239). These are far-reaching definitions which require detailed examination of every point. Mazrui believes the word civilization can be applied to the Western and Islamic as well as 'indigenous legacies' but cautions that the term is 'always relative and somewhat hyperbolic'. Exactly what constitutes a civilization may be debated, but cultures, when viewed as different systems of values, can often clash with each other, particularly if those values are in competition for authority and control. Ultimately, Mazrui asserts, one culture will establish a 'clear ascendancy' which essentially forces the 'more vulnerable culture to surrender.' Subsequently, cultural confusion emerges among the dominated culture leading to a process of first 'cultural surrender' followed by 'cultural alienation' and then 'cultural revival', meaning a return to traditionalism. In essence, Africa has a 'triple heritage of indigenous, Islamic and Western forces – fusing and recoiling, at once competitive and complementary' (ibid.: 239, 21).

During the latter years of the colonial period the intellectual political climate within nationalist movements in Africa was dominated by Marxism, variant forms of socialism and notions of self-determination.[2] The path to the future was to be secular and independent. While some Pan-African Congress resolutions stressed the need for 'freedom, democracy and betterment', others highlighted that Africa was prepared to fight for liberation: 'If the western world is still determined to rule mankind by force, then Africans, as a last resort, may have to appeal to force in the effort to achieve Freedom' (Mazrui and Tidy 1986: 22). Essentially, the African struggles against colonial rule were waged to end European dominance. Goran Hyden argues that African post-colonial leaders created an 'informal context' in which they could ignore formal rules by promoting the idea that the 'essential experience during the colonial period was exploitation of the local people' by outsiders. 'Formal rules' would include the performance of certain basic tasks, such as promoting political freedoms and economic prosperity, but Africa's new political elite managed to construct an overarching objective: ending colonial rule (Hyden 2006: 32). Since the perceived purpose of colonialism was to oppress politically and to exploit economically, it was expected that decolonization would bring freedom and prosperity to Africa. It certainly brought freedom of a kind but prosperity is still awaited by many Africans. Politically, for the masses it often brought military government, the one-party or no-party state, the dominant ruler and until quite recently the 'president for life.' Table 1.1 outlines the political longevity of some African leaders.

The patriarchal political environment of many African states gave rise to ethnic clashes with rival groups fighting for control of government and access to resources. See Map 1.2 for an outline of some ethnic groups across the continent. The increasing lack of legitimacy and economic development has led to the politicization of ethnicity. As Patrick Chabal asserts, the incidence of violence in Africa is often attributable to 'bad government' (Chabal 1992: 34). The Charter of the Organisation of African Unity (OAU) at its inception in 1963 asserted that its members are 'Determined to safeguard and consolidate the hard won independence as well as the sovereignty and territorial integrity of our states and to fight against neo-colonialism in all its forms.' However, by 1991 the OAU referred to the need for African states to democratize and take seriously 'the expansion of liberalism' and the adoption of multi-party politics (Deegan 1996: 32). For Nelson Mandela, who addressed the OAU summit in 1994, Africa had to 'put its house in order': 'We must face the matter squarely that where there is something wrong in how we govern ourselves, it must be said that the fault is not in our stars but in ourselves that we are ill-governed' (Deegan 2001: 56).

For Ali Mazrui (1986: 11–12), 'Africa is at war. It is a war of cultures. It is a war between indigenous Africa and the forces of Western civilisation. It takes the form of inefficiency, mismanagement, corruption and decay.' In fact, the whole process of attempted modernization is a form of 'unnatural dis-Africanisation',

Table 1.1 Political longevity of selected African leaders

Political leader	Years served	Country
F. Houphouet-Boigny	1960–93	Côte d'Ivoire
J. Nyerere	1961–86	Tanzania
M. Traore	1968–91	Mali
A. Ahidjo	1960–82	Cameroon
L. Senghor	1960–80	Senegal
M. Kerekou	1972–91	Benin
D. arap Moi	1978–2002	Kenya
R. Mugabe	1980– Still in power	Zimbabwe

Map 1.2 A selection of ethnic groups.

1. Afikpo Ibo
2. Azande
3. Baule
4. Dassanetch
5. Dogon
6. Fang
7. Frafra
8. Kikuyu
9. !Kung San
10. Lele/Bushong
11. Lese/Efe
12. Luo
13. Mbuti
14. Nuer
15. Suku
16. Tallensi
17. Tiv
18. Tswana
19. Yoruba

which is effectively tearing Africa away from its indigenous roots. Yet can economic progress take place without a massive shift in societal values? And should improvements in welfare, education and literacy determine a new cultural enlightenment?

Traditional theories of culture and development

For over a century the relationship between developmental and cultural change has been much debated. It was assumed that as countries developed there would be a shift towards the adoption of scientific knowledge, an evolution from subsistence farming towards commercial production of agricultural goods and a move towards industrialization. Yet such changes involved great social and cultural alteration. Hence, this process of structural differentiation marked a break in established norms of social and economic life. Consequently, during periods of development, familial, kinship, religious and cultural ties would be undermined and regarded as largely restrictive traditional forces (Smelser 1966: 29). For some political participation was seen as a key which opened the door to development, thus distinguishing the traditional society, which separated people 'by kinship into communities isolated from each other and from a centre', from an advancing modernizing state (Lerner 1958: 48–50). Other analysts, however, believed that developing nations initially faced a 'cruel choice' between rapid, self-sustained expansion and the introduction of democratic processes. As Western patterns of capital accumulation were seen as crucial for development, it was argued that authoritarian states would be more adept at extracting surpluses from their populations. Economic progress, then, would have to precede moves towards democratization: 'development first, democracy later' was the theme (Bhagwati 1966: 53; see also revised version, Bhagwati 1995). S. M. Lipset (1960: 71) explained: 'Men may question whether any aspect of this interrelated cluster of economic development . . . gradual political change, legitimacy and democracy is primary, but the fact remains that the cluster does hang together.'

Inevitably, attitudes towards social activities and societal change would vary between different cultures depending on their values and beliefs. Also, societies were composed of structures whose 'cultural systems' exercised organized patterns of influence over the whole community, sometimes irrespective and independent of particular individuals (Billington *et al.* 1991: 4). In general, then, cultural factors serve an overall integrative function in society. Yet often a complex relationship exists between culture and a social structure. According to Emile Durkheim, societal values constituted the component which reached the highest level of generality, for they were 'conceptions of the desirable society that are held in common by its members' (Wolff 1960: 122). Values and norms were specified within the cultural system and determined the manner in which 'people behave as they are expected to in a given situation' (Parsons 1968: 399). A 'well-defined system of values shared to some degree with other members of the community' is necessary (ibid.). Yet modernization as a complex process of social change has the capacity to dislodge previous cultural systems and value structures (Deutsch 1953: 35).

The straightforward division between agricultural/agrarian and industrial societies provides a clear illustration of the differences between these forms of states as seen in Table 1.2. The shift from what can be regarded as a semi-feudal society to one that is differentiated and essentially class-based suggests that a stage has been reached when common values are expressed in conformity with the universal principle that 'everybody be judged on the same fundamental bases' (Sutton 1963: 67). But how is it possible to move from one typology to another? Certainly, several technical, economic and ecological processes that frequently accompany development can be isolated:

- in the realm of technology: the shift from simple and traditional techniques towards the application of scientific knowledge;
- in agriculture: the evolution from subsistence farming towards commercial production of agricultural goods, i.e. the introduction of cash crops, purchase of non-agricultural products and the introduction of wage-labour;
- in industry: the transition from the use of human/animal power toward industrialization/factory production led by the market mechanism;
- ecologically: the move from farm and village towards urban centres.

(Smelser 1963: 32–33)

As development demanded urbanization, improved literacy rates, expanding economies and exposure to mass communications, it subjected the institutional framework of a society to continual challenges to adapt in the face of rapidly developing productive forces. Economic modernization, associated with ideals of progress and rationality, was intended to sweep away traditional beliefs, ways of life and patterns of authority. Obviously, the process presented difficulties, particularly in traditional societies where value systems tended to be 'prescriptive' (Bellah 1966: 188). A prescriptive system was characterized by 'the comprehensiveness and specificity of its value commitments and by its consequent lack of flexibility. Motivation is frozen . . . through commitment to a vast range of relatively specific norms governing almost every situation in life.' Whereas in a modern society a degree of flexibility had to be introduced in economic, political and social spheres, in 'prescriptive' societies a religious system would attempt to regulate all those areas. 'Thus changes in economic or political institutions – not

Table 1.2 Typologies of societies

Agricultural society	Industrial society
• Predominance of particularistic relationships	• Predominance of universalistic achievement norms
• Stable local groups	• High degree of social mobility
• Limited social mobility	• Well-developed occupational system
• Relatively simple and stable occupational differentiation	• Open class system based on achievement
• A deferential stratification system	• Prevalence of civic organizations

to speak of family and education – in traditional societies tended to have ultimate religious implications' (ibid.: 189). In fact, in certain societies, notably Muslim, it was believed that traditional culture was synonymous with religion and rested 'everywhere on an Islamic basis' (Rustow 1970: 452). The relationship between religion, tradition and development becomes more complicated, especially so if culture has the capacity to inhibit modernization.

R. B. Bellah's research explored how the organization of a value system had to alter so that economic development could take place. He concluded that the value system or culture of a society had to 'change from a prescriptive type to a "principial" mode.' The rigidity of traditional societies had to mutate into flexible environments in order for economic, political and social change to take place. The real distinction between prescriptive and principial societies rested in the societies' belief systems. In a principial state the religious system would not attempt to regulate all aspects of economic, political and social life in great detail. This is not to say that religion would disappear from the culture of a society, merely that its function would alter: 'In modern society there is a differentiation between the levels of religion and social ideology which makes possible greater flexibility at both levels' (Bellah 1966: 188). With such a separation, social, economic and political reformers could engage with secular ideas without being regarded as cultural religious heretics.

The question that posed considerable debate was that of how social systems changed and developed. Table 1.3 identifies two models of change: the developmental and organic models. The developmental model is predominantly economic and planned and coordinated by the state. Often quasi-ideological in approach, the model has a heavy emphasis on industrialization and controlled phases of change. By contrast the organic model responds to societal or external pressures and influences. It is capable of adaptation and moving towards a gradual process of change.

A distinction was drawn between the educated classes and upper reaches of officialdom, for whom progress meant 'opportunity for social mobility and economic success' including all the material utilities of the West, and the peasant confronted by disease and poverty, who viewed progress in terms of 'land distribution, schools, free medical facilities and an increased income' (Bellah 1966: 188). Although rural communities were ready to welcome progress they expected the government or external agency to bring it about and, therefore, did nothing to advance progress themselves: 'instead, they passively accept the innovation

Table 1.3 Models of change

Developmental model	Organic model
• State driven	• Emergent
• Planned	• Adjustment
• Phases	• Adaptation
• Economic	• Response to societal pressures
• Industrialization	• External push
• Controlled	• Gradual change

and once the agency of change is removed, they lapse as often as not into the old way of doing things' (ibid.: 53–54). Yet in underdeveloped areas production was usually located in kinship units. Subsistence farming predominated while other industry was supplementary and still attached to kin and village. Therefore the 'pull of the past' affects modernization: 'tradition mediates between the forces of change and the acceptance of change' (Welch 1967: 20). Traditional and local lore may continue to lie at the roots of peasant life, giving 'shape to and preserving the village pattern' (Fuller 1969: 115).

Some economies, however, adopt a lineal approach to economic transition and differentiation, in that, for example, migratory labour may be a form of compromise between full membership in a wage-labour force and at the same time maintaining an attachment to an old community life (Smelser 1966: 31). The reasons for this partial differentiation may rest in the resistance of sections of the population to surrendering traditional economic modes of production. Yet at some stage the role and economic centrality of the family has to diminish. This process may be gradual but it is an essential requirement of progress. For Emile Durkheim institutions and the rule of law were important guiding principles within society. The need for a 'regulatory system of rules, explicit or implicit, legal or customary' was necessary to constrain social action into behaviour that was in conformity with the wider system. Rules would be manifestations of the common value system of the community and, therefore, they could exercise 'moral authority' over the individual. Social institutions would be appropriate vehicles in the exercise of this 'moral authority' (cited in Parsons 1968: 407).

Social change and tradition

The family and extended kinship groups often operate economic functions for their own benefit and such ties are a major basis for labour recruitment. Ascribed systems of social stratification focus primarily on those aspects of human experience which centre on kinship, gender, ethnicity and territorial locality. Life chances depend upon the status accorded by birth into a particular family or tribe. Under a simple form of economic organization, for example subsistence agriculture or household industry, there is little differentiation between economic roles and family roles. Pre-modern societies fuse social and political integration with kinship position, control of land, chieftainship or powerful culturally significant groups. Often peoples' sense of self is bound up in the actualities of blood, race, language, locality, religion and tradition (Geertz 1967: 168). According to one theorist, these deep-rooted sentiments stem from the feeling that, whatever may be the momentary economic advantages of the larger sphere, ultimate security, not necessarily dominated by economic forces, exists and persists within the village orbit:

> Here there are always kinsmen and people of one's own blood to whom the
> peasant may turn. Here is the plot of land enduring through generations. Here
> is the familiar world which, through lore and tradition, has nourished the

peasant since childhood. Here within the village is an emotional form of security not found elsewhere.

(Fuller 1969: 116)

These primordial instincts can be powerful and resistant to change. As Max Weber claimed, social action includes both 'failure to act and passive acquiescence'
(Roth and Wittich 1968: 22).

When industrialization occurs only in villages or when villages are built around
paternalistic industrial enterprises 'many ties of community and kinship can be
maintained under industrial conditions' (Smelser 1966: 35). The difficulty with
such communities is that political authority is coterminous with kinship relations
and, therefore, can inhibit reform and development. Although men can be affected
by their economic participation in the wider world, on return to the village from
beyond its borders they 'easily fall back into the general pattern of village ways'
(Fuller 1969: 117). According to a seminal work by Edward Shils, economically
underdeveloped countries are also 'consensually underdeveloped' in that their
'belief patterns have not coalesced to the point where it is believed that central
institutions are capable of acting justly in the allocations of rewards and opportunities' (Shils 1975: 179). Consequently, there is a lack of 'civil affinity' and a
disinclination to look beyond primordial associations.

Traditional standards have been identified as the 'most intransigent obstacles'
to modernization and when threatened can arouse serious dissatisfaction and opposition to change (Smelser 1966: 37). However, the whole nature of 'tradition'
and 'traditional' forces has been examined by Edward Shils. He argues that those
who would explain why a particular action is performed or a belief accepted say
'there is a tradition' which motivates the desire to act or believe in that way.
'Traditional' is used to designate whole societies which change relatively slowly
or 'in which there is a widespread tendency to legitimate actions by reference to
their having occurred in the past.' But Shils questions this approach arguing: 'The
substantive content of traditions·has been much studied but not their traditional-
ity.' The modes and mechanisms of the traditional reproduction of beliefs require
close examination: 'traditions are beliefs with a particular social structure; they
are consensus through time' (Shils 1975: 183–86). He maintains that the 'sequen-
tial structure of traditional beliefs and actions can itself become a symbolized
component of the belief and its legitimization or the grounds of its acceptance.'
In other words, he explains, the past becomes a model: 'We should do as we have
done before' or 'We should do now what we did previously because that is the
way in which it has always been done' (ibid.: 186). For the past to have continual
relevance in the present, a process of 'handing down' or 'filiation' must occur.
This process permits the transmission of beliefs that were previously accepted by
others. In their most elemental form, traditionally transmitted beliefs are recommended and received 'unthinkingly'; they are 'there':

no alternatives are conceived; there is nothing to do but to accept them. Traditional beliefs are those which contain an attachment to the past, to some

particular time in the past, or to a whole social system, or to particular institutions which allegedly existed in the past.

Beliefs which assert the moral rightness or superiority of a past society and which assert that what is done now or in the future should be modelled on past patterns of belief or conduct are traditional beliefs (ibid.: 196). Equally, Shils argued, they 'express an attitude of piety not only toward earthly authorities, toward elders and ancestors, but also to the invisible powers which control earthly life.' It is interesting that even within the last decade or so there have been calls to 'let Africa be Africa again', meaning that the modern world sits uncomfortably with African culture and endeavours to marginalize it.

> Centuries of forced integration have not succeeded in blowing out our age-old heritage of knowledge, both practical and theoretical. If this had been the case, we should no longer have any handicraft, any weaving, any pottery, any basket-making, any cooking, any metallurgy, any rain-making technique, any 'traditional' medicine, any divination system or any counting system.
>
> (Hountondji 1995: 7)

For Max Weber, however, it was the issue of authority and how it came to be maintained in different societies that was of significance. Authority, he claimed, 'will be called traditional if legitimacy is claimed for it and believed in by virtue of the sanctity of age-old rules and powers' (Roth and Wittich 1968: 226). He regarded this type of organized rule as the simplest, with the commands of the ruler being legitimized in two ways:

- Partly in terms of traditions which themselves directly determine the content of the command and are believed to be valid
- Partly in terms of the traditional prerogative which rests primarily on the fact that the obligations of personal obedience tend to be unlimited.

(ibid.)

Society and religion

Under a simple kind of economic organization, such as subsistence farming or household industry, there is little differentiation between economic roles and family roles, as all reside in the kinship structure. However, as an economy develops, several kinds of economic activity are removed from the family–community complex. In agriculture, for example, diversification of production involves a differentiation between consumption and community. Goods and services which may previously have been exchanged on a non-economic basis are pulled progressively into the market. One consequence of the removal of economic activities from the kinship nexus is the family's loss of some of its previous functions (Smelser 1966: 31). Following from this change several related processes accompany the differentiation of the family from its other involvements. The direct control of elders and kinsmen over the family weakens and relationships within the family alter. When differentiation has begun the productive roles of family members are isolated 'geographically, temporally and structurally from their distinctively familial roles' (ibid.: 35). According to Weber, 'collective self-help is for the kin group the most typical means of reacting to infringements upon its interests' (Roth and Wittich 1968: 366).

The structural changes associated with modernization are disruptive to the social order. Differentiation demands the creation of new activities, norms, rewards and sanctions, for example money, political position, prestige based on occupation. These often conflict with old modes of social action, which are frequently dominated by traditional, religious, tribal and kinship systems. As traditional beliefs are deferential, communities have a tendency to express attitudes of piety towards earthly authorities as well as otherworldly spheres. Therefore, 'holy men and priests are prized by traditional attitudes, as is sacred learning: the learning of sacred texts.' Shils believed a sense of 'awe' occurred in respect of these sacred beliefs, for they represented that which was considered to be 'the most vital and most basic to existence'.

> Sacredness can be a property of individuals or of collectivities or of the external physical, non-human world; what is important is that these properties embody and represent symbolically or are connected with symbols which are essential in our image of life and the universe and their right order. The sacredness of things can be timeless, continuously operative; it can be so while still having a temporal component, in which the past or the future has a special significance.
>
> (Shils 1975: 197–98)

The two categories of religious phenomena, beliefs and rituals, were fundamental, the former being concerned with thought and the latter with action or practices. Durkheim's emphasis on the importance of ritual in religion was necessary in identifying social unity: society was to Durkheim 'the reality underlying the symbols of religious ritual' because it was the only 'empirical reality which, as of a moral nature, could serve as the source of the ritual attitude'. Talcott Parsons interpreted this behaviour as 'an expression of the common ultimate-value attitudes which constitute the specifically "social" element in society' (ibid.: 433). He regarded Durkheim's proposition as one of 'profound insight'. Certainly, it represented an important strand in his analysis of the social importance of religion in providing a common value system that underpinned the foundation of society: 'for without a system of common values, of which religion is in part a manifestation, a system adhered to in a significant degree, there can be no such thing as society' (ibid. 434). The primary sense of moral obligation created a sense of social constraint based on the observance and maintenance of a system of rules that rested on a set of common values. For Durkheim, the object of religious life, in all its forms, was 'to raise man above himself and to make him lead a life superior to that which he would lead if he followed only his spontaneous desires'

(Lukes 1988: 474). In a sense, these were the objectives of Christian missionary groups who sought to convert Africans.

Weber considered the origins of religions to be governed by a form of 'charismatic powers'. The term 'charisma' could be applied only 'to a certain quality of individual personality by virtue of which he is considered extraordinary and treated as endowed with supernatural, superhuman qualities' often regarded as of 'divine origin' (Roth and Wittich 1968: 241–42). In primitive environments he believed these aspects rested on magical powers and prophets, and were supported by followers or disciples. For Weber charisma was directly linked with legitimacy but he took the concept further by associating it with social change:

> The prophet is thus the leader who sets himself explicitly and consciously against the traditional order, or aspects of it, and who claims moral authority for his position . . . such as divine will. It is men's duty to listen to him and follow his commands or his example.
>
> (Parsons 1968: 663)

In contemporary states, then, there are both structural and cultural components of development. Structural transformation is, perhaps, more obvious, for without such change, social, political and economic development cannot emerge. The cultural component, however, is more complex. At times modernization may be thwarted by political elites or by the wider society, which may still be attached to traditional, fragmentary or inconsistent norms of behaviour. In these circumstances, although modernity may be regarded as good in itself it may not be perceived as an actual material form of life. In other words, people may believe in modernity as an abstract concept without acknowledging the need for actual social change. Values, beliefs and behaviour all inform and to a degree delineate developmental potential. National integration refers to the 'process of bringing together culturally and socially discrete groups', whereas 'integrative behaviour' relates to 'the readiness of individuals to work together in an organized fashion for common purposes and to behave in a fashion conducive to the achievement of these common purposes' (Weiner 1967: 150). Increasing urbanization, improved literacy rates, expanding economies and exposure to mass communications all combine to mobilize the population and increase demands for government services.

Africa today

So where does Africa stand now? And what does 'Africanness' seem to represent in the contemporary world? Well, today, 'Africa' is almost used as a 'brand name' to identify, market, promote, condemn, herald, or indeed call attention to any facet of the continent which may concern the international, globalized environment. If it is not violence, conflict, poverty, rape or HIV/AIDS that is grabbing the headlines, it is political mismanagement, arms dealing, corruption or terror. Africa, then, is associated with a maelstrom of problems and difficulties and viewed as, in the former UK Prime Minister Tony Blair's strident phrase, 'a scar on the conscience of the world' (*The Times*, 25 March 2005). Africa seems to be tarred with the brush of incompetence, a region which Richard Dowden, Director of the Royal African Society, pithily described as 'the hopeless Continent' (Dowden 2000). But what of 'Africanness'? Does it represent a tangible prospect of hope or optimism?

If 'Africanness' represents the vibrancy and vitality of a body politic, with good opportunities and life chances, then Tables 1.4, 1.5 and 1.6 make sobering reading. 'Africanness', of course, is not homogeneous, as an inspection of these socio-economic tables indicates, but the figures reveal disturbing insights. Infant mortality in Angola, for example, a state rich in oil wealth, is 140 per 1000 births. In Botswana, one of the highest male/female secondary education enrolment rates (of 70 and 75 per cent respectively) is marred by the HIV/AIDS pandemic, which makes life expectancy for males and females 38 years and 40 years respectively.

Table 1.4 Mortality and literacy indicators

Country	Infant mortality (total per 1000 live births)	Life expectancy (years)		% illiterate (older than 15 years)	
		Male	Female	Male	Female
Burundi	107	40	41	42	56
Eritrea	73	51	54	-	-
Ethiopia	100	44	46	52	66
Kenya	69	43	45	10	21
Malawi	115	37	37	24	51
Mozambique	122	36	39	38	69
Somalia	118	46	49	-	-
Uganda	86	45	46	21	41
Tanzania	100	42	44	15	31
Zambia	105	32	32	14	26
Angola	140	38	41	-	-
Cameroon	88	45	47	23	40
Chad	115	43	45	46	63
Botswana	57	38	40	24	18
Namibia	60	42	45	16	17
Benin	93	48	53	45	74
Burkino Faso	93	45	46	82	92
Gambia	81	52	55	-	-
Ghana	58	56	59	18	34
Mali	119	48	49	73	88
Niger	126	45	46	75	91
Nigeria	79	51	51	26	41
Senegal	61	50	55	51	70

- Data not available.

Table 1.5 Demographic, social and economic indicators

Country	Total population (millions) 2004	Average population growth rate (%) 2000–2005	% urban	Urban growth rate (%) 2000–2005	Expenditure on primary education (% of GDP per capita)	Health expenditure (% of GDP)
Burundi	7.1	3.1	10	6.5	11.6	2.1
Eritrea	4.3	3.7	20	5.8	-	3.7
Ethiopia	72.4	2.5	16	4.1	-	1.4
Kenya	32.4	1.5	39	4.4	0.9	1.7
Malawi	12.3	2.0	16	4.6	-	2.7
Mozambique	19.2	1.8	36	5.1	-	4.0
Somalia	10.3	4.2	35	5.7	-	1.2
Uganda	26.7	3.2	12	3.9	-	3.4
Tanzania	37.7	1.9	35	4.9	-	2.0
Cameroon	16.3	1.8	51	3.4	8.5	1.2
Chad	8.9	3.0	25	4.6	9.5	2.0
Gabon	1.4	1.8	84	2.7	4.7	1.7

Sudan	34.3	2.2	39	4.6	-	0.6
Botswana	1.8	0.9	52	1.8	6.0	4.4
Namibia	2.0	1.4	32	3.0	22.1	4.1
South Africa	45.2	0.6	57	1.4	14.3	3.6
Benin	6.9	2.6	45	4.4	10.1	2.1
Côte d'Ivoire	16.9	1.6	45	2.6	14.9	1.0
Gambia	1.5	2.7	26	2.6	-	3.2
Ghana	21.4	2.2	45	3.2	-	2.8
Guinea	8.6	1.6	35	3.8	9.2	1.9
Guinea-Bissau	1.5	2.9	34	5.4	-	3.2
Mali	3.0	3.0	62	5.1	14.4	1.7
Niger	12.4	3.6	22	6.1	16.8	1.4
Nigeria	127.1	2.5	47	4.4	-	0.8
Senegal	10.3	2.4	50	3.9	13.8	2.8
Sierra Leone	5.2	3.8	39	5.6	-	2.6
Togo	5.0	2.3	35	4.0	11.0	1.5

- Data not available.

Table 1.6 Education and reproductive health indicators

Country	Secondary school enrolment (%)		Births per 1000 women aged 15–19	Contraceptive use (%)	
	Male	Female		Any method	Modern method
Burundi	12	9	50	16	10
Eritrea	33	22	115	8	5
Ethiopia	23	15	100	8	6
Kenya	34	30	78	39	32
Malawi	39	29	163	31	26
Mozambique	16	10	105	6	5
Rwanda	15	14	50	13	4
Uganda	19	15	211	23	18
Tanzania	-	-	120	25	17
Zambia	27	21	145	34	23
Angola	21	17	229	6	5
Cameroon	36	29	121	19	7
Chad	17	5	195	8	2
Sudan	34	30	55	8	7
Botswana	70	75	91	40	39
Namibia	57	65	78	29	26
South Africa	83	90	66	56	55
Benin	35	16	107	19	7
Burkina Faso	12	8	136	12	5
Gambia	40	28	125	10	9
Ghana	41	34	76	22	13
Mali	-	-	191	8	6
Niger	8	5	233	14	4
Nigeria	-	-	103	15	9
Senegal	22	15	86	13	8

In Burkino Faso, 82 per cent of men and 92 per cent of women over the age of 15 years are illiterate. In Somalia, a country with one of the highest population growth rates, 4.2 per cent, health expenditure is a mere 1.2 per cent of gross domestic product, in part because of the country's appalling political, economic and security situation. Even Nigeria, the most populous country, of 127 million inhabitants, and oil rich, spends only 0.8 per cent on health provision. Life expectancy across the countries listed reaches a peak of only 59 years for women in Ghana and is at its lowest for men in Zambia at 32 years. Births per 1000 women aged between 15 and 19 years is 233 in Niger, which indicates almost a quarter of all births are born to teenagers, suggesting why the secondary school enrolment figure for girls is so lamentably low at 5 per cent. Contraceptive use is almost negligible in Mozambique with 6 per cent using any method and a mere 5 per cent using modern methods.

If these figures are anything to go by it really does look as though, in Ali Mazrui's potent phrase, 'Africa is at war.' But now it seems to be at war with itself and the continent's populations. Socio-economic progress is necessary today but it is not enough. Now the contemporary focus has shifted to good governance, sustainability, transparency, human rights, probity and gender equality. Economic, political and social inequalities stifle progress for generations and looking backwards for some form of cultural authenticity may not be the best way forwards – although the acclaimed writer Aimé Césaire (1956) thought otherwise: 'La voie la plus courte vers l'avenir est celle qui passé par l'approfondissement du passé.' (The deeper you look into the past, the shorter your way to the future.) Yet the present state of African affairs in economic, political, social and cultural spheres has been viewed as potentially leading to fatalism and despair (reported discussions between government, civil society and private sectors at the UN Conference on Good Governance 2007; see EISA 2007b).

No-one, of course, is offering an apologia for Western colonialism or the excesses of World Bank and International Monetary Fund Structural Adjustment Programmes in the 1980s and 1990s, which attached their lending to economic liberalization policies, with attendant debt and financial crises for many African countries. Similarly, the recent Arab cultural impact on the continent has been far from benign. Although Mazrui maintained that such an impact 'in non-Muslim areas could be increased' in pursuit of cultural assimilation, he imagined it could take place in the sphere of 'architecture' rather than within the context of a radicalizing, Middle East funded, Islamist agenda (Mazrui 1986: 258). In short, Africa's 'triple heritage' is as relevant and concerning today as it has ever been. The question now is: will it stand in the way of progress?

2 Religion

The force of religion in global affairs is now the preoccupying concern of the international community. More specifically, the growth of Islam, particularly outside the Middle Eastern area, together with the violence that has occurred between Muslims and Christians, has threatened to destabilize countries and regions, few more so than in Africa. But neither Islam nor Christianity is a new faith in Africa; their heritage is both deep and profound. This chapter considers these two monotheistic religions and the way in which they have interacted with the continent. A case study focuses on the conflict between Muslim and Christian groups in Kano, northern Nigeria, based on research in the area, and a separate analysis on Islam, law and society aims to provide a preliminary understanding of Islam.

Islam and Christianity

The association between Arabs and Africa has been one of long standing. In fact, the origins of present-day African–Arab relations are rooted in the early history of mankind and civilization. Arabs had settled in East and Northeast Africa, establishing strong trading links with Yemen and Oman, before the emergence of Islam as a religion. The Islamic presence in North Africa appeared when the Arab empire extended its conquests in AD 656. Islamic states also emerged in other areas including Ghana and Mali (Yousuf 1986: 13). Exposure to Islam varied according to region and accessibility to trade routes, with early Muslim settlements in East Africa developing into small dynasties along the coast. Differences in the penetrative effect of Islam partly reflected the degree to which settlement took place and the extent to which intermarriage occurred. Besides the North African Muslim countries of Morocco, Algeria, Tunisia, Libya and Egypt, Africa is predominantly Muslim above the tenth parallel, which cuts through the northern regions of Sierra Leone, Côte d'Ivoire, Ghana, Togo, Benin, Nigeria, Cameroon, Central African Republic, Ethiopia and Somalia. The same line roughly separates Muslim from non-Muslim in Sudan and Chad; to the north of it, the Gambia, Senegal, Mali, Niger and Mauritania are preponderantly Muslim (Barrett *et al.* 2001). (See Map 2.1.)

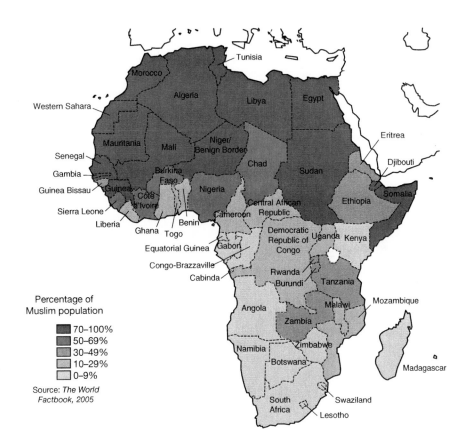

Map 2.1 Muslim population in Africa.

The connection between Middle Eastern Arabs and indigenous Africans has been seen as not entirely harmonious: 'the Arabs infiltrated Africa, enslaved its peoples and imposed Islam on them' (Wai 1985: 62), whereas Africans did not infiltrate the Arab region apart from their enforced presence as slaves. Consequently, tensions existed between Arabs and Africans who, with value systems stemming from very different social and environmental backgrounds, have little in common (Wai 1985: 62). These views, however, have been refuted by others who seek to establish a much closer linkage between Arabs and Africans, maintaining it is completely erroneous to look at Africa on 'a linguistic basis as Arab Africa north of the Sahara and purely African in the south' (Musa 1985). The two areas of the African continent cannot be distinguished ethnically and culturally:

> Population movements between the regions have been continuous over many centuries and human, linguistic, intellectual, religious, economic and social interaction has persisted. Both Africa north of the Sahara and south of it, together with the Horn of Africa and East Africa, constitute a single cultural region reinforced by Islam and the Arabic language.
>
> (Musa 1985: 70)

Although Islam has been regarded as inspiring a 'certain cultural uniformity' in some emergent modern states of the western Africa region, doubts have been raised about the existence of wider commonalities between Africans and Arabs across the continent (Grove 1978: 88). One view suggests 'it would be more appropriate to admit that the Arabs have a separate identity from Africans than to rule out any such distinction', concluding 'it is not accurate to consider African cultures or the cultural development of African peoples as being identical with Arab culture' (Zebadia 1985: 81). The major points of contact between Arabs and Africans in the evolution of the continent's African Islamic heritage were 'trade, war and proselytism' (Yousuf 1986: 13). Certainly, Nigerians have been critical of the 'alien influences via Muslim trans-Saharan trade' which left 'indelible marks on local traditions and cultures' and tried to 'make Nigerians black Arabs'. By the middle of the nineteenth century 'trans-Saharan influences had successfully conquered and displaced the kings of Hausaland and in their places had set up a theocratic empire' (Ugowe 1995: 94). In fact the Church Missionary Society hoped but failed to convert the Hausas, whom they regarded as 'only nominally Muslim' (Walsh 1993: 13). Currently research is being undertaken in northern Nigeria by an NGO, the Centre for Hausa Cultural Studies, and Bayero University in Kano, to reclaim the Hausa language from its Arabic influences (Muazzam interview 2005).[1] Many different 'socio-political organisations existed in pre-colonial Africa' (Cammack et al. 1991: 34). Studies using linguistic evidence suggest that the people of Burundi, for example, 'participated in a regional trade system that was much older and broader in scale than was previously thought' and such practices were well established before the arrival of the Arabs. Burundians participated in a 'multiplicity of exchange relations' with a wide range of goods over considerable distances, but when the Arabs arrived their trading practices were superimposed on existing procedures. Sometimes the traders complemented each other, for example in the boosting of the metals and salt trade, but at times they competed, as in the garment trade, to the disadvantage of the indigenous Burundians (Wagner 1993).

The connection between Islam and Africa raises several interesting points and, according to Louis Brenner, poses some difficult questions. In the first place, Islam challenges the pan-African view of a secular, politically unified Africa forged in the post-independence era; second, it undermines the Afrocentrist school of thought, which asserts a black cultural identity and history, not associated with either the West or, indeed, Islam; and third, it attacks the political/economic imperatives of African development rooted in the Marxist tradition (Brenner 1993). Certainly, Africa's history is complex and multi-dimensional and does not lend itself easily to narrow interpretation: 'Across the vast tropical and southern regions of the continent the black peoples of ancient times progressed from one phase of development to another' (Davidson 1994: 3. See also Nugent 2004; Gordon and Gordon 2001). Yet one perspective on the conjuncture between East and West in Africa accuses European aggrandizement and colonialism of attempting to 'sever the links between Arabs and Africans by all possible means' (Zebadia 1985: 180). If European expansion is considered from the Portuguese explorations of the fifteenth century, parallels have been drawn between Portuguese settlements on the west coast to those of the early Arab traders on the east coast, in that towns sprang up around trading posts and intermarriage occurred. In tracing a continent's heritage, however, very different influences are brought into play, which may not be homogeneous. The colonial experience was conducted through the policies and practices of many European powers, each with different approaches to the exercise of government and administration. Equally, missionaries represented a broad spectrum of denominations: Catholic, Methodist, United Presbyterian and Anglican. African Christianity south of the Sahara has moved through phases: pre-colonial, colonial and post-colonial. Portuguese Catholics were the first Europeans to move into the region when they traversed the western seaboard. Christianity was introduced at Benin in Nigeria in the fifteenth century by Portuguese Roman Catholic priests who accompanied traders and officials to the West African coast. Several churches were built to serve the Portuguese community and a small number of African converts but, when the Portuguese withdrew, the influence of the Catholic missionaries waned. In fact, some Nigerians regarded Christian missions in much the same way they viewed Islam: as 'alien' forces determined to 'fashion Nigerians into black Europeans' (Ugowe 1995).[2] Although the Kingdom of Kongo became a Christian kingdom in the 1490s, by the beginning of the nineteenth century very few people in Africa were practising Christians, apart from Ethiopians, Coptic Egyptians and people living in the remnants of the Kongolese Empire (modern-day Congo-Brazzaville and western Democratic Republic of Congo; see www.bethel.edu/~letnie/AfricanChristianity/).

During the 1800s, missionary work increased in significance. Although Catholic missionary expeditions were active in West Africa, particularly Senegal and Gabon, and Protestant missionaries took up work in Sierra Leone in 1804, two factors were especially important: the abolition of slave owning in 1807 and of slave trading in 1834. Outlawing the slave trade and the conversion of freed slaves were significant factors, as some of the earliest Protestant missionaries were former slaves who had been liberated from slaving ships along the west coast of Africa. In Sierra Leone, former slaves established the nucleus of West African Protestantism. Meanwhile, during the 1840s there was a resurgence of Catholic activity as various missionary groups of priests and religious sisters were formed to spread the faith. Three in particular played major parts in establishing the Church in Africa. In 1845 the Congregation du Saint Coeur de Marie was founded and then merged with an older mission order of priests and became known as the Congregation des Pères du Saint-Esprit (Holy Ghost Fathers); the Societé des Mission Africaines (Society of African Missions) was founded in 1856 and the Societé des Missionaires de Notre Dame d'Afrique (known as the White Fathers) in 1868 (Walsh 1993: 7). In fact, both the Holy Ghost and White Fathers are active within Africa today.

The first half of the twentieth century witnessed the pace of growth of Christianity in Africa outstripping that of Islam. However, this was to change in the latter part of the century. Numbers of Christians increased from around 10 million in 1900 to more than 250 million in the early 2000s, but the number of African Muslims was greater: 34 million in 1900 and nearly 300 million by 2000 (Barrett *et al.* 2001). The political scramble for Africa was 'echoed in the Catholic Church' as the Society of African Missions extended their activities in Lagos, Nigeria; the Gold Coast in 1884; the Ivory Coast in 1895; Liberia in 1906 (Walsh 1993: 15). One of the keys to the success of Christian missions was education. Jeff Haynes explains that missionaries

> were aware that teaching a love of Christ was insufficient on its own, realising that many Africans regarded themselves as in need of material as well as spiritual assistance. It was, therefore, in the missionaries' interest to seek to improve the material knowledge, skill and well-being, via African converts' ability to read and write.
>
> (Haynes 2007: 304)

Certainly, it has been recorded that 'new ideas (including Christianity) are acceptable only when the African sees that they are obviously useful . . . to anything beyond that they are not receptive' (Ayandele 1966: 505). Colonization led to a great demand for education and a proliferation of schools. Protestants had stressed literacy, education and reading the Bible from the beginning of their missions but the advent of colonial power meant that literacy also gained social, political and economic importance. Catholic and Protestant schools spread rapidly and became a major conduit for new mission converts. The new generation of school-educated Christians was different from the first generation of former slave converts in that they were young and educated and had the opportunity of employment, probably of a clerical nature, within the bureaucracy. The Annual Reports of the Society of African Missions during the 1950s pinpoint three fundamental reasons why children were increasingly being released from their farming duties and sent to school. First, the children who were sent to school took up jobs that brought them money and a higher social status. Second, government offices and firms needed trained clerks and staff and these could only come from schools. Ability to speak and write English could result in gaining an individual the job of interpreter. Third, a government job carried an aura of responsibility and respectability, and enhanced a person's position in the home village (Annual Reports from the Diocese of Jos 1955–57 cited in Walsh 1993). Many African Catholics owed their conversion to black African catechists, persons who were largely untrained and unordained, but who were able to preach the gospel. Catechists were largely responsible for an increase in the numbers of Christians, particularly in Igboland, southern Nigeria, where the Catholic community grew from 5000 in 1900 to 74,000 in 1912 (Walsh 1993). Ali Mazrui (1986: 285–86) maintains that a large majority of the first generation of African leaders were educated in mission schools.

Relations between colonial authorities and missionary groups were varied. Some groups were close to the colonial power, as in the Belgian Congo and for a while in French West Africa. Bayart suggests that Christian conversion may have resulted from the strong association between church and state. He points to the example of Rwanda where the Catholic Archbishop of Kigali sat on the central committee of the ruling party until 1985 (Bayart 1993: 189). But this was not the case everywhere. The political institutions of colonialism and the structures of indirect rule were thoroughly secular in that the ultimate source of legitimacy was not the church but the colonial authority. In northern Nigeria, for example, under the control of the British, missionaries of any persuasion were not viewed in a favourable light:

> The records show that from 1906 onwards the Residents would like to keep missionaries out of their districts for various reasons . . . some had become autocrats dictating to the emirs . . . A missionary was likely to be a rival to the Resident's influence and, as a man close to the poorer classes, was likely to be the tribune of the oppressed.
>
> (Ayandele 1966: 515)

Northern Nigeria was divided into 14 provinces with a Resident in charge of each. Sometimes it was helpful if missionaries were not identified as being too closely associated with the colonial power, as was the case when France ended diplomatic relations with the Vatican, expelled religious orders from France and ended subsidies to missionaries in the colonies. The missionaries were permitted to remain in the colonies and found their distance from the colonial administration helpful. One Catholic priest wrote: 'The blacks are far from ignoring that the colonial authorities are hostile to us and that our religion is not that of the whites who live in the French Sudan' (Hastings 1994: 431).

Although the progress of Islam tended to follow pre-existing trade routes sometimes conversions were made via *jihad* (holy war); see Box 2.1. It is argued there are various 'versions' of Islam within Africa, as outlined in Box 2.2. Sufi or-

Box 2.1 Islamic conversion via *jihad*

In 1804, Sheikh Usman dan Fodio led the *jihad* against Hausa kings who failed to abandon traditional religious practices and fully devote themselves to Islamic religion. Aided and supported by local chapters of Fulanis and disgruntled Hausa peasantry in the years between 1804 and 1812, the *jihad* established political and religious control over the Sokoto area, Katsina, Kano, Zaria, Kazaure, Nupe, Katagun, Adamawa, Gombe, Bauchi, Daura, Jamare and Ilorin. Each of these areas was constituted into an Emirate headed by an Emir to whom Sheikh dan Fodio issued a flag of authority from Sokoto with the injunction to rule his people in accordance with the Kuran (*Qur'an*), under the authority of the Caliph, from his capital in Sokoto. Thus was inaugurated the Fulani Empire of the Sokoto Caliphate.

Source: Ugowe (1995).

Al-Hadji Umar Tal led his first major *jihad* in the Senegal area out of the Fouta Djallon (in present-day Guinea) and defeated the Bambara kingdom of Karta in 1854. Tal's *jihad* was based on the purification of Islam, the establishment of the 'real' faith and expulsion of the perversions he saw in the 'so-called' Islamic states he was attacking. In this respect his *jihad* bears a strong resemblance to that of Usman dan Fodio, by whose teachings he was certainly influenced.

Source: Callaway and Creevey (1994: 21).

Box 2.2 Versions of Islam in Africa

1   Islam in the emirates of northern Nigeria, northern Cameroon and the sheikdoms of northern Chad
2   Sufi brotherhoods in West and East Africa: Senegal, The Gambia, Niger, Mali, Guinea, Kenya and Tanzania
3   Muslims fragmented by ethnic and regional concerns, and politically marginalized: Ghana, Togo, Benin and Côte d'Ivoire

Source: Haynes (2007).

ders have received considerable attention since the 1960s with a view developing that they are the 'most important form for the practice of Islam in Africa' (Soares 2007a: 320). Benjamin F. Soares analyses the research undertaken in Senegal and questions this assumption (Soares 2007a: 319–26; cf. Cruise O'Brien 1971; Gellner 1980). The Muridiyya brotherhood was founded by Ahmadu Bamba (also spelt Mourides and Amadou Bamba), who was born Muhammad ibn Muhammad ibn Habib-Allah in Senegal *c*. 1850. He travelled to Mauritania, was initiated by

Sheikh Sidia and founded his own order in 1886. The Mourides followed complete allegiance to their *khalif* and were distinguishable from other brotherhoods by their 'blind obedience and hard labour' (Callaway and Creevey 1994: 22). The Mourides, then, have been viewed as hard-working and pious but not necessarily interested in *jihad.* Work is not a substitute for prayer but the Mourides laid 'unusual stress on work as the form taken of the submission which is required of the follower *vis-à-vis* the leader'. Ernest Gellner regarded the Mourides and their well-organized agricultural labour as 'something very similar to the Zionist movement' (1980: 111–12). It is intriguing, Soares argues, that they have been judged to represent 'a supposedly authentic African Islam of Sufi orders'. The 'diversity of historically specific Islamic discourses and practices within Muslim societies in sub-Saharan Africa' should not be overlooked (2007a: 325). Basil Davidson asserts:

> Whether through its historic brotherhoods such as Qadiriyya and the Tiyaniyya, or in the famous schools of Islamic learning in cities like Timbuktu and Djenne, African Islam upheld and defended the teachings of the Prophet Muhammad, and of the *sharia* that is believed by Muslims to be the constitutional and legal system divined by God . . . many Muslims in Africa believe that salvation must lie in the strict return to the ancient beliefs and practices of Islam.
>
> (Davidson 1994: 274)

Yet the question must be posed: what are the 'ancient beliefs and practices of Islam?' The Chapter 2 Analysis: Islam, Law and Society outlines some of the historical and contemporary discourses within the religion.

Independence

The independence of many African states in the 1950s and 1960s raised a new set of dynamics which preoccupied emergent nation states. The difficulties were essentially twofold: how to construct national unity and thus integrate peoples within a sovereign state, whilst simultaneously undermining ethnic and religious divisions. As the first election manifesto of Ghana's socialist Convention People's Party (CPP) under the leadership of Dr Kwame Nkrumah stated:

> The party system has come to stay. The CPP, in accordance with progressive forms of government everywhere, is opposed to the formation of political parties on the basis of racialism, tribalism and religion, and will make use of every legitimate means to combat it. In our country, with its tradition of religious tolerance and respect for all faiths, it is highly undesirable that a religious association or denomination should take on itself the character of a political party. If it does so, the public is liable to associate its religious tenets, be they Christian or Muslim, with its political aims, and to withhold from such a religious movement the tolerance which is given to purely religious sects. Down with politicians who are exploiting religious fanaticism.[3]

The manifesto of the Belgian-Congolese Elite in 1956 also proclaimed the need for national union in which it would be possible for 'pagans, Catholics, Protestants, Salvationists, Mohammedans to agree on a programme of common good' (Okuma 1963: 70). However, whereas Patrice Lumumba, then President of the Congo, described those Africans of Arab descent as 'uncles of the Congolese' (ibid.), the situation in northern Nigeria, home to the Hausas and Fulanis, was rather different. These peoples were judged to be anti-Western and 'extremely fanatical about Islamism. They have an open contempt for those who do not share their religious belief' (Awolowo 1965). Certainly, the concept of nation-state building through a national consensus was not the priority of the party, the Northern People's Congress, who spoke of 'One North, One People' (Clapham 1985: 33). Racial tensions between Africans and Arabs in Zanzibar became intense in the 1950s and 1960s as the island was proclaimed an independent African state to be merged with Tanganyika (as Tanzania) under the socialist leadership of Julius Nyerere. Yet civil conflict in Sudan between the Muslim north and the largely Christian and Animist south actually began before independence was declared in 1956. Religious, ethnic, territorial and political difficulties confronted the whole of sub-Saharan Africa during those early years of independence.[4] French-speaking West and Equatorial Africa had separate political movements. The conference of the Rassemblement Democratique Africain (RDA) held in 1946 in French Sudan (now Mali) offered political ideas informed by a Marxist analysis, rather than Islamic belief, that would be unconstrained by territorial boundaries. The goals of this widely based multi-state association were: 'The emancipation of our different countries from the yoke of colonialism through the affirmation of their political, economic, social and cultural personalities, and the freely agreed union of countries and peoples, founded on the equality of rights and duties' (G. D'Arboussier cited in Emerson and Kilson 1965: 79).

The Kenyan experience, on the other hand, raised the spectre of racial tension when the Kikuyu tribe launched a movement known as the Mau Mau in the early 1950s. The Swahili Arabs, who were linked to the Africans racially and culturally, gave an ambivalent response to the movement. Although allegedly sympathetic to African aspirations, they were concerned about the threat to their own interests. African leaders responded with recriminations about the Arab role in the slave trade and relations deteriorated (Throup 1998). Racial issues in Uganda arose when accusations were levelled against Arabs and Arab-Africans of supporting President Idi Amin simply on the grounds that he was a Muslim. Libya and Saudi Arabia also supported his regime and when he was overthrown a bloody campaign was fought. Certainly, clear tensions were apparent both at the time of independence and during the years which followed. Whether the interests of Muslim Africans could be identified as the same as non-Muslim Africans is difficult to answer. The communities were essentially schooled in very different traditions. Independence and nation-building, however, was a challenge to everyone and perceptions differed. Whereas predominantly Muslim northern Nigeria was viewed as 'dragging behind' when it came to 'Western European civilisation' and militating against any quest for national unity (Deegan 1996: 20), the Christian and Animist peoples of southern Sudan 'lagged far behind in terms of every index of provision' and were vulnerable to an explicit policy of Islamization and Arabization imposed by the north of the country (Nugent 2004: 82).

It is necessary to mention Egypt at this point because the country underwent an anti-colonial revolution in 1952 led by Gamal Abdel Nasser. Nasser recognized the relevance of sub-Saharan Africa:

> We cannot, under any conditions, relinquish our responsibility to help spread the light of knowledge and civilisation to the very depth of the virgin jungles of the continent. Africa is now the scene of a strange and stirring turmoil. We cannot stand as mere onlookers, deluding ourselves into believing that we are in no way concerned.
>
> (cited in Deegan 1996: 21)

After 1952, African nationalist leaders were invited to Egypt and solidarity was expressed between Nasser and various African political figures. However, an element of caution existed regarding the assistance Egypt was prepared to provide to African Muslims. Egypt resisted any secessionist movements by sending troops to the Congo in favour of President Lumumba and by supporting the federal government of Nigeria. Egypt also supported the unification of Zanzibar and Tanganyika, which essentially implied the disappearance of an Islamic state. On the one hand, then, Islam was a guiding cultural force in Egypt's relationship with emergent African nations, providing educational missions, Quranic and Arab language education, scholarships, building *madrasas* (Islamic schools) and mosques, etc.; but on the other, Egypt made little attempt to create Islamic blocs or to nurture Muslim groups which might undermine national unity in the newly established African states. That was to come from other Middle Eastern states later, as discussed in Chapter 9.

Traditional religions

The spread of Christian and Islamic religions in Africa must be seen in the context of conversion and both faiths continue to disseminate their beliefs through this process. Yet there were a range of divinities, spirits and cults within Africa's traditional religions: in Nigeria, for example, the 'word for God in the Ibo language is "Chukwu", the Greatest, the Highest of the spirits or of the spiritual forces, or "Chineke", the Creator' (Ugowe 1995: 45). Religious conversion encountered resistance in a number of African states. The Goemai people of Nigeria were particularly resistant to attempts by Muslim groups and Christian missionaries to convert them to Islam or Catholicism. According to Jarlath Walsh, former Director of the Institute of Pastoral Affairs in Nigeria, the reason for the Goemai's steadfastness rested upon their satisfaction with the traditional religion of their forefathers. Consequently, they 'saw no reason to abandon it and follow religions they did not know' (interview 1998). The Goemai religion was founded on the desire to protect the lives and welfare of the people. Two deities, 'Karem' and

'Matkarem' (male and female, respectively), were believed by the people to be responsible for most events of human concern, and rituals were performed to appease these gods. Christianity was seen to be concerned not with life on earth but with an afterlife in a world beyond. Therefore, for the people of Goemai new religions had little meaning beyond any possible material benefits that might be accrued. This independent, so-called 'pagan' people had been under the nominal authority of the Muslim Emir of Wase since 1820; then, as a continuing part of the *jihad* of Usman dan Fodio, Yakubu of Bauchi conquered the territory and placed it under control of his follower, Hassan. 'It was not a control that the Goemai recognised and it had to be enforced on many occasions by the Emir of Wase' (Walsh 1993: 25). Subsequently, although the community was friendly to Catholic priests and allowed them to settle, they remained resistant to conversion.

Interestingly, Christian missions operating in Nigeria in the 1990s reported that the Ibo ethnic group, who had formerly largely converted to Christianity, were becoming 'more occultist', performing magical rituals and searching for an 'authentic spiritual identity in keeping with their culture' (Connolly interview 1998). The Islamic Sufi orders in Senegal are seen as 'allowing much greater emphasis on magic, mysticism and personal attachment to a leader' (Callaway and Creevey 1994: 4), which might accord with African traditionalist beliefs. Prevalent among African traditionalists is the belief in ancestor spirits, 'called "vadzimu" among the Shona people of Zimbabwe or "amadhozi" among the Zulu/Ndebele traditions. These are spirits of the deceased mothers and fathers who are recognised in a special ceremony, held usually a year after they have died' (Moyo 2001: 303). Witchcraft beliefs are widespread in Africa and 'witches, sorcerers and angry ancestor spirits are usually identified as the major causes of misfortune' (ibid.). Assumptions have been made that magical ritual is sustained by belief and emotion and performed by 'pre-logical people with no true knowledge of the world around them; people who are quite unable to distinguish between a natural cause and a supernatural one' (Yinger 1970: 73). However, the recourse to magic practices may demonstrate that societies are struggling to deal with contemporary problems in a traditional form. Bayart maintains that the popularity of religious cultism may result from the powerful impact Islam and Christianity had on the African state. In a sense, it is an attempt by Africans to reclaim their cultural heritage (Bayart 1993: 187–89). Magical ceremony, witchcraft and occultist activity do represent an important aspect of Africa's historicity and despite suggestions that such practices are both irrational and unscientific they continue to have legitimacy in African societies. Mission groups reported a decade ago that increasing numbers of priests and religious figures were also dabbling in occultist rituals as such practices were regarded as 'truly African' (Connolly interview 1998). Even Joseph Kony, the head of the notoriously violent Lord's Resistance Army, which caused a 21-year civil war in Uganda, who was charged by the UN International Criminal Court in 2005, allegedly communicates with 'spirits' in his bid to turn the country into a theocratic state based on the Ten Commandments.[5] For Ambrose Moyo (2001: 325), the combined efforts of early missionary and colonial powers to destroy African cultures and religions have led to a crisis of identity that, ironically, has promoted the continued practice of African Traditional Religions as a major aspect of African cultures.

Case study: clashes between religious groups in Kano, Nigeria[6]

Between 1987 and 1993, 3000 people died in Nigeria as a result of growing tensions between Muslims and Christians, and most of the 'overt cases of religious violence' occurred in the northern states of the country (Haynes 2007: 213; Wakili 2001). This case study considers metropolitan Kano as it suffered conflict between Muslims and Christians in the 1990s. Kano is an important northern city which has a long and interesting history (see Box 2.3). During the period of British colonial rule and until the 1930s, Christian missionary groups were discouraged on the grounds they could 'infect' or 'corrupt' Muslim and traditional culture. Yet, as migrants from southern Nigeria settled in Kano, Christianity began increasing in the city. The 'Catholic Church faced problems similar to those of the Protestants' when trying to establish themselves in Kano, and the church of St Elizabeth was established in 1925 in the Sabon Gari area on the basis that its 'activities would be confined to Southerners and [it] would not try to evangelise the Muslims'. Sabon Gari was 'established outside "pagan" and Muslim settlements, for the Europeans, Southerners and missionaries'. Islam proved to be a 'formidable obstacle to Christianity in the north', and the Catholic Church did not attempt to evangelize Islamic areas. This was in contrast to the activities of Protestant churches, which engaged in evangelization but whose 'attempts to convert the Muslims proved to be of no avail' (Walsh 1993: 58–59, 172).

However, this is not the view of Nigerian analysts, some of whom consider the foundations of the inter-religious conflict as being laid during the colonial period when Christian evangelism in the Muslim emirates was eventually permitted. 'From that period onwards Christianity and Islam became engaged in a battle for new converts among the pockets of non-Muslim communities' (Wakili 2001: 46). Others see it differently:

> Christian Missionaries operating in Nigeria saw themselves engaged in two wars both aimed at bringing about religious change designed to make Nigeria part of Christendom. One was the war against traditional religion, and the other was the war against Islam.
>
> (C. N. Ubah cited ibid.)

So the conflict in 1991 was seen as just another example of the continuation of this long-standing rivalry between two universal religions:

> Thus, the attempt by the Christians to host the biggest evangelist meeting in the predominantly Muslim city of Kano in October 1991 was interpreted as

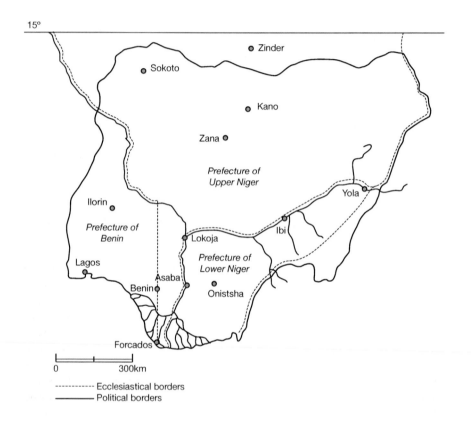

15°

Zinder

Sokoto

Kano

Zana

*Prefecture of
Upper Niger*

Yola

Ilorin

*Prefecture of
Benin*

Ibi

Lokoja

Lagos

*Prefecture of
Lower Niger*

Asaba

Benin

Onistsha

Forcados

0   300km

--------- Ecclesiastical borders
——— Political borders

Map 2.2 Ecclesiastical map of Nigeria 1894.

Box 2.3 Short history of Kano, Nigeria (see Map 2.2)

Kano lies within the Hausaland plateau or the Sudan Savannah and its written history can be dated to 999 BC when the first king, Bagauda, started his reign. During the reign of Yaji (1301–40) Islam became a state religion as a result of the massive influx and influence of Wangarawa migrants from Mali who settled and became integrated with the indigenous inhabitants through intermarriage to create a Kanawa identity as distinct from a Hausa or Fulani identity. The peak of Kano's expansion and rapid institutional development crystallized during the reign of Muhammad Rumfa (sixteenth century AD), who gave support to Islamic scholars and built the renowned Kurmi market and the palace known as Gidan Rumfa, which are still in existence. It was during his reign that Kano developed a written constitution, *Taj ad din Fima Yaqib Ala'al Maluk* (The Crown of Religion Concerning the Obligation of Princes). The constitution was written by Sheikh Muhammad al-Maghili and became an important text in Kano's political and religious institutions. Other migrations from North Africa and the Sahara region made and still make Kano a melting pot socially, culturally and linguistically. Kano in the nineteenth century was acting as the commercial centre of the emirate and Sokoto Caliphate, where traders brought new techniques and influences. In one ward, Makwarari, for example, there is a mixture of Hausa and the descendants of a Sudanese migrant, Mallam Ali Jallaba, who specialized in the trade of Farin Kano (white cloth) and whose name is still used to describe the long flowing garments worn in the region and in Sudan. Kano was economically important to the region with an extensive hinterland and large plantations of cotton, tobacco, indigo and grains. The town was also known for its trade and production in cloth, leather, kola, slaves and salt. The indigo wells, the making of cloth, traditional dyeing and agricultural production are still in existence and the Kurmi market still bustles with trade.[a] Peoples from Syria and Lebanon arrived in the nineteenth century and still play a prominent role in the economy as hotel, bakery and café owners, and are an important sector of society. There is also a parallel international currency exchange market which operates in Fagge, outside the traditional city, but to the visitor this foreign exchange market seems invisible and inaccessible except through an intermediary.

Kano has 44 local governments and a population of between 7 and 9 million people.[b] It is a growing urban centre and continues to attract migrants from southern Nigeria, as well as neighbouring Niger and Sudan.

Source: Muazzam interview 2005.

a The author visited the indigo wells and Kurmi market in 2005.
b Current estimate from 1991 census.

meaning yet another Christian offensive against Islam. It was regarded as an attempt by the Christians to penetrate into Muslim territory.

> (Kano State of Nigeria, *Report of Kano Disturbances, October 1991*,
> cited ibid.: 47)

But exactly what was the nature of the event? According to official reports a German evangelist, Reverend Reinhard Bonnke, proposed a 'crusade' which was to take place in Kano between 15 and 20 October 1991 and expected to be attended by 'over 500,000 delegates and participants'. The Muslim population was opposed and organized a 'peaceful protest march'. Haruna Wakili maintains there were two stages in the incident:

> The first phase occurred in the early hours of Monday, 14 October 1991 when a group of a few thousand Muslims converged at the Kofar Mata open air praying grounds to say *Salatul Hajah* (a special Muslim prayer offered at critical periods of need). The short prayer was meant to ask for God's intervention to prevent the hosting of the proposed Christian crusade. The prayer was followed by a peaceful procession to the Palace of the Emir of Kano in order to seek the Emir's assistance in this serious religious matter. Some young radical Muslim Scholars cutting across all the major religious sects and groups in Kano led the protest march.
>
> (ibid.: 42)

The Emir responded by agreeing to do all he could to prevent the crusade and the demonstrators dispersed. However, the second stage 'took a different dimension from the first phase'. Eyewitness reports assert the peaceful demonstration was later 'hijacked, transformed, and escalated into a violent religious conflict between Muslims and Christians'. This outcome occurred 'as the tail of the procession' moved into the opposite direction and, after passing through Fagge, 'went straight into Sabon Gari' (ibid.: 42). As previously mentioned, Sabon Gari was a predominantly Christian area. This group enlarged and began chanting: '*Allahu Akbar* (God is the greatest) and *Ba ma so* (we do not want)' as they converged in these areas:

> The rioters carrying dangerous weapons attacked economic targets, places of worship, and men and women in the street who appeared to them to be Christians. Several shops and stalls mainly belonging to Igbos were looted and destroyed. Churches, beer parlours, hotels were also destroyed and several people were attacked, molested, injured or killed on both sides during the violent crisis.
>
> (Police investigation report, *KIIB Kano, October 1991*,
> cited ibid.: 43)

The following day the violent conflict resumed with Christian Sabon Gari residents embarking on a counter-offensive against Muslims, their mosques and property.

Meanwhile, Muslim groups formed into 'militias' and paraded other parts of the city 'hunting for Christians and their property to attack'. Finally, the crisis ended only when the police and a section of the Nigerian Army 'became determined to put down the violent conflict' (ibid.).

Many Nigerians were outraged:

> What is disconcerting in the contemporary religious scene in Nigeria is that religious differences are being used as a cloak for political factions, arson, burning down of places and objects of worship, contrary to the traditional heritage of religious freedom and tolerance.
>
> (Ugowe 1995: 106)

In fact, when the Baptist minister Reverend Bitrus Joshua Fraps arrived in Kano in 1993 the response was 'negative'. He was 'ejected from his premises again and again' and ultimately had to set up the Baptist Church in mobile barracks for safety (interview 2005). The loss of life in 1991 was considerable. Although official sources estimated 200 lives, the real figure could not be known as many 'victims were burnt or thrown into unused wells and ponds. A total of sixteen churches and three mosques were destroyed, 558 shops were looted, damaged or burnt down, over 200 vehicles were burnt or damaged and 192 houses were partly or completely destroyed during the violence' (*Report of Kano Disturbances* cited in Wakili 2001: 43–44). Not surprisingly, many left the region; not only 'Southerners or the Igbo but also people from the Middle Belt and non-Muslim Northern minorities' (ibid.: 44). Wakili found the nature of the violence strange and not part of previous patterns of rioting in Kano. For example, Christian minorities had formerly been allies of the Muslim Hausas whereas now they were the 'targets of religious violence'.

Reasons for religious conflict

In attempting to explain and understand the reasons for the violent outbursts, four possible triggers can be identified: socio-economic problems; weaknesses of state mechanisms in dealing with potential clashes; religious rivalry and radicalization; and external factors. In regard to the possible first cause, there is no doubt that the socio-economic environment of Kano had caused concerns and many were referring to 'dark spots' within society:

> The failure to organise and plan for the youth has brought about a fine revenge on the society. Youths get cooped up in the confused atmosphere of the growing metropolis and take to idling, rambling the streets or resorting to violence.
>
> (Muazzam interview 2005; cf. Umar interview 2005)

Certainly, the profile of over 100 persons arrested in the 1991 riots revealed that the majority were 'children and youths aged between the ages of 13 to 30 years', many of whom were unemployed. These profiles were similar to those who were arrested in the religious riots which occurred in Katsina in March 1991 (Police investigation report cited in Wakili 2001). One large community-based organization (CBO), Yakasai Zumunta (meaning Yakasai Brotherhood) has recognized the need for training through apprenticeships but some young people lack even basic skills. Although levels of education have increased many are not fully served. There has also been a 'crisis' identified within the traditional Quranic school (TQS) system. The *Almajirai* (the term used to describe pupils of TQS) are sent away to learn about the Islamic faith but in practice have been 'turned into street juveniles . . . beggars and hawkers of petty commodities'. Economic problems are seen as contributory factors in these outcomes and contribute to 'social explosions' and 'incidences of riots and mob actions' (Sule-Kano 2004: 9).

If socio-economic difficulties are the first cause of violence then attention has turned to the second possible trigger, the weakness of local state structures in delivering appropriate levels of education, health care and general public services. In this climate, CBOs operate on an almost parallel level providing public goods in place of the local authority. The Yakasai Zumuntu CBO actually covers 44 local governments and provides clinics, hospitals and even food: 'the aim is to have people look to the organisation for assistance' (Umar interview 2005). This may fill a gap in provision but others observe that these types of organization 'tend to have their particular clientele' (Muazzam interview 2005) and are often regarded as 'too close to government and its political dispensation' (Kawu interview 2005). Yet Yakasai Zumuntu has received funding from the UK's Department of International Development and from Unicef, so its role in the community is becoming internationally recognized. The government of Kano is under the authority of the *Shari'a* Commission, which implements *shari'a* law, and the *Hizlah* Board guides morality within the area. As such, permission must be granted by the Commission for any activity, including public festivals.[7] The implementation of *shari'a* law has raised concerns. Some maintain that Christian and Islamic relations within an unsympathetic state can often be tense and uneasy, whereas others argue that its introduction has affected business and led to the withdrawal of investment from southern and eastern Nigeria (Kukah 1993; Fraps interview 2005). Many people supported *shari'a* at first because they assumed that through *zakat* (almsgiving) the rich would give to the poor and they would share their wealth with the needy. Although the Emir of Kano donates to Islamiyya schools, more generally there has been little transfer of resources.

The third cause, religious rivalry and radicalism, is seen as emanating from both Islamic and Christian groups. Although counter-claims have been made there does seem to be a direct 'relationship between religious conflict and violence of the 1980s and 1990s and the upsurge of both Islamic and Christian revivalism and fundamentalism of the period' (Wakili 2001: 45). It was generally acknowledged internationally that 'A popular fundamentalist current was making a comeback in northern Nigeria due to economic problems and largely financed by Iran' (BBC Summary of World Broadcasts AL/2116 3 October 1994 cited in Deegan 1996: 120). This would have been in Katsina, where religious conflict broke out in March 1991 led by Mallam Yakuba, a follower of Mallam Ibrahim

Yakuba El-Zak-Zaky, the national leader of the Muslim Brotherhood Movement in Nigeria (Wakili 2001: 39). Yet Christian acts of provocation and aggression against Muslims were cited by Muslim leaders when relations between the communities became increasingly tense over the role played by the Organisation of the Islamic Conference (OIC) in pressurizing Nigeria to join (cf. Deegan 1996 and Chapter 9 in this volume). But what were the Christian 'provocations' and 'aggression' in the context of the trigger for the Kano riots? In a sense, this must be viewed through the prism of religious freedom. 'Provocation' was identified as synonymous with a Christian religious group holding a 'Gospel crusade under the banner "Kano for Jesus". It was seen as a deliberate Christian provocation directed against Muslims and their religion' (Kano State of Nigeria, *Report on Kano Disturbances, October 1991*).

Yet, interestingly, both the Catholic community and the National Council of Muslim Youth Organisations believed there was a correlation between the prevailing socio-economic distress, youth unemployment and the outbreak of the Kano disturbances (cf. Wakili 2001: 47–48; Musa interview 2005). One salient factor seems to have emerged, however, and that is the differential toleration of various denominations of Christianity within the city. Whereas the Catholic Cathedral in Kano is large with a convent attached, evangelical Protestant groups are less welcome. Protestant groups are seen as more 'fundamentalist' than the Catholic community. This has raised the issue of religious rights and freedom of worship, which are provisions in the Nigerian constitution of 1979. Evangelists of any religion, it could be argued, were permitted under the constitution to exercise their rights to freedom of expression and worship. Muslims, on the other hand, viewed the pasting of posters and banners in the locality, some of which depicted a 'Muslim seeking salvation from Christ', as 'highly provocative and inciting' (Kano State of Nigeria, *Report on Kano Disturbances, October 1991*). Revealingly, the trigger for religious clashes in Katsina was the 1990 publication in a comic magazine, *Fun Times*, of a cartoon captioned 'Would you marry a known prostitute . . . ', which made references to both the Prophet Muhammad and Jesus Christ. In echoes of the recent outcries about the Danish cartoons and the Sudanese teddy bear called Muhammad, Muslims, led by a branch of the Islamic Movement in Nigeria, organized a protest march against the publication of the cartoon on the grounds that it 'ridiculed and insulted the Prophet' (Wakili 2001: 39).[8]

The Islamic Movement in Nigeria claims it recognizes neither the Nigerian constitution nor the laws of the country. Mallam Yakubu Yahaya, the leader of the Islamic Movement in Katsina, asserted: 'I am a Muslim under Muslim rules and I do not recognise any authority over me but that of the Holy *Qur'an*. I do not recognise the Federal Government, I do not recognise the State Government and their laws' (*African Concord*, 22 April 1991: 26 cited ibid.: 55). In Kano, 'both radical and moderate Muslim groups were united on the supremacy of *shar'ia* law over secular laws of the Nigerian state' (ibid.: 55). However, perhaps this is changing, as no posters or declarations proclaiming *shar'ia* appeared in 2005 as had been the case previously. Essentially, when religion combines with politics many believers take a pragmatic view about the delivery of benefits. That is why brotherhood organizations such as Yakasai Zumunta recognize the importance of providing schools, clinics, jobs, food etc. to local communities. Lack of sanitation, open toilet facilities and inadequate water supplies are just some of the concerns identified by a community empowerment project when researching four communities in Kano State (Salihu 2003: 31). At some point, these very real needs of people must be addressed by political representatives. The upholding of *shari'a* law will not automatically meet these urgent requirements.

Finally, it is necessary to consider the external environment. International events were also significant as problems developed in the Middle East following Saddam Hussein's invasion of Kuwait in 1990. Abiding by UN resolutions, the 1991 Gulf War, aimed at removing Iraq's military presence from Kuwait, was raging. One contemporary report asserted at the time:

> Nigeria's security agencies stopped demonstrations by Muslims in the northern part of the country after the influential Muslim leader, Abubakar Gumi, declared that Iraq was fighting the Muslim's cause and urged every Muslim to support the country. Leaders of the Christian Association of Nigeria appealed to the nation's citizens not to allow the Gulf crisis to mar or disrupt peace in the country.
>
> (cited in Deegan 1996: 112)

More worrying were the responses to the attacks on the United States on 11 September 2001:

> There is a huge demand for the image of Osama bin Laden and a seemingly insatiable market . . . this infatuation has more to do with ideology than adoration. To most Muslims here, bin Laden is a hero: an Islamist, who looked the United States straight in the face and said 'Go to hell.'
>
> (Muhammed 2002: 51)

Yet the Muslims of Kano also recognize the benefits of USAID and other resources the United States bestows on the region, and welcomed the country's representatives when they subsequently drove through the streets of Kano in cars decked with Stars and Stripes flags (Aulam interview 2005). What the future holds for Islamic–Christian relations in northern Nigeria is open to question but on one issue there seems to be a degree of consensus at the national level: politically Nigeria does not wish to suffer the same experiences as Sudan.

ANALYSIS: ISLAM, LAW AND SOCIETY

> [S]*haria* is Islam's comprehensive and systematic legal code, developed by Muslim jurists of the 8th and 9th centuries AD, and derived by them from the *Qur'an* and the Sunna of Muhammad. But in all that time since then, great controversies and schisms have divided Muslims as to what lawful behaviour really is or should be. Since then, too, Muslim authorities have introduced many reforms of their law, many tolerances, many reconciliations with fellow-citizens who are not Muslims. Yet modern Fundamentalism has set its face against these reforms and tolerances and has insisted, for example, that the extremely harsh punishments laid down in the *sharia* code, long ago in medieval times, such as the amputation of the right hand for theft, severe lashing or even stoning to death for fornication or adultery, be still applied.
>
> (Davidson 1994: 274–75)

In order to explore further the assertions contained in this quotation it is necessary to examine dimensions of the faith.

The early Islamic period

Islam regards itself as a religion, a polity and a total way of life; therefore its relationship with society is all-powerful. In theory, the Islamic state is communal rather than territorial in scope, with the capacity of *shari'a* law to extend over both public and private matters. Political, economic and societal affairs all fall under the jurisdiction of this religious law. Under certain conditions it may appear resistant to innovation and determined to retain the status quo in every sphere. Islam, it has been argued, has the ability to actually freeze the basic pattern of societies; in practice meaning 'what does exist "ought" to continue to exist' (Pfaff 1967: 106).

Islam must also unify Muslims over and beyond the confines of the nation-state. 'Islam has no territorial boundaries', asserted one religious leader at a Friday sermon (Ahmad 1991), and Sudan's Hasan Turabi stated in the late 1990s: 'The ideal of Islam is one of freely associating social groups united by common descent, custom, domicile, interest or moral purpose' (interview 1997). The political form this structure would take is one in which the Caliphate would be re-established and restored, upholding one centre of authority and uniting the Muslim community. In other words, a unified Islamic order would be created under which a political system conformed to *shari'a*. The Caliphate would serve as the central institution of the Islamic *umma* (community), preserving the deeply entrenched Islamic tradition of free migration and reminiscent of classical Caliphates. The ideal human community is the *umma muhammadiyya*, 'a group of disciples, initially small, weak and threatened, that grew larger thanks to the direct help of God and the action of the Prophet' (Arkoun 1994: 53). See Boxes 2.4 and 2.5.

Table 2.1 outlines the relationship with fellow creatures according to Islam, which is 'absolutely essential for human happiness, peace, progress and prosperity' (Surty 1995: 16). There is also a strong emphasis on brotherhood, *al-ukhuwwah*:

The bond of Islam can unite strangers into a brotherhood stronger than that of blood relations.

Brotherhood is one of the great blessings of Allah through which two hearts are reconciled and it cannot be attained without His grace even if whatever exists in the world be spent. (8:63)

With this noble relationship two aliens can be united like the teeth of a comb. It creates mutual love, a spirit of cooperation, sharing, sacrifice, understanding and tolerance. (49:10; 3:103; 33:5)

(ibid.)

According to Mohammed Arkoun, notions of ideal communities are partly un-real. Mythical visions are presented and sustained by an idealized transmission of all events and words by a privileged generation: the disciples and companions who define the condition and spiritual quality of the ideal community (Arkoun 1994). Ideas need to connect with contemporary realities. The Islamic practice of *al-shura* (consultation) is presented as a means of connecting the wider Mus-lim community, one that should be united and balanced between the 'immediate local community, the intermediate regional composite and the distant universal collectivity' (Turabi 1993; cf. Turabi interview 1997). According to Islam 'all members of the society, locally and internationally, are tied strongly with the bond of brotherhood'. Yet some form of government is intrinsic to human society because a society which is 'totally uncontrolled, unguided and unregulated is a contradiction in terms' (Dunleavy and O'Leary 1991: 1). Within Islam, although the fabric of society is 'woven by the Divine law', the rights and obligations of each member of society are 'assigned by Divine sanction, on the basis of justice, equity, harmony and natural requirements' (Surty 1995: 20). Mohammed Arkoun believes Sura 9 of the Qur'an illustrates the theological and socio-political context for applying rights and duties to all human beings in society, including 'believers among themselves, believers and non-believers and, believers and *ahl al-kitab*' (people of the book, i.e. Jews and Christians) (Arkoun 1994: 55).

However, the early Umayyad rulers developed a strong, centralized, dynastic kingdom, an Arab empire.

The more advanced government, institutions and bureaucracy of Byzantium (the eastern flank of the Roman Empire and Persian provinces) adopted and adapted to Arab Muslim needs. Native civil servants and ministers were re-tained to guide and train their Muslim masters. In time through a process of conversion and assimilation, language and culture, state and society were Arabized and Islamized. Arabic became the language of government as well as the lingua franca of what today constitutes North Africa, much of the Mid-dle East and areas of Africa.

(Esposito 1994: 42)

Although the Umayyads used Islam as a means of legitimizing their activities, the Caliphs were the 'protectors and defenders of the faith charged with extending the

Box 2.4 The Prophet Muhammad

The Prophet was born in AD 570 in Makkah, Arabia into the clan of Banu Hashim, the descendant of the Prophet Ishmael. Before his birth his father, Abdullah, died and his grandfather, Abdul Muttalib, looked after him. He lost his mother, Aminah, at the age of six and a year later, his grandfather. It was finally his uncle, Abu Talib, who provided him with assistance.

Khadijah, a wealthy widow of Makkah, engaged him in trade which the Prophet carried out honestly. She eventually offered him her hand in marriage which the Prophet accepted. The polytheism of Makkah, its social customs and injustices concerned the Prophet. In search of peace, it became his practice to leave Makkah for the solitude of Hira, a cave on the Mountain of Light in Makkah. It was in this cave at the age of 40 that he received the first revelation of the Qur'an through the angel Gabriel and from that time he began promoting the message of Islam.

The people living in Makkah viewed the Islamic message as a threat to their religion, prestige, rank and authority. The spread of the message aroused anger and hostility and Muslims migrated to Madinah where they could practice their faith. The Makkans were very disturbed by this development and plotted to kill the Prophet. When he learnt of this conspiracy he migrated from Makkah to Madinah in AD 622. This, migration of the Prophet, was the turning point in the history of Islam and from that day the Islamic calendar began. The Prophet was welcomed in Madinah where he constructed a mosque and a home within its courtyard where he stayed in absolute simplicity till his death. He is buried there.

He established an Islamic State in Madinah and united Muslims under the Divine code of law. Under his political and religious authority the Prophet combined legislative, judicial and executive functions. The Prophet led a simple and frugal life.

He was a modest, truthful, trustworthy, considerate and affectionate person. He was very fond of children. He was courteous. His speech was sweet, clear, brief, full of thought and wisdom and heart penetrating. He possessed a good memory, practical wisdom and inventive genius. The rich and poor, black and white, the powerful and the weak were all treated equally by the Prophet. He did not hesitate to risk his life in the defence of truth and the administration of justice.

Source: Surty (1995).

Box 2.5 An historical view of the Prophet Muhammad

The Prophet Muhammad was an illiterate Arab, aided by a shrewd business head and a rich widow's fortune, who was converted in mature life to the consciousness of a religious vocation. He preached a faith that ethically was far in advance of the Arab code. He became the political leader of Arabia, founded a world religion and inspired his followers with a fiery zeal that enabled them to conquer half the Roman empire and many lands beyond it. Circumstances such as unrest in Arabia and the presence of vague national aspirations conditioned the process, forcing Muhammad to become a political ruler, outside his original purpose.

In his teaching he borrowed from Jewish and Christian sources, accepting the Old Testament and holding Christ to be a human prophet with a divine mission. But this hardly accounts for his ethical and religious doctrine. The personality of the man was the determining factor throughout. He had rare gifts of insight into human character and skill in managing men; his sincerity is beyond dispute; he was without fanaticism and without fraud.

Source: Bury (1921).

Table 2.1 The relationship with fellow creatures according to Islam

Love, mercy and forgiveness	POLITICAL LIFE	Justice, equality and brotherhood	ECONOMIC LIFE	Kindness, peace and thanksgiving	PRIVATE AND SOCIAL LIFE	Allah consciousness, trust in Allah and patience

Source: Surty (1995).

rule of Islam' (ibid.). Inevitably, as in any empire, society was divided and unequal with non-Arab Muslims and non-Muslims feeling unfairly treated, as in parts of Africa, but trade was both important and necessary. In neither the Qur'an nor the sayings of the Prophet is there any prohibition on trade with infidels (Horden and Purcell 2004: 156).

Ultimately the Umayyad dynasty, which lasted from AD 661 to 750, fell when Damascus surrendered and the Abbasids claimed the Caliphate. Shi'i opposition to Umayyad rule spread to Persia (Iran), where another kind of sentiment bred discontent. The Persians, 'a vigorous and martial peasantry of Indo-European stock' (De Burgh 1961: 29), had become Muslim and had a long history of high civilization stretching back to Cyrus, who belonged to the clan of Achaemenids, conquered Babylon and called himself king of the Persians in AD 553. However, the 'Abbasids were not Shi'is, who claim leadership of the Muslim community belongs to the Prophet's descendants through his daughter, Fatimah, but they were opposed to the Umayyads' (Sonn 1990: 37). The Abbasids established their capital in Baghdad and from there ruled the eastern areas, whereas the Umayyads maintained control of Andalusia (southern Spain) and parts of West Africa. The triumph was that of 'Persian over Arab; of religion over political, Arabian nationalism' (De Burgh 1961: 418). By the ninth century the Mediterranean world contained four great powers, two in the west and two in the east:

> In the West were the Christian empires of the successors of Charles the Great, and the Mohammedan kingdom of the Umayyad emirs of Cordova (Spain) . . . in the East were the Christian empire, ruled from Constantinople, and the Abbasid caliphate of Baghdad.

The force of political gravity tended to bring together in alliance 'the eastern empire and the Spanish Mohammedans on the one hand, the western empire and the Abbasids on the other' (ibid.: 419). Certainly, the Abbasid Caliphate has been regarded as 'the flowering of Islamic Civilisation' with the early period of rule associated with 'unparalleled splendor and economic prosperity' (Esposito 1994: 52). As well as art, Islamic scholarship, schools, mosques and culture, the Abbasids further developed *shari'a* law. The Umayyad dynasty was criticized for its failure to implement an effective Islamic legal system, but the Abbasids, with their wealth and resources from trade, commerce, industry and agriculture, could offer considerable support to its development. As John Esposito makes clear, the *ulama* (religious scholars) became a far more influential 'professional elite of religious leaders, a distinct social class within Muslim society. Their prestige and authority rested on a reputation for learning in Islamic studies: the *Qur'an*, traditions of the Prophet and law.' As such they became jurists, educators and interpreters and guardians of Islamic law and tradition: 'The *qadi* (judge) administered the law as it was developed by the early jurists, thus, firmly establishing the Islamic court system' (ibid.: 54). During the Abbasid period

> Islam – the offspring of Arabia and the Arabian Prophet – was not only a system of belief and cult. It was also a system of state, society, law, thought and art – a civilization with religion as its unifying, eventually dominating factor.
>
> (Lewis 1966: 133)

However, the next Islamic empire, led by the Turkish Ottoman Sultans, made serious inroads into Islamic codes of conduct. The Ottoman Empire, with its large numbers of non-Muslims, found it particularly difficult to subject these communities to a legal framework that had a strictly religious base. Consequently, dual legal systems evolved, one governed by *shari'a*, the other based on custom. Within the empire the corporate organization of society was not compatible with national identity. Each religious community or *millet* formed a juridical and political entity in itself. Citizens of the empire were subject to public law but each *millet* was autonomous with respect to matters of personal status and family law. Such a system tended to lead to social fragmentation and by the eighteenth century the empire's power and prosperity was being seriously challenged by the economic, military and political authority of a modernized West. Ultimately, the empire collapsed during the First World War. Yet notions of Islamic society were being interpreted. The Egyptian intellectual, Rifa'a Badawi Rafi' al-Tahtawi, stressed the purpose of society was to 'do God's will by striving to establish *maslaha* (social well-being) in this world, which will assure happiness in the next'. However, as Tamara Sonn explains, al-Tahtawi's description of *maslaha* was of 'a just and progressive society founded not only on religious training, but also on the economic activities which lead to wealth and the improvement of conditions and contentment among the people as a whole' (1990: 37). Al-Tahtawi also mentioned the word *watan* (locality), which referred to a geographical area rather than a community of believers as expressed by the term *umma*:

> For there is a national brotherhood among members of the same *watan* over and above the brotherhood in religion. There is a moral obligation on those who share the same *watan* to work together to improve it and perfect its organisation in all that concerns its honour and greatness and wealth.
>
> (Al-Tahtawi cited in Hourani 1970: 79)

These sentiments were to become prominent among the brotherhoods in Senegal, especially the Muridiyya Brotherhood (see above in Chapter 2).

During the declining years of the Ottoman Empire, the Arabs wanted to escape from its authority. Some turned to religious revivalism and hoped to establish a true Islamic caliphate whereas others sought independence through nationalism. Jamal al-Din al-Afghani called for Islam to renew itself by reclaiming science and reason. Thereby, he argued, it would be able to repel the West. Islam was a comprehensive way of life, encompassing worship, law, government and society. It was essential that a real Islamic identity and solidarity be asserted. Afghani criticized the religion's stagnation and called for *ijtihad* (independent analysis/interpretation of Islamic law). Yet although he called for pan-Islam he recognized the need for national independence. Some nationalists hoped that a political formula of constitutionalism might forge together into one 'national' community the disparate peoples of the empire, but world events were to provide the backdrop to the future development of the dismembered former authority. After 1920 Turkey, severed from its Arab regions, turned to Mustafa Kemal Atatürk and a different approach towards progress. The other areas of the Middle East were confronted by the force of European colonialism. John Esposito believes that those who re-interpreted Islamic sources in order to obtain new approaches and to consider some Western notions made a contribution towards modernism (Esposito 1994: 155). Other analysts, however, have been less convinced: 'despite voluminous theoretical discussions, no workable model of a modern society organized on the principles of Islam has been created' (Banani 1961: 151).

The distinction between state and society found in most accounts of modern political communities rests in part on the analytical separation of social relations in respective spheres. The state exercises authority over individual actions that are guided by belief in the legitimate order of power, which political leaders and officials maintain. The concept of legitimacy is shared by those who exercise authority and by those who are subject to it. In customary and traditional societies, however, relations are typically based on affinities of interests, be they tribal, familial, kinship or religious; in other words primordial loyalties. In modern states, access to positions of public authority has gradually become separated from primordial loyalties. Decision making at legislative, judicial and administrative levels has become subject to impersonal rules and attained a level of independence from social interests. Under absolutist forms of rule, the legitimacy of the regime involves state officials rather than the wider population. Political stability depended upon those officials convincing local powers that it was in their interests, and in accordance with their values, that the regime should continue to function without major disturbance. However, with the development and demands of bourgeois political claims, the notion of a wider community as properly influencing state policy became more acknowledged. This constituency would not simply be ruled; rather it would be represented in a participatory system. Equally, the state itself was increasingly regarded as a new element of society: a structure of authority as well as a mechanical organization of society. The impersonal abstract state, which controls a consolidated territory and possesses a system of offices that is differentiated from those of other organizations, became synonymous with modernity. Constitutions would be designed to reflect the need for laws that would not only protect the autonomy of the market and the privileges of the propertied but also articulate the idea of the state, with categories that provided coherence and consistency in the exercise of power and the maintenance of social order. Emile Durkheim presented two contrasting types of society. The first type, 'mechanical', is a small, simple, undifferentiated society in which the basic conditions of its members' lives are homogeneous and largely dependent upon subsistence agriculture. The second society, 'organic', is united into a single functioning whole, with each part dependent upon the whole. He viewed the function of the state to be an agency of rationalization which would free individuals from social groups and customs (Durkheim 1982: 53). Weak states in Africa make religion and its formal structures of control important. Within Islam, the traditional view emphasizes that no distinction can be drawn between religious and secular affairs. However, in practice in the Middle East and Africa, this picture is complicated by nationalism, secularism and sectarianism. Religious interests and concerns to some degree compete with those based on national and economic development.

Islam and liberalism

As liberalism developed during the nineteenth century it became more than just economic individualism; it was also concerned with moral and social freedom. Individuals had the right to question traditional values. Liberal democracy conceived as universal suffrage and citizenship rights did not become fully established in many Western democracies until well into the twentieth century. Yet the market society itself produced a pressure for democracy because liberalism had always justified itself as providing equal individual rights and equality of opportunity. Democracy was demanded and largely admitted on liberal grounds, as an extension of rights to individuals, rather than classes, prepared to accept, in exchange, both the existence of the state and the responsibilities associated with citizenship. A system of pluralism is identified with liberalism and the accept-ance of certain values: the rule of law which separates the legislative function from the executive one; the preservation of the liberties of the people – freedom of speech, freedom of association, freedom of press and freedom of assembly; political tolerance and the right of opposition; an accountable government that is subject to regular elections and the political equality of one person, one vote and equal sized constituencies. A pluralistic society represents competition between diverse groups but, although diversity and opposition are stressed and groups are encouraged to disagree on particular issues, there must be an overriding commit-ment from all groups to the rules of society. Should a group, party or organization hold deeply antagonistic ideas about the functioning of the political system, it would be regarded as a threat to that society. Opposition, then, is the central fea-ture of a liberal, pluralistic society but only so far as it does not seek to undermine, terrorize or eliminate the structures of the state.

But what is the relationship between Islam and liberalism? According to one analyst there are two kinds of Islamic liberalism:

> The first finds the idea of a liberal Islamic state possible and desirable not only because such a liberal democratic state accords with the spirit of Islam, but especially because, in matters political, Islam has few specific requirements . . . The second form would justify the establishment of liberal institutions (parliament, elections, civil rights) and even some social welfare policies, not on the basis of the absence of any contradictory Islamic legislation, but rather on the basis of quite specific Islamic legislation, which they are inclined to deduce from canonical sources and from the available anecdotal histories of the early caliphate.
>
> (Binder 1988: 243–44)

Other commentators, however, offer a different perspective:

> Although most Muslim countries adopted Western models of political, economic, educational and legal development, their citizens have not fully appropriated intellectually and psychologically their implicit values. While an elite minority has accepted and become fully acculturated to a Western secular worldview and system of values, the majority has not internalized a secular, rationalist outlook.
>
> (Esposito 1994: 195)

Liberal institutions are based on certain principles: pluralism, individualism, capi-talism, agnosticism, empiricism, pragmatism, utilitarianism and tolerance. The important issue is the kind of relationship that exists between the state and religion. In liberalism, the state is separated from religion.

Liberalism has had its critics in the West especially when viewed in the context of development. Pluralist systems have been regarded as sectional and sterile, and strong centralized states advocated. Equally, democracy has been seen as only tangentially linked with liberalism; 'competitive capitalist individualism' should be rejected in favour of 'moral worth, dignity and humanity'. The problem with liberalism was its emphasis on 'possessive individualism' and the assumption that society was little more than a series of market relations between individuals (Macpherson 1973: 165). These views were only part of a discourse and others found: 'The process by which democracy is "liberalized" is a key one, for it ties together notions of capitalist development, class formation and class conflict, as well as such essentials of liberalism as competitive parties and majority rule' (Joseph 1987: 20). Africa, it could be argued, has not fully embraced liberalism; rather it is nationalism that has found more fertile ground.

The late Edward Said pointed to the writings of Nasr Abu Zeid, who refused to believe there was a distinction between 'moderate' and 'extreme' Islamists, and sought to scrutinize the ideological bases of their pronouncements. Abu Zeid criticized Islamist statements on the grounds that they were based on:

- An identification of 'thought' with 'religion' and an elimination of the distance between 'subject' and 'object'.
- An explanation of all phenomena by reducing them to a single first principle or a single cause. This explanation includes all scientific as well as social phenomena.
- A reliance on the tyranny of either the 'past' or 'tradition', by converting secondary traditional texts into primary ones, which are endowed with a sanctity that in many instances is scarcely less than that of the primary texts.
- An absolute mental certainty and intellectual derisiveness that refuses to brook any disagreement at all, except in negligible details.
- Avoidance or ignorance of the historical dimension which manifests itself in weeping over the wonderful past embodied in the golden age of the Caliph Haroun al-Rashid or the Caliphate of the Ottoman Empire.

(Zeid cited in Said 1994: 409–10)

Said believed Abu Zeid represented a 'rising new critical consciousness' within the Islamic world. His approach, although reflective of European modes, is conducted 'entirely within the Arab and Islamic domain', addressing problems that are both local and universal. Above all, he 'exemplifies an investigative attitude that is both skeptical and affirmative and that has, in fact, existed for many centuries in the Muslim tradition' (Said 1994: ibid.). Mohammed Arkoun's objective is not the establishment of an Islamic state, but rather a democratic state in which the distinction between Islamic reason and philosophical reason will disappear. He calls on Muslim intellectuals to contribute to Islam by considering questions of ethics and politics in the contemporary world: 'What are the blind-spots, the failings, the *non sequiturs*, the alienating constraints, the recurrent weaknesses of modernity? Protest must reach every form of activity, every point of intervention, every logical structure' (Arkoun 1994: 119).

So what of notions of Islamic liberalism? If Charles Kurzman is correct, three strands can be distinguished:

1   Islamic teachings are essentially liberal.
2   Islamic teachings are neutral towards liberalism.
3   There exists a conflict between liberalism and traditional Islam but this can be reconciled through a process of mutual re-interpretation.

(Kurzman 1999)

In a sense, the interpretation of Islam is the key to the way in which it deals with both the past and the future. Binder (1988: 357) makes the observation that 'fundamentalist and liberal' strands of Islam 'draw on the same religious sources, they often employ the same types of reasoning, they usually concentrate on the same authoritative pronouncements, and in some cases the differences between the two may be difficult to discern.' Yet for the Sudanese former diplomat Abdelwahab El-Affendi (2005), the 'question of whether liberal democracy can be given a "truly" Islamic basis, is unanswerable'.

Nevertheless, the varied nature of the recent Islamic resurgence has created tensions and contradictions within the religion. One analyst asserts that historically 'during periods of political decline the ideals of Islam have been stressed in order to combat the threat of change'. Abubaker Bagader (1994: 118) cites four factors which he believes partly explain the rise in significance of Islam in the 1980s and 1990s: (1) the success of the Muslim Brothers and the Islamic revolution in Iran, which confronted the modern world with a new set of ideas; (2) the decline of Arab nationalism, continuous social and economic crisis and the diminishing legitimacy of the ruling elites; (3) the uneven modernization process in the Arab world, which dislocated traditional groups and created differentiated social classes; and (4) the increasing spread of secularization among the elites of most Arab Muslim societies.[1] Islamic responses to these challenges, however, manifested themselves in different groupings, some revolutionary, some spiritual, some ritualistic, some intellectual. Bagader sees a distinction between traditionalist groups which emphasize religious faith, piety and codes of dress and behaviour; the Muslim Brotherhood parties that present an overtly political view; and the radical groups which reject gradual change in favour of extreme confrontation, at times with other Muslim groups, in order to establish an Islamic state. Certainly, some intellectuals and writers refer to Islam as dynamic and malleable, open to interpretation and carrying a propensity for conflict between traditionalists and reformers within the religion itself (Goytisolo 1996).

However, behind these pluralist elements lies the belief that, to a greater or lesser extent, Muslim societies have forgotten *taqwa* (fear of Allah and righteousness). Once *taqwa* is lost, a condition of disobedience and transgression appears within societies. The great problem for Islam is how to conduct a return to a state of *taqwa* (Ahmad 1991). There are also concerns about *al-'adl* (justice) contained within Islamic scripture.

Shari'a law

Notions of justice often invoke discussions of legal systems and they can vary in form, structure and objective. When viewed more generally in the context of the question 'What is law?', the answers may seem contradictory:

1 the formal expression of conventional morality, or of that part of it the state should enforce;
2 a system of rules by which the interests of a dominant class are safeguarded;
3 a system of rules held to be binding or obligatory;
4 a system of rules aimed at realizing justice;
5 a system of rules discoverable by reason;
6 the commands of the sovereign authority;
7 what judges decide in the courts;
8 a system of rules backed by coercive sanctions.

[handwritten: no mention here of popular sovereignty; (common law)]

Islamic *shari'a* law connects to the idea of 'spiritual law' and a 'system of divine law' and a 'way of belief and practice' in the Qur'an (Abdul Mannan Omar, *Dictionary of the Holy Qur'an*, cited in http://en.wikipedia.org.wiki/Sharia). Yet it, too, has aroused much debate, with some legal scholars asserting that its basic concept has been 'thoroughly confused in legal and common literature', the basic difficulty being the conflation of that which is revealed within Islam and that which is not (L. Ali Khan cited ibid.). Tables 2.2 and 2.3 outline the Foundation of Islam and the individual's essential relationship with Allah.

The Foundation of Islam includes two aspects:

• the authoritative sources: the Qur'an and the *Sunnah*;
• the three basic concepts: *al-Tawhid* (the Oneness of Allah), *al-Risalah* (Prophethood) and *al-Akhira'* (the life hereafter).

Tables 2.4 and 2.5 set out the two authoritative sources of Islam, the Qur'an and the *Sunnah*. The fundamental concept of *al-Tawhid* (the Oneness of Allah) emphasizes the 'pivotal place' Allah has in a Muslim's life, which means 'sovereignty belongs only to Allah'. The 'unity of mankind' is stressed, which 'opens up the horizons of universalism'. *Al-Risalah* (the Prophethood) demands obedience

Table 2.2 The Foundation of Islam

Life hereafter	The *Sunnah*	The Prophethood (divine guidance)	The Qur'an	Oneness of Allah

Source: Surty (1995).

Table 2.3 The individual's relationship with Allah

Pilgrimage	Self-purification and pleasure of Allah	Fasting	Supplication	Welfare due	Repentance	Prayer	Remembrance of Allah	Faith

Source: Surty (1995).

Table 2.4 The authoritative sources of Islam – the Qur'an

The Qur'an literally means 'the reading' and 'the collection'. It is the collection of the essence of all revealed scriptures of the past

It is the Word of Allah and a universal message containing final guidance to mankind for all times

It was revealed to the Prophet Muhammad during some 23 years of his prophetic mission in the Arabian peninsula. It has been preserved in original Arabic both in writing and in memory throughout the last 1400 years

The Qur'an contains 114 suras (chapters), 6616 ayahs (verses), and 77,934 words. It is regarded as an undisputed authority from which laws, ethics and other Islamic concepts emerge

Faith and performance of righteous deeds stem from the Qur'an

The Qur'an lays down that all human beings are born innocent and are accountable for their deeds

The Qur'an prohibits intoxicants, interest, gambling, adultery, oppression and corruption

The Qur'an commands that the followers of other faiths must be tolerated and treated with kindness

Source: Surty (1995).

Table 2.5 The authoritative sources of Islam – the *Sunnah*

The conduct, example, actions and sayings of the last Prophet and Messenger of Allah, Muhammad, are considered as his *Sunnah*

The Qur'an assigns to the Prophet four distinct roles:

1 He is the expounder of the Qur'an (16:44)
2 He is the legislator (7:157)
3 He is to be obeyed (3:32, 132; 4:49, 64, 80)
4 He is the model for Muslim behaviour (33:21; 59:7; 4:65)

The Qur'an regards obedience to the Prophet as obedience to and love for Allah (3:31). Whatever the Prophet regards lawful and whatever he prohibits must be followed (59:7; 24:51).

The Prophet is extremely concerned for the welfare of all mankind. He is compassionate and merciful (9:128; 33:45; 34:28).

The Prophet does not conceal any revelation of his Lord and he is the first to surrender to the Divine will (5:67; 6:14).

The Qur'an is also a book of principles and translated in the *Sunnah*, which serves as the commentary on the Qur'an. It is the record of the implementation of Qur'anic teachings. Hadith literature reflects the method the Prophet adopted in order to change the course of the lives of his companions for the upliftment of human rights, values and virtue on the foundation of equality, justice, truth and Divine law.

Source: Surty (1995).

to the Prophets, whose aims were to 'establish a proper relationship between man [*sic*] and Allah'. Muhammad was the last Universal Prophet. The *al-Akhirah* (life hereafter) emphasizes 'the paramount importance of life hereafter for mankind'. Human beings must be aware of their duties to Allah 'and fellow creatures in the temporary worldly life'. The eternal life, the hereafter, includes:

- the Day of Resurrection;
- the Day of Judgement;
- Paradise;
- Hell.

Death finally closes the worldly period and the journey begins to the life hereafter (Surty 1995: 7–11).

The comprehensive nature of *shari'a* law is due to the belief that it must provide all that is necessary for a person's spiritual and physical well-being (http://wikipedia.org/wiki/Sharia; see Table 2.6). Yet the conception of law in Islam appears to be authoritarian: 'The Law, which is the constitution of the Community, cannot be other than the Will of God, revealed through the Prophet.' According to one analyst, this is an Islamic version of a Christian principle, namely, that 'the will of the sovereign is law' since God is the sole Head and Legislator. Consequently, 'to violate the law, or even to neglect the law, is not simply to infringe a rule of social order – it is an act of religious disobedience, a sin and involves a religious

Table 2.6 Shari'a law

The acts of worship, *'ibadat*	Human interaction – worldly transactions, *mu'amalat*
1 Ritual purification (*wudu*)	1 Financial transactions
2 Prayers (*salah*)	2 Endowments
3 Fasting (*sawm* and Ramadan)	3 Laws of inheritance
4 Charities (*zakat*)	4 Marriage, divorce and child care
5 Pilgrimage to Mecca (*hajj*)	5 Foods and drinks, including ritual slaughtering and hunting
	6 Penal punishments
	7 Warfare and peace
	8 Judicial matters

penalty' (Gibb 1950: 4–5). H. A. R. Gibb believes the *shari'a* was never 'erected into a formal code' as such because in origin it was based upon heterogeneous legal practices: 'Arab customary law, the commercial law of Mecca, the agrarian law of Medina, elements of Syro-Roman law taken over after the conquests, supplementing or accommodated to the Qur'an' (ibid.).

By the tenth century, however, Islamic legal thought had evolved into four official schools which had each developed around a leading jurisprudent in various regional centres of the empire. They differed from each other in methodology and degree of flexibility of interpretation of the *Sunnah*. The legal scholars, *fuqaha* (*fiqh*, jurisprudence), decided upon *ijma'*, which was effectively an agreement between themselves. *Ijtihad* (interpretive thinking) had been long associated with Islamic law but at this time it was narrowed so that only the *fuqaha* could practise it authoritatively. The historian Ibn Khaldun (1332–1406) described this development as a door being closed to further analysis: 'There was no new *fiqh* (legal thinking) and anyone who claimed he was capable of *ijtihad* was excluded and discriminated against. All of Islamic law now consisted of these four' (cited in Sonn 1990: 40). Saudi Arabia's interpretation of *shari'a* law as guided by Wahhabism, a form of Islam that is spreading in Africa, is illustrated in Box 2.6. The notion of 'law' can be problematic in African states with authoritarian political structures and leadership. Under these circumstances, *shari'a* law, with its formal rules and duties, may seem acceptable and perhaps even necessary. For example, the introduction of strict Islamic courts in Somalia in 2007 was welcomed by many because they imposed a form of law on a chaotic society.

Punishment and *jihad*

A focus on the position of women reveals a 'widely prevalent tendency to subsume the identity of women underneath the shibboleth of a heavily patriarchal construct of the Muslim "self"' (Chatterjee 2006: 61).[2] Yet according to Al-Sadeg Al-Mahdi, the President of Sudan's Umma Party and one-time leader of the country, this tendency is not connected to Islam. The Qur'an, he argues, is concerned with 'diversity and humanity' and seeks to 'empower the human being'. From an Islamic perspective he itemizes its 'true vision':

Box 2.6 The origins of the judicial system of Saudi Arabia

Origins

The administrative and application of the judicial system of Saudi Arabia illustrates the importance of the *ulama* (religious leaders). When King Abdul Aziz extended his rule over the western part of the kingdom, the Hijaz, he was faced with the existence of three separate judicial systems:

1   Hijaz, an Ottoman orientation;
2   Najd, in which an Amir would act as final arbiter of the law;
3   tribal law.

In 1927 a Royal Decree aimed at unifying the judicial system and classified its institutions into three hierarchical categories:

1   Courts of Expedition;
2   *Shari'a* Courts;
3   Commission of Judicial Supervision.

The Wahhabi movement

Muhammad bin Abdul Wahhab travelled through Arab lands during the period of the Ottoman Empire and became aware of the deviations from the true Islamic faith. His purpose was to re-establish Islam in its pure form. The Wahhabi movement is associated with the formation of Saudi Arabia by King Abdul Aziz Al Sa'ud, who claimed the Wahhabi creed was not a new sect but was based on the Qur'an and the *Sunnah*. However, that first alliance between Sa'ud and Wahhab was both political and religious in nature, that is, the state and religion in Saudi Arabia are inseparable; it is an example of an Islamic state governed by the Qur'an. The *ulama* play an influential part in the following fields of government:

1   the judicial system of Saudi Arabia;
2   the implementation of the rules of *shari'a*;
3   religious guidance groups that have affiliated offices across the country;
4   Islamic legal education and theology at all levels;
5   religious jurisprudence;
6   preaching and guiding the nation;
7   supervision of girls' education;
8   religious supervision of all mosques in the country;
9   preaching of Islam abroad;
10   scientific research;
11   the handling of legal cases in courts according to Islamic law.

Source: al-Farsy (1990: 36).

- There is a need to understand Islam. Muhammed was a messenger of humanitarianism not sectarianism.
- There must not be confrontation. There must be co-existence and a pluralism of religion.
- Islam must not exclude the 'other'; it should agree terms with others.
- The Qur'an cannot be a country's constitution. There needs to be a more nuanced interpretation of the Qur'an.
- *Jihad* is not a form of attack.

(Al-Mahdi 2006)

Interestingly, Al-Mahdi's brother-in-law and political opponent, Hasan al-Turabi, has shifted from his former hard-line stance on Islam to one that is more nuanced and 'contextualized' in its understanding of the 'power of texts in modern Islamic thought' (Tayob 2006: 13).

Certainly, real concerns have been expressed about the manner in which Islam is being represented. It has been argued that Islam could be 're-constituted' within the Middle East and North Africa region, the centre of the faith, which would send a message to co-religionists elsewhere and would clearly have a significant impact on African Muslims. The Qur'an 'can be a reference for a constitution as it has laid down some values'; but, Al-Mahdi (2006) emphasized, the Qur'an 'is interpreted by the human mind'. The whole process of energizing a contemporary discourse within Islam is currently being initiated by analysts in Turkey, who are considering the earlier writings of jurists and academics. If Islam is to be a dynamic and evolving faith, contradictory texts require attention. For the late Asaf A. A. Fyzee (2007: 154) the theology of Islam had to be 're-examined in all its aspects' and modern philosophy, ethics, psychology and logic should be applied 'to formulate and restate its essential dogmas'. Others argue, however, that each era in human history has its own predominant logic and rationale that 'manifests itself in the philosophy, culture, art and law' of that period. Consequently, 'Islamic law is not an exception. Islamic law is not a sacred or a mystic science, but a human science that is produced and developed by people and influenced by the predominant culture and rationale of each era in Islamic history' (Guney-Ruebenacker 2006). The variation in the interpretation and implementation of Islamic law in contemporary Muslim societies is attracting interest, not least because the punishments prescribed under *shari'a* can be seen as cruel and barbaric. For example, the penalty for theft, in accordance with the Qur'an and several *hadith*, is the amputation of hands or feet, or cross-amputation, in which both a leg below the knee and an arm below the elbow are amputated, depending on the severity of the offence. In Sudan, hospitals carry out cross-amputation and the practice has been defended by the ruling elite and judiciary.[3] The stoning of women accused of adultery, domestic punishments, gender differentiation and the execution of Muslims who have converted to other faiths have also taken place in Nigeria. However, some are beginning to engender a critical engagement with Islam by reclaiming its intellectual inheritance. The indispensable role of *ijtihad* (independent legal reasoning) has been invoked as a means through which the religion can evolve, through communication and open-minded discussion (bin Talal 2006). There are also calls for the restoration of the separation between the 'timeless (ethical–moral) and changing (society-related) elements' within Islam. By taking the former out of the sphere of politics, religious ideas can become 're-sacralized and freed from the secular constraints of social reality' (Hamzawy 2001: 22).

Notions of a 'progressive' Islam have been revisited and renewed with an emphasis on pluralism, social justice and human rights. Muslim progressives draw on the 'strong tradition of social justice from within Islam' (Guney-Ruebenacker 2006), for example in sources such as the Qur'an and *hadith*. There is also an interest in the roles human beings have played in historical periods and their relationship to Islam: 'religious ideas evolve, moving in time and space, through history and place' (Chebel 2006). The charge has been made that militants have 'distorted the image of Islam' by creating 'movements of terror' and seeking to 'silence' anyone who disagreed with their religious interpretation (Al-Ashmawi 2007: 180). Central to this discourse is an analysis of *jihad* (to strive or struggle) and its understandings within modern Islam. Although Max Weber referred to Islam as a 'warrior religion' (Roth and Wittich 1968a: 573) and, historically, aggressive warfare has occurred in the name of the religion, the actual status of *jihad* now requires re-examination. In fact, some analysts have called for *jihad* to be 'declared useless and obsolete' as it must be possible to replace 'war with peace' (Chebel 2006). *Jihad* has been viewed as a 'process of revolutionary struggle initiated to achieve the objectives of Islam' (S. Abul A'la Mawdudi cited in Choueiri 1990: 138). Yet the environment that existed both before and at the time of the Prophet Muhammad must be seen in context. Early reports of Arabs describe their weaponry as 'a bow, carried at the right side – a long bow, which assumed a reverse curve when unstrung' (Herodotus 2003: 440). They were viewed as 'predatory' and the 'ability to get the better of others by taking their camels, abducting their women, killing their men or slitting the throats of their defenceless slaves was highly prized' and 'boasted of' in poetry (Crone 1998: 3). In fact, the depiction of Arabs in both their own writings and that of Romans in 700 BC was one of preparedness for conflict: 'all alike are warriors of equal rank, half nude . . . ranging widely with the help of swift horses and slender camels'; 'we returned home with women captive behind us on our camel saddles, and with a booty of camels'. Another Arab poet referring to raids against other tribes asserts 'we slew in requital for our slain an equal number of them, and carried an unaccountable number of fettered prisoners' (cited ibid.: 4–5; see also Horden and Purcell 2004). Muhammad's monotheism 'transcended tribal divisions and called upon the Arabs to unite in a single community, worshipping the same God, following the same law and fighting the same holy war (*jihad*)' (Crone 1998: 10). Yet the word *jihad* does not mean war in the sense of 'launching an offensive'; it essentially means undergoing a 'struggle'. One analyst argues it is important to remember that in the time of Muhammad 'an atmosphere of militancy prevailed in Arab society', yet the Prophet always sought to avoid conflict (Khanam 2007). During the post-Muhammad period classical jurists divided *jihad* into two forms: 'aggressive' and 'defensive', the former seeking to conquer and control, the latter only prepared to defend Muslim lands from invasion (Jackson 2007: 399). However, Sayyid Qutb (1906–66) reasserted the notions of militant *jihad*, looking to the Qur'an for guidance:

> They ought to fight in the way of God who have sold the life of this world for the life of the Hereafter; and whoever fights in the way of God and is killed or becomes victorious, to him shall We give a great reward. Why should not you fight in the way of God for those men, women and children who have been oppressed because they are weak.
>
> (3:74–76, cited in Donoghue and Esposito 2007: 415)

Other analysts, however, call for a 'revival' of the 'old' Islam and a rejection of 'militant and political' interpretations of the religion in favour of 'a version of Islam based on *Qur'anic* notions of peace, mercy and the love of mankind' (Khanam 2007: 2):

> and God calls to the home of peace.
>
> (10:25)

It is clear that interpretation is the key to discovering the essential qualities of Islamic teaching. The imam Ibn al-Qayyim distinguished three aspects of *jihad*:

1 *Jihad* against one's soul
2 *Jihad* against the devil
3 *Jihad* against infidels and hypocrites

(cited in Al-Farag 2007: 422)

It is, of course, for contemporary Muslim jurists to analyse those precepts in the light of human values which are widely shared in today's world. Africa has long been the receptacle for different modes of Islamic expression. Perhaps the time has come for African Muslims to speak up and contribute to the debate about the nuanced interpretations of their religion as African Christians have done. The potential impact on Islam in Africa could be profound and far-reaching.

3   Development

The marginalization of the African continent over the past three decades has been characterized by slower economic growth than in other developing regions together with lower and less efficient investment levels. As Table 3.1 demonstrates, sub-Saharan Africa lags behind other developing nations in Central and Latin America as well as in Asia.

Major international statements on African development have been made in recent years. In the 1990s, for example, the then Secretary General of the United Nations, Boutros Boutros-Ghali, asserted that economic progress in Africa was dependent on cooperation and investment in human resources. The solution to Africa's problems would be found in debt reduction, regional integration and the diversification of economies. These main objectives could be achieved as part of patterns of coordination and regionalization with national and international agencies. The United Nations Focus on the New Agenda for Development in Africa stressed that regional aid was preferable to bilateral aid because water, electrification, air transport, communications, hospitals and health delivery systems all called for region-wide solutions. Economic progress demanded both access to information and an informed population (United Nations 1993). The International Development Association (IDA), an affiliate organization of the World Bank, focused its attention on the 'world's poorest nations' and US$22 billion were made available for aid between 1993 and 1996 (World Bank 1993). Its policy was to build on poverty reduction, economic reform, sound management and environmentally sustainable development. The IDA's approach to poverty reduction was twofold: first, it supported a pattern of economic initiatives which attempted to provide efficient employment and income opportunities for the poor; second, it supported investment in people in the areas of primary health, education and nutrition. Investments in family planning and increasing women's access to education were also highlighted. Countries also received assistance, for example a revamped management structure for Guinea's power utility and an autonomous electricity corporation in Guinea-Bissau.

Yet it was not long before Boutros-Ghali was cautioning against 'grandiose schemes' and African leaders were warning that 'underdevelopment in productive forces, i.e. science, technology, managerial capacity and skilled labour', would inhibit any real economic progress in the continent (President Museveni of Uganda cited in Deegan 1996: 165). These were prescient views but not necessarily ones that Western donor communities wanted to hear. 'Transparency' and 'governance' were the keynotes of the decade, combined with the push for elections. South Africa's transition from apartheid to democratic rule in 1994 gave international observers considerable encouragement and fostered a belief that Africa as a whole could adopt political reforms. Yet views differed between the World Bank's notion of 'good governance', France's support for 'participative democracy' and Britain's emphasis on neo-liberal democracy. For the World Bank, 'good governance' implied sound public management conducted within a legal framework, with development and accountability to be included in economic and financial spheres. Although all donors recognized the importance of the 'rule of law' France and Britain stressed civil and political rights from slightly different angles: decentralization favoured by the French and greater openness in government desired by the UK.[1] Nevertheless, by the 2000s, although numerous elections had taken place

Table 3.1 Values and shares of merchandise exports and imports (%)

Exports	1980	1985	1990	1995	2000	2004	2005	2006
Sub-Saharan Africa	3.7	2.5	1.9	1.4	1.5	1.7	1.8	1.8
Developing economies: America	5.5	5.5	4.1	4.4	5.6	5.1	5.4	5.7
Developing economies: Asia	18.0	15.6	16.9	21.0	23.8	26.0	27.6	28.3
Developing economies excluding China	28.5	24.0	22.4	24.7	27.9	27.2	28.6	28.7
Imports								
Sub-Saharan Africa	3.1	2.0	1.5	1.4	1.3	1.5	1.5	1.5
Developing economies: America	6.0	4.1	3.5	4.8	5.9	4.7	4.8	5.0
Developing economies: Asia	13.1	15.1	15.9	21.4	20.8	23.4	24.2	24.8
Developing economies excluding China	22.8	20.9	20.8	26.1	25.3	24.5	25.2	25.6

Source: www.unctad.com/en/docs/tdstat31.

across the African continent, many states still lacked transparency, accountability and economic progress.

Clearly, it was time the United Nations reviewed its 1991 New Agenda for Development policy. As one UN official claimed in 2003: 'In spite of all its words, nothing had been achieved.' So what had gone wrong? Three critical spheres were identified as having undermined the UN's strategy in Africa:[2]

- Peace and security within Africa were essential for development to take place.
- The reliance on free market economics had been unwise – African states had to decide which economic policy to adopt.
- There had been an absence of African 'ownership' of policies in that strategies were seen to be imposed externally.

From the failure of the 1991 UN New Agenda emerged a new creation jointly devised by certain African states and the G8 countries: the New Partnership for Africa's Development (Nepad).

New Partnership for Africa's Development (Nepad)

Launched in 2001 and enthusiastically embraced by the British government, Nepad focused on a number of sectors: education; health; regional infrastructure including transportation links; agriculture; market access; and preservation of the environment. The Initial Plan of Action announced in Abuja outlined a series of measures for mobilizing and utilizing resources, which included paying attention to public resource management and improving the performance of Africa in global trade.[3] Japan took the first initiative to organize the dialogue between leaders from the G8 (UK, Canada, France, Germany, Italy, Japan, the Russian Federation and the United States) and the South on the eve of the Okinawa Summit held in July 2000, by inviting three presidents from African countries: South Africa, Nigeria and Algeria. This new dialogue between African leaders and the G8 continued during the Genoa 2001 summit. It was the proposed 'development partnership' between the world's richer, donor nations and those of the African continent that was the basic attraction of the Nepad project.[4] It was actively promoted by South Africa's President Thabo Mbeki and co-sponsored by Presidents Olusegun Obasanjo of Nigeria, Abdelaziz Bouteflika of Algeria, Abdoulaye Wade of Senegal and Hosni Mubarak of Egypt. African leaders acknowledged that the continent faced 'grave challenges', the most urgent of which were the 'eradication of poverty and the fostering of socio-economic development, through democracy and good governance' (Nepad Secretariat 2002: 3–4).

Yet the 'African condition', long acknowledged by members of Africa's political elites, was defined as 'drought, debt, desertification, disease and death' (Nigeria's President (formerly General) Obasanjo cited in Venter 2003: 22). If meaningful development was to be achieved, key constraints to economic, social and political progress had to be recognized:

- Africa's climate and geography, particularly for landlocked, natural resource-poor economies with high transport costs and vulnerable, semi-agricultural economies;
- limited diversification, leaving Africa largely dependent on economically volatile primary commodities for export;
- negative perceptions by investors who tend to extrapolate damaging media information about any individual country to all countries in a region;
- high levels of indebtedness which can lead to human capital flight and, consequently, limited capacity, both physical and human;
- weak governance, lack of accountability and transparency, which can lead to patronage and short-term focus on control of resources rather than delivery of public goods;
- conflict, which causes instability and hampers growth.[5]

These problems are still challenging but the emphasis of Nepad was on African 'ownership' of policy, that is, Africa would take possession of the strategy and engage more pro-actively in the global environment. In order to achieve this Africa needed to implement a series of reforms which would be supported by the G8 through a combination of external debt relief and improved access to markets in the developed world. The African Union (formerly Organisation of African Unity) adopted Nepad as a framework for development. So what were the key reforms that African countries were urged to uphold? See Box 3.1.

Certainly, Africa's position in the world has been of concern with some prominent figures declaring ominously that 'without solving the Africa issue there will be no global success in the 21st Century' (Domichi 2003). The rationale for this view was based on a number of facts: sub-Saharan Africa constitutes 10 per cent of the population, 20 per cent of the land surface and a quarter of the countries of the world (Africa Insight 2002). But it is not only the issue of economic growth that worries the international community; the post-9/11 problems of global security have meant that regional conflicts, political instability and collapsing states create a breeding ground for terrorist activity especially in a continent where Islamic extremists had been active long before the events of 2001 (see Chapter 9). Clearly, then, Africa is a source of anxiety. The question is: can it become a source of hope and potential? There was much expectation of Nepad and many leading business executives were 'very enthusiastic' about the policy (Stuart 2003). Yet the demands on African states are considerable, none more so than in the political measures that Nepad recommended be adopted in order to ensure the promotion of democracy and good governance. African states signing up to Nepad had to demonstrate that their political systems included the points outlined in Box 3.2.

Political reform was only one dimension of Nepad; other important elements identified as preconditions for sustainable development included peace and security, improved economic and corporate governance, and the importance of sub-regional and regional integration for development. Regional coordination between groups of countries within the continent was viewed as a hopeful way of motivating and encouraging regeneration and change. There were some indications of improvements in gross domestic product growth rates as outlined in Table 3.2. The Common Market for Eastern and Southern African States (COMESA) – including countries such as Angola, Eritrea, Ethiopia, Kenya, Malawi and Uganda – had the objective of expanding its economies in Africa through regional cooperation. South Africa is a key player within the Southern Africa Development Community (SADC), which includes Malawi, Mozambique, Tanzania, Zimbabwe, Namibia, Botswana and Angola.

Nepad also identified certain priority sectors that African states should address:

- improvement of infrastructure, such as general transport infrastructure and energy; access to information and communication technology; and water and sanitation;
- human resource development, including poverty reduction, improved access to education and measures to reverse the brain drain;
- improvement of all health services;
- improvement of the performance and productivity of the agricultural sector to ensure food security and general economic development;
- protection of the environment.

Nepad's Africa Peer Review Mechanism

One very important feature of Nepad was the voluntary Africa Peer Review Mechanism (APRM), established in April 2003, which can be adopted by any member of the AU as a self-monitoring instrument. Initially, 16 African states signed up to the APRM, which aimed to 'ensure that the policies and practices of participating states conform to the (mutually) agreed . . . values, codes and standards contained in Nepad's Declaration on Democracy, Political, Economic and Corporate Governance' (Nepad Secretariat 2002: 9). Operationally, the APRM was directed and managed by a five- to seven-member Eminent Persons' Panel, to be appointed by the heads of states and government of participating countries.

Box 3.1 Nepad's key reforms for African states

- The establishment of civil order and more democratic government
- The prevention and reduction of conflict throughout Africa
- Wider respect for human rights
- Increasing investment in human resources, especially in the health and education sectors
- Policies aimed at diversifying African economies and boosting trade with the rest of the world
- Ensuring that Africa is in a position to adopt new technologies and able to combat disease, e.g. HIV/AIDS, malaria

Members of the Panel serve for a period of up to four years, retiring on rotation. Its members are Africans with expertise in political governance, macro-economic and public financial management, and corporate governance (ibid.: 9). Four types of review existed:

1   The base review is carried out within 18 months of a country becoming a member of the APRM process.
2   A periodic review takes place every two to four years.
3   Additionally, a member country can request a review that is not part of the periodically mandated reviews.
4   Early signs of impending political or economic crisis in a member country would also be sufficient cause for instituting a review.

The peer review process should spur countries 'to consider seriously the impact of domestic policies, not only on internal political stability and economic growth, but also on neighbouring countries' (ibid.: 10). African countries, of course, are at different levels of development and on joining the APRM process are initially assessed and given a timetable for a programme of action. The programme takes into account the circumstances of the country and consults with a range of people from government, business, politics, academic, trades unions, professional and civic communities. The review team's draft report is first discussed with the government concerned with regard to the accuracy of the findings and how identified shortcomings might be addressed. At this critical stage, the report needs to be clear on a number of points. First, does the government have the will to take the

---

Box 3.2 Nepad's good governance

All states must:
- uphold the rule of law
- adhere to a governmental separation of powers, including an independent judiciary and an effective legislature
- promote the equality of all citizens before the law, including equality of opportunity for all
- safeguard individual liberties and collective freedoms, including the right to form and join political parties and trade unions
- acknowledge the inalienable right of the individual to participate, by means of free, credible and democratic processes, in periodically electing leaders for a fixed term of office
- uphold probity in public life
- combat and eradicate corruption
- ensure free expression including media freedom
- facilitate the development of vibrant civil society organizations
- strengthen electoral commissions, administration and management

Table 3.2 Annual average growth rates of real gross domestic product (%)

African economic regional groupings	1980–90	1990–2000	2000–2005	2005–6
COMESA	4.0	3.1	4.4	7.8
ECOWAS	3.6	2.0	5.1	4.6
SADC	1.9	2.1	3.9	5.6
UEMOA	2.8	3.7	3.3	3.2

Source: UNCTAD (2007).

COMESA: Common Market for Eastern and Southern African States; ECOWAS: Economic Community of West African States; SADC: Southern Africa Development Community; UEMOA: West African Economic and Monetary Union (eight-member Francophone economic grouping within ECOWAS).

necessary steps and decisions to remedy the situation? Second, what resources are necessary to take corrective action? Third, how much of these can the government itself provide, and how much is to come from external sources? Fourth, given the necessary resources, how long will the process of improvement take? Ultimately, the report is formally and publicly tabled within the committee structure of the African Union.

The APRM was hailed as a 'made in Africa' approach and a means by which the continent could find 'African solutions to African problems.' The 2006 APRM report on Kenya identified a number of concerns it recommended the country address: 'poverty and wealth distribution; land reform; corruption; constitutional reform; gender equality and youth unemployment' (EISA 2008b). Countries should be able to learn from the experiences of other neighbouring or regional states when they require support and guidance, but, equally, they must be prepared to enact the recommendations. Kenya's failure to do so contributed to the violence following the 2007 elections. Zimbabwe, for example, after President Mugabe, will need to re-establish itself economically and socially. In 2007, the country's inflation rate stood at a 'staggering 7,635 per cent'. Escalating prices and shortages of food then resulted in people being killed in stampedes following the 'frenzied storming' of a truck carrying sugar (Ndebele 2007: 71–74). Economists have outlined ways in which the Zimbabwean economy could be reformed as outlined in Box 3.3. The APRM may result in the engagement of constructive dialogue between states and offers of practical advice to countries struggling with economic and governance shortcomings. But if it is to address the very real political, social and economic practices of political elites some straight talking is required. The APRM Kenyan report was prepared to call for 'transformational leadership' that recognized the 'need for a dramatic change in society' and was generally regarded as a hard-hitting analysis of the challenges facing the country. But if political elites fail to listen the whole question of development is undermined, especially now that political reform is viewed as the *sine qua non* for economic regeneration.

The African Union's adoption of Nepad and its promotion of conflict resolution, governance and reform are ambitious and potentially far-reaching. However,

Box 3.3   Zimbabwe: possible economic reforms

- A revival of the agricultural sector: agriculture is important both for domestic consumption and the generation of foreign exchange. Zimbabwe has produced well qualified graduates in agriculture who, together with farmers, know what is required to improve productivity.
- Resuscitate the manufacturing sector; a lack of foreign exchange has stunted growth in recent years, despite the fact that Zimbabwe boasts a highly educated and flexible labour force.
- Adopt a more efficient trade regime: bottlenecks and impediments to trade need to be removed; simplification of duties and tariffs will stabilize prices and help to bring down the cost of goods.
- Emphasize tourism; this is a quick route to foreign exchange and job creation, with benefits across the services industry. Zambia and South Africa have benefited from the demise of tourism in Zimbabwe over the last decade; political stability would help the country to recover this lost lucrative market.

Source: Nothando Ndebele, Zimbabwean economist, cited in Moyo and Ashurst (2007: 75).

in this call for a new economic and political future for Africa there exists one fundamental problem, that of implementation. What might be the obstacles? First there is the basic issue of sovereignty and the extent to which African states will cede it to regional organizations and the AU. Second is the question of whether or not there is sufficient political will within African states for reforms to be welcomed. Third, what role will be played by the existing ruling elites, many of whom have been seduced by power and wealth for generations and have little concern for democratic legitimacy? In other words, how might the AU tame its political leaders? Ghana was the first country to be peer-reviewed with Kenya following in 2006 and both nations were congratulated for their willingness to submit themselves to such an audit. The process involved countries developing a self-assessment report and a programme of action based on a questionnaire that looked at four themes: democracy and political governance; economic management; corporate governance; and socio-economic development (see Box 3.4).

The embryonic nature of civil society within many African states tends to undermine public participation and engagement in political life. Far too many passive subjects of states need to be transformed into active citizenry who call their governments to account. Interestingly, the governments of only 12 African states discussed Nepad and its potential role with their populations; and even then there have been mixed receptions. The South African National NGO Coalition was pretty scathing about Nepad:

Box 3.4 Countries that have acceded to the African Peer Review Mechanism (APRM)

Ghana, Rwanda, Kenya, South Africa, Algeria, Benin, Burkina Faso, Lesotho, Mauritius, Uganda, Nigeria, Tanzania, Angola, Cameroon, Congo, Egypt, Ethiopia, Gabon, Malawi, Mali, Senegal, Sierra Leone, Sudan, Zambia, São Tomé

> Nepad is the high point of the ideological conversion of African leaders to liberalization. They actually seem to think that globalization is helping Africa, even in the face of all evidence to the contrary. Their answer is that insofar as globalization has not benefited Africa, the fault lies with the Africans themselves. Africans have not put their economic and political governance in place so as to attract a sufficient amount of foreign capital to put Africa on the road to sustainable development. The victims are authors of their own victimization. . . . Nepad not only misses the whole historical experience of Africa, but it also misunderstands the politics of international economics.
>
> (South African National NGO Coalition 2002: 15)

Certainly, Nepad looks to the business sector to energize aspects of African economies which would require governments to introduce reforms to improve their business climate. This would include liberalization of investment, trade and prices; promoting competition; creating deeper and broader financial markets; tax reforms; and ensuring that commercial law protects property rights (Nepad 2005: 7). As Sir Nicholas Stern (2005) asserted, 'sustained economic growth is driven by the private sector' and centres on how the public and private sectors relate to each other. Public/private partnership is crucial to economic development, which will then lead to human development. The objective of a 7 per cent economic growth rate would meet the Millennium Development Goals by 2010 and US$20 billion would be invested in Africa's infrastructure. Four areas of infrastructure have been identified as priorities: energy, sanitation, transport and ICT, because they have such a crucial role in the continent's development (see Box 3.5). A short-term action plan for infrastructure was developed between the African Development Bank, the European Union and the African Union, which highlighted specific needs:

- building a framework for investment, for example, regulations and governance;
- capacity building within African societies;
- implementation of agencies that deal with poverty alleviation, as some states are too poor to integrate;
- encouragement of the private sector.

> **Box 3.5   Significance of infrastructure in African development**
>
> - Regional and international trade are central to economic growth and development.
> - Efficient infrastructure network has the effect of generating new investments in other sectors.
> - African countries, individually, are too small to generate economies of scale found in larger markets.
> - Weak infrastructure linkages condemn the African region to low competitiveness in the global market.
> - Regional infrastructure leads to larger project sizes capable of attracting more private sector investments.
> - Bridging the infrastructural gap will help promote regional integration.

Interestingly, the biggest investor in Africa from within the continent is South Africa but at times even that expansion has been resented by other countries and viewed as curtailing their own industries, e.g. beer production, supermarkets etc. Major corporations are already involved in Business Action for Africa, an umbrella organization designed to unite business interests. It was put together by Shell and includes Rio Tinto, Anglo American, Unilever and De Beers, all of which are major players within Africa. However, it is hoped that indigenous private sectors will also take off. Certainly, a range of countries are now benefiting from high oil prices, e.g. Nigeria, Angola, Equatorial Guinea, Sudan. If Nepad is to succeed in the long term it will have to be paid for and a figure of US$64 billion a year has been flagged. Although the bulk of this huge sum will have to come from outside Africa, domestic resources are also essential and the considerable capital flows out of the continent will have to be stemmed. South Africa and Nigeria have taken a lead regionally but trade must increase between African states as well as with international partners. If words are to be put into action Africa faces enormous challenges but, equally, may benefit from renewed opportunities. However, the extent to which economic reform will be accepted by the peoples of Africa is open to question. When Afrobarometer surveyed attitudes towards market pricing and privatization their respondents were significantly against changes, as outlined in Table 3.3.

Millennium Development Goals (MDG)

At the United Nations Millennium Summit of September 2000 a set of development goals were agreed. The targets, outlined in Box 3.6, are to be achieved by 2015. In 2002 a report prepared by the UNDP and UNICEF at the request of the G8 Personal Representatives for Africa considered whether or not progress had been made in moving towards MDG's objectives. A list of 'targets' and 'indicators' was used to determine if changes had occurred (see Table 3.4). The Report

Table 3.3 Attitudes to economic reform

Reform	In favour (%)	Against (%)
Market pricing	37	54
Privatisation	35	57

Source: Bratton *et al.* (2005).

found that 'inadequate' movement had been made: 'Twenty-three sub-Saharan countries are failing in half or more of the goals; twelve do not have enough data to be assessed. This leaves a mere ten countries on track to meeting half the goals or more' (www.undp.org/mdg/report). By 2005, Kofi Annan, then UN Secretary-General, was more optimistic. The MDGs were different from former policy objectives in that they were:

- People-centred, time bound and measurable
- Based on a global partnership, stressing the responsibilities of developing countries for getting their own house in order, and of developed countries for supporting those efforts
- Received unprecedented political support, embraced at the highest levels of developed and developing countries, civil society and major development institutions such as the World Bank
- Achievable

(www.unstats.un.org.mdg.report2005: 33)

Certainly when viewed globally, poverty rates were falling but this development was being led by Asia. When considering sub-Saharan Africa the picture seemed less encouraging and had deteriorated further with 'millions more' falling into 'deep poverty'. The number of underweight children increased from '29 million to 37 million between 1990 and 2003' (ibid.: 8). Although it was acknowledged that some states had made progress in enrolling more children in primary school, sub-Saharan Africa as a whole 'still has over a third of its children out of school' and in some countries, for example Mali, 'almost none of the 61% of children out

Box 3.6 Millennium Development Goals
- Eradicate extreme poverty and hunger
- Achieve universal primary education
- Promote gender equality and empower women
- Reducing child mortality
- Improve maternal health
- Combat HIV/AIDS, malaria and other diseases
- Ensure environmental sustainability and access to safe water
- Develop a global partnership for development

Table 3.4 Targets and indicators of Millennium Development Goals

Target	Indicators
Halve, between 1990 and 2015, the proportion of people whose income is less than $1 a day	• Proportion of the population below $1 a day
Halve, between 1990 and 2015, the proportion of people who suffer from hunger	• Prevalence of underweight children under 5 years of age • Proportion of population below minimum level of dietary energy consumption
Ensure that, by 2015, children, boys and girls alike, will be able to complete a full course of primary schooling	• Net enrolment ratio in primary education • Literacy rate of 15- to 24-year-olds
Eliminate gender disparity at all levels by 2015	• Ratio of girls to boys in primary, secondary and tertiary education • Ratio of literate females to males among 15- to 24-year-olds
Reduce by two-thirds, between 1990 and 2015, the under-5 mortality rate	• Under-5 mortality rate • Proportion of 1-year-old children immunized against measles
Reduce by three-quarters, between 1990 and 2015, the maternal mortality ratio	• Maternal mortality rate • Proportion of births attended by skilled health personnel
Ensure environmental sustainability	• Proportion of people with sustainable access to an improved water source
Reverse, by 2015, the HIV/AIDS pandemic	• HIV prevalence rates

Source: adapted from www.undp.org/mdg/basics.shtml.

of school have ever attended school consistently' (ibid.). Forty-two per cent of the population of sub-Saharan Africa does not have access to safe drinking water but the real hindrances to development were identified as 'conflict, political instability and the low priority assigned to investments in water and sanitation'. These factors were then exacerbated by high population growth rates (ibid. 10–11).

An initiative by President Bush of the United States, the Millennium Challenge Account (MCA), was described as 'groundbreaking' in that it utilized an 'entire toolbox' of measures to promote political and economic change in Africa: 'diplomacy, development and democracy, assistance, intelligence, sanctions, incentives and trade policy' (www.usembassy.org.uk/forpo551.htlm). Certainly, it offered a new American strategy: a harsher, more businesslike inventory of 'good practice' expected from African states with targets set for economic/political progress. Various benchmarks were set for countries to reach in governance, limits on corruption, increasing political participation, accountability and private sector growth. Any state sponsoring terrorism would not qualify. Among the 16 indicators required for MCA funding are civil liberties, political rights, voice and accountability, rule of law, anti-corruption, primary education completion rates, improvements in health and immunization, trade policy and the institution of regulatory authorities.

The MCA policy represented a rather more direct approach to African states, who would increasingly find themselves forced to adopt responsibility and accountability. As a unilateral American development initiative it is distinct from Nepad. Although the US would like to see Nepad succeed it is fully aware of the deficiencies in the capacity of the AU to deliver on the policy. For MCA, democratic accountability means that African governments must have the capacity for change and accept the existence and viability of legitimate political opposition. In 2007, the US government was providing assistance to 47 countries in Africa and USAID had 23 bilateral missions in Africa. The focus of US foreign assistance to the continent is broadly in line with the Nepad's objectives and the Millennium Development Goals: 'helping African governments, institutions and African-based organisations incorporate good governance principles and innovative approaches to health, education, economic growth, agriculture and environment programmes.' US$519.1 million has been budgeted for 2008 to encourage Africa's economic growth by building on the African Growth and Opportunity Act and the Africa Global Competitiveness Initiative. This initiative seeks to end the cycle of recurrent food crises (www.usaid.gov/sub-saharan_africa). The emphasis in economic terms is on increasing African trade competitiveness and integrating African nations in the global economy. Trade is increasingly being seen as the potential route through which Africa can be reformed politically and economically. To achieve the Millennium Development Goals, 'increased aid and debt relief must be accompanied by further opening of trade' (Annan 2002: 255).

Aid and trade

2005 was viewed by the then UK Prime Minister, Tony Blair, as the 'year of Africa' and he instituted the Commission for Africa (see Box 3.7). The Report of the Commission for Africa stated that in order for income growth to increase towards 7 per cent and to encourage progress towards the Millennium Development Goals, both 'the volume and quality of external aid' to the continent 'must change radically'. Although the report recognized that aid in the past had been 'used badly' it argued that 'strong and measured' aid could be targeted and had to be accompanied by 'continued improvements in governance' (Commission for Africa 2005: 331).

Box 3.7 Membership of the Commission for Africa

Tony Blair, Fola Adeola, K. Y. Amoako, Nancy Kassebaum Baker, Hilary Benn, Gordon Brown, Michel Camdessus, Bob Geldof, Ralph Goodale, Ji Peiding, William Kalema, Trevor Manuel, Benjamin Mkapa, Linah Mohohlo, Tidjane Thiam, Anna Tibaijuka, Meles Zenawi

Undoubtedly, the issue of aid has become contentious with some sceptics viewing the doubling of aid to Africa from US$23 billion in 2004 to US$50 billion annually by 2015 a 'questionable proposition' (Mistry 2005: 665). Yet the Commission wanted to 'radically improve the quality of aid' by:

- Strengthening the processes of accountability to citizens in aid-recipient countries;
- Allocating aid to countries where poverty is deepest and where aid can be best used;
- Providing much stronger support to advancing governance where conditions for effective use of aid are currently weak;
- Channelling more aid through grants, to avoid the build-up of debt;
- Aligning more closely with country priorities, procedures, systems and practices;
- Providing aid more predictably and flexibly over the longer term;
- Protecting countries better against unanticipated shocks.

(Commission for Africa 2005: 301)

Although some of these priorities may seem vague, the Commission accepted that more aid without better governance was actually detrimental to poorer nations (Walton 2005). According to Organisation for Economic Cooperation and Development (OECD) reports, Africa received almost '$1 trillion (in 2005 dollars) in aid between 1965 and 2004. It has paid back $400 billion in debt service, still leaving a net $600 billion or so in aid received over forty years' (cited in Mistry 2005: 666). Although at an aggregate level there seems little to show for it in terms of development, the Commission pointed to Mozambique in the 1990s when 'aid accounted for about 50 per cent of Gross Domestic Product (GDP)' as an example of aid creating growth: 'GDP growth reached an astonishing 12 per cent' (Commission for Africa 2005: 308). P. S. Mistry is a harsh critic of aid and believes that Africa's 'development deficit' has resulted not from a lack of money but rather from the 'the chronic inadequacy of human, social and institutional capital.' If those weaknesses are not addressed 'development in Africa will not occur, no matter how much aid is thrown at it' (Mistry 2005: 666). Certainly, one of the major challenges for the developed world concerns the 'design of aid in order to assure effectiveness within a country.' Unfocused aid works badly in 'weak and unequal settings' and could 'undercut the need to build a domestic government–citizenry contract' (Walton 2005). However, if used as part of poverty reduction strategies, aid can encourage better institutions capable of supplying education and health care, which ultimately develops society. The G8 summit in Edinburgh in 2005 announced the intention to increase aid by US$50 billion per annum in real terms between 2004 and 2010 with annual aid for sub-Saharan Africa doubling from its 2004 level of US$25 billion. There are doubts whether these objectives will be met and warnings were made in 2007 that aid would have 'to increase very substantially in 2008 if there is to be a realistic prospect of meeting the 2010 targets' (http://uk.oneworld.net/guides/aid?gelid=CITLZZiak). UNCTAD's 2006 report on economic development in Africa cast a critical eye over the international aid system and identified flaws including 'high transaction costs; politicisation; lack of transparency; incoherence; unpredictability; and excessive demands placed on the weak institutions of recipient countries.' Far greater 'multilateralization of aid' was called for which would 'reduce unnecessary and costly competition among donors and, thus, greatly reduce administration costs' (www.unctad.org//en/docs/gdsafrica2006la_en.pdf).

In parallel with announcements of increased aid, trade has also been rightly identified as a way in which African states can fully enter the globalized market. The continent accounts for only 3 per cent of world trade and less than 2 per cent of global GDP. Yet trade is important to Africa and represents a trade-to-GDP ratio of 60 per cent (African Development Bank 2005: 6). However, it generally relies on the export of primary sources: crude petroleum, mineral products, natural gas, gold, diamonds, cotton, cocoa, coffee, wood etc. – commodities that are priced on international raw material markets, which operate on supply and demand and are subject to price fluctuations. In 2007 some price fluctuations were significant. The price for crude petroleum, for example, reached the unprecedented figure of US$120 per barrel in May 2008 and some analysts have already commented on the economic potential that high levels of income could give oil-producing states in Africa (Dowden 2007; see Box 3.8). Sub-Saharan Africa produces almost 12 per cent of the world oil supply and accounts for around 19 per cent of US net oil imports (http://tonto.eia.doe.gov/dnav/pet/pet_move_neti_a_epoo). The region's output has increased by 36 per cent during the past 10 years and it is estimated that by 2020 Equatorial Guinea could become Africa's third largest producer with 740,000 barrels a day. Clearly, resources resulting from oil and gas could generate economic growth but, of course, only if there is appropriate financial, accounting and political transparency.

For some analysts Africa must 'learn to exploit global market forces and hitch them to the domestic economy' (Mittelman and Pasha 1997: 244). An obvious example of this would be the financial sector 'call centres' in Kenya which have sprung up over the last decade. Or the niche trade in tropical flowers, exotic fruit and fine wine that has become prevalent in some African states, e.g. South Africa. The Africa–EU Strategic Partnership Strategy outlined at the Lisbon meeting in 2007 aimed to bridge the development divide between Africa and Europe through 'economic cooperation and the promotion of sustainable development in both continents, living side by side in peace, security, prosperity, solidarity and hu-

---

Box 3.8 Oil-producing states in sub-Saharan Africa

Angola (OPEC member, joined December 2006); Cameroon; Chad; Congo; Equatorial Guinea; Mauritania; Nigeria (OPEC member); Sudan; São Tomé and Príncipe; Gabon

man dignity' (EU–Africa Summit 2007: 2). It called for the strengthening of ties between the African Union and the European Union in order to deal with the 'common challenges' of 'peace and security, migration and development, and a clean environment'. The 'political dialogue' between Africa and the EU needed to be 'upgraded' and civil society 'empowered'. Whereas the statement reiterated the need for the continent to meet the MDGs by 2015 it also outlined 'new approaches' that would provide a strategy in the priority areas of:

- peace and security – support the AU Peace and Security Council/counter terrorism and human/drugs trafficking;
- governance and human rights – support the APRM/strengthen the rule of law in Africa;
- trade and regional integration – promote regional economic communities/ improve productive capacities/attract investment/promote business-friendly environment/ develop private sector;
- key development issues – accelerate progress towards MDGs.

The 'new approaches' were intended to change the relationship between the EU and Africa by stressing contemporary mutual concerns rather than former relationships of colonial rule and authority. For the strategic partnership to be successful certain political challenges had to be confronted as outlined in Box 3.9.

When one considers long-term economic growth within African states, however, its record of 'slow and volatile growth reflects a pattern of alternating, identifiable accelerations and declines.' In a revealing study J. S. Arbache and J. Page considered factors which contributed to this trend and found that, 'contrary to the common wisdom, African countries have experienced numerous growth acceleration episodes in the last 30 years, but have also gone through a comparable number of growth collapses that cancelled out most benefits of growth' (Arbache and Page 2007: 21). There was also an 'asymmetry between how growth accelerations and decelerations affect human development outcomes'. Whereas during periods of growth there are relatively small improvements in human development, decelerations have 'important negative impacts on education and health outcomes'. If the Millennium Development Goals are to be achieved Arbache and Page warn that 'preventing growth collapses is essential'. But what causes these downturns? 'Doing the wrong things – poor macroeconomic management, poor structural policies and institutions, and poor governance – appears to be a relatively broadly based predictor of a descent into bad times' (ibid.: 22). Conflict is also a factor in the downturn of a country's growth rate and may also distort economic patterns.[6] Ultimately, however, the 'keys to better long economic performance are both more growth *and* fewer collapses' (ibid.).

One of the more dynamic aspects of African economics now is its trade with China, which has increased at an exponential rate over the past few years and is widely predicted to grow even further (see Table 3.5) This trade is driven by China's need for raw materials and energy in order to forge its economic growth.

Box 3.9 New approaches between Africa and the EU

In order for the Africa–EU Strategic Partnership to be successful it would have:

a To move away from a traditional relationship and forge a real partnership characterised by equality and the pursuit of common objectives
b To build on positive experiences and lessons learned from past relationships
c To promote accurate images of each other, in place of those that are dominated by inherited negative stereotypes
d To encourage mutual understanding between the peoples and cultures of the two continents
e To recognise and fully support Africa's efforts and leadership to create conducive conditions for sustainable social and economic development; implement partner-supported development programmes; underline the importance of strong African political commitment and responsibility
f To work together towards adapting relevant policies and legal and financial frameworks
g To ensure bilateral relations, dialogue and cooperation continue
h To integrate common responses to global challenges
i To encourage the full integration of members of migrant communities/ diasporas in their countries of residence while promoting and facilitating links with the countries of origin in order to provide contributions to the development process

Source: http://ec.europa.eu/development/icenter/repository/EAS2007_joint_strategy, pp. 3–4.

Table 3.5 Africa–China trade

Year	Amount of trade
1999	$2.0 billion
2004	$29.6 billion
2005	$39.7 billion
2007	$42.0 billion
2010 (projected)	$100 billion

Oil, of course, is a major area of expansion but China is also interested in bauxite, uranium, iron ore, aluminium, manganese, cotton etc. It is involved in textile production and manufacturing and 2006 was designated the 'Year of Africa' by the Chinese government. (See Table 3.6.) As a consequence of this trade many Chinese multi-nationals operate within Africa (see Box 3.10). China's expand-

Table 3.6 African exports to China in 2005

Commodity	Exporting country	Amount
Crude oil	Angola	$6.6 billion
	Sudan	$2.6 billion
	Congo	$2.1 billion
	Equatorial Guinea	$1.4 billion
Iron ore	South Africa	$705 million
Cotton	Burkina Faso; Benin; Mali; Côte d'Ivoire; Cameroon; Tanzania	$677 million (total)
Diamonds	South Africa	$502 million
Logs/timber	Gabon; Congo; Equatorial Guinea; Mozambique; Cameroon	$495 million (total)

Source: Sandrey (2006).

Box 3.10 Chinese multinationals operating in Africa

Sinopec; State Gride; China National Petroleum; Industrial and Commercial Bank of China; China Mobile Communications; China Life Insurance; Bank of China; China Southern Power Grid; China Construction Bank; China Telecommunications; Baosteel Group; Sinochem; Agricultural Bank of China; China Railway Engineering; COFCO; China First Automotive Works; Shanghai Automotive; China Railway Construction; China State Construction.

Sources: http://money.cnn.com/magazines/fortune/fortune_archive/2007/08/06; http://money.cnn.com/2007/08/06/news/international/Sudan_khartoum.

---

ing economic relationship with Africa has aroused interest in the West, not least over the situation in Sudan,[7] and China's avowed antipathy to mixing business with politics. Whereas, on the one hand, Chinese-owned firms have been viewed as exploitative, on the other, money is being invested in areas considered too risky or politically unpalatable by Western investors. Certainly, China's reopening and investment in textile manufacturing in Nigeria was welcomed along with other Asian commercial involvement. Yet often it is Chinese workers who are employed by these concerns, not Africans (confidential interview, Kano, 2005). Is this another form of economic colonization? Probably, if African nations become passive participants in the trade. China's multi-nationals, entrepreneurs, investors and workers are ultimately motivated by their own aspirations, which they will work long and hard to achieve. At some stage Africa needs to consider exactly what its own economic aspirations are.

So what of the future development of Africa? Nepad and MDGs may be different ways in which the international community can engage in the development process but ultimately policies must be accepted and implemented by Africans themselves. Lists of priorities may be all very well but will come to naught if not acted upon. Equally, unrealistic or unrealizable goals will remain just that. If African leaders do not accept the challenges of development 'Nepad will merely be added to the other failed initiatives on the scrap-heap of the continent's history' (Loots 2006: 24); a harsh comment but also a sobering one.

4 Democracy

Democracy is not African, European or Asian . . . it is universal.

(Walubiri 2008)

A popular government exists when all the power is in the hands of the people.

(Cicero, *De Re Publica* 1.42)

The masses are a feckless lot – nowhere will you find more ignorance or irresponsibility or violence.

(Herodotus, *The Histories* 2003: 3.81)

leadership based on greed and ambition . . . (by) men committed to the power struggle . . . (who) treated as their prize the public interest to which they paid lip service and, competing by every means to get the better of one another, boldly committed atrocities

(Thucydides, *History of the Peloponnesian War* 3.82)

It is clear that since the sixth century BC, when the first concepts of democracy were born in Athens, its character and form have been much contested. Kleisthenes' reforms in 510 BC proposed that every community would have a formal structure and recognized rights and be represented on a central council. He hoped to bring to Athens *isegoria* (equality of speech) and *isonomia* (equality in law) (Osborne 2005: 299–304). Yet it is perhaps interesting that many communities in Africa today are still awaiting those political privileges despite being subject to various forms of government over decades. While some African states have witnessed reform over the past 15 years, others have lapsed into dysfunction, with the 'public interest' overlooked in favour of antagonistic ethnic, religious or political cliques. Yet democracy continues to be commended and research indicates it is desired by Africans. The Afrobarometer studies measured public attitudes towards democracy, markets and civil society in Botswana, Ghana, Malawi, Namibia, Nigeria and Zimbabwe, and found that democracy 'broadly defined' attained 'wide legitimacy' with 'more than seven out of ten respondents naming it as their preferred form of government' (Afrobarometer 2006). This seems encouraging evidence that a swathe of indigenous Africans is keen to maintain democratic governance. However, as Bratton, Mattes and Gyimah-Goadi emphasize: 'While perhaps a mile wide, support for democracy in Africa may only be an inch deep.' Why? An 'extremely vague understanding of democratic values and procedures' prevails within Africa, together with dissatisfaction with the 'practical performance of elected governments' (Bratton *et al.* 2005: 94).

Such attitudes are concerning for the sustainability of democracy. John Stuart Mill, the nineteenth-century theorist, whose views continue to be relevant, maintained that democracy was inexplicably linked with three fundamental conditions:

> People should be willing to receive it; they should be willing and able to do what is necessary for its preservation; and they should be willing and able to fulfil the duties and discharge the functions which it imposes on them.
>
> (Mill n.d.: 68)

How many polities in Africa are able to meet these conditions today? Did Kenyan ethnic groups protest to defend their democracy after the 2007 elections? Maybe, but they also turned on each other with the loss of over 1000 lives. Have voters in Zimbabwe been empowered over the past 28 years? No, they have been bludgeoned and imprisoned by malign political leadership which has left them fearful and impoverished. For Mill, of course, the participation of a country's citizenry in communal activities, and specifically political affairs, was crucial to the development of representational government. To be denied active participation and be consigned to a life of passivity created a sadly impoverished people deprived of intellectual stimulus and lacking 'any potential voice in their own destiny' (ibid.).

The need for 'voice in their own destiny' should be the preoccupying facet of African politics and be finding expression in strengthened and re-engaged parliamentary sessions; in renewed constitutions; and in active civic organizations and political parties. Robert A. Dahl (1989: 221) believed democracy or 'polyarchy' essentially required extensive competition among individuals, organized groups and political parties for government positions; political participation in the selection of candidates and potential leaders through regular and fair elections; and a level of civil and political liberties that provides a framework for society and permits citizens to express themselves without fear of punishment.

Although elections were vital in that they should reveal the general interests of the community at large and render society more cohesive, Dahl's conditions were far wider than simple electoralism. People were granted rights and responsibilities, freedoms and duties to exercise in a legitimate manner and within agreed boundaries. These views echo those of John Stuart Mill, for whom voting, although a key to participation, was not to be a carefree act of indulgence: the voter was under an absolute 'moral obligation to consider the interests of the public, not his private advantage and to give his vote the best of his judgement' (Mill n.d.).

Voting, or any form of political activity, had to be informed, impartial, thoughtful and self-improving.

Undoubtedly, both structural and cultural components of democracy are necessary. Structures provide the actual institutional mechanics of government without which representative democracy cannot emerge. Yet the cultural component is more complex and may be traditional, fragmented or inconsistent. It is at this point that divisions between 'normative' and 'empirical' accounts of democracy emerge. Normative accounts stress the notion of a 'good' society which looks to human capabilities, potentialities and aspirations, whereas empirical approaches emphasize the applicability and efficacy of political practices in the real world. But how can African politics be conducted in the real world? If political participation is solely confined to electoral choice the result will be 'little more than a series of market relations between individuals' (Macpherson 1973: 158). As Cohen and Arato assert (1995: 7):

> By restricting the concept of democracy to a method of leader selection and to procedures regulating the competition and policy making of elites . . . all criteria are lost for distinguishing between formalistic ritual, systematic distortion, choreographed consent, manipulated public opinion and the real thing.

The 'real thing' would be participatory and politically significant. Equally, if democratic exercises are confined to a periodic vote few opportunities will exist for citizens to act as citizens, that is, to be participants in public life. David Held (1996: 7) elaborates a view of 'democratic autonomy':

> Persons should enjoy equal rights and, accordingly, equal obligations in the specification of the political framework which generates and limits the opportunities available to them; that is, they should be free and equal in the determination of the conditions of their own lives, so long as they do not deploy this framework to negate the rights of others.

Tiro Seeletso of the Independent Electoral Commission in Botswana agrees that civil society should be neutral but recognizes that, in reality, 'NGOs tend to be partial and sometimes linked to political parties' (Seeletso interview 2004). In Botswana's neighbour, the South African National NGO Coalition (SANGCO) accepts that these organizations can be political but maintains that they are making 'a critical contribution' especially with regard to the 'gap between policy and policy implementation'. Nevertheless, there is a need for civil society to take a 'responsible' line: 'they can't simply be oppositionists; they must provide some constructive suggestions or policy proposals' (Farred interview 2002). This often can be difficult in the context of violent elections. For example, during the 2007 presidential electoral campaign in Nigeria there was much criticism by civil society of electoral practices but, as one analyst asserted:

The Parties waged war against one other it was not just electoral fraud. Politicians were gunned down on the streets of Lagos; an Imam was killed in a mosque in Kano . . . there was a crisis and if the cleavages had corresponded to ethnic and religious divisions, the country would be finished.

(Mustapha 2007)

One presidential candidate concluded that invariably Nigerian politics were centred on 'power, corruption and personalities' (Utomi 2007).

So notions of the state and civil society operating under a set of general conditions which would include the open availability of information to ensure informed decisions in public affairs may seem overly optimistic, to say the least, in certain African instances. In these conditions, perhaps Jurgen Habermas's views are more pertinent:

I can imagine the attempt to arrange a society democratically only as a self-controlled learning process. It is a question of finding arrangements which can ground the presumption that the basic institutions of the society and the basic political decisions would meet with the unforced agreement of all those involved, if they could participate, as free and equal.

(Habermas 1979: 186)

Within this form of democracy, there is no onus on individuals to participate directly in the policy-making process so long as they can identify it as legitimate. The question of legitimacy is crucial in any democratic order. According to Jean Blondel (1990: 54), legitimacy stems from individual support when members of the polity 'are favourably disposed towards the political system'. Support may be diffuse and may vary in strength over time. Passive support is widespread, argues Blondel, as large segments of the population often have little contact with national authorities. Seymour Lipset, in a seminal work, maintained that the 'stability of any given democracy depends not only on economic development but also upon the effectiveness and the legitimacy of its political system' (1960: 77). Legitimacy was defined as the capacity of a system to engender and maintain public confidence in its efficacy. Yet the legitimization of political institutions required a degree of knowledge and understanding among the wider population which again recalls John Stuart Mill's conditions for democracy.

The contemporary focus has shifted to the issue of good governance, that is, administrative competence, probity and accountability. This shift is partly conditioned by a combination of factors: the demands of international aid agencies, the changed global political scene and the increasing unacceptability of unelected authoritarian forms of government. So can countries move forward democratically and what role should the international community play? Larry Diamond lays down a 13-point guide to the principles which should underpin development assistance policies and donors. 'A country's development performance' should be linked to its demonstrations of 'political will for reform and good governance'. Countries should be rewarded for demonstrating a 'respect for democratic procedures and freedoms and a willingness to undertake and see through difficult political and economic reforms'. If this is not the case, international donors should 'suspend most governmental assistance and work only with nongovernmental actors'. Corrupt and repressive political elites who misappropriate a country's resources should suffer targeted sanctions while 'advanced industrial countries should work vigorously to negotiate an end to agricultural subsidies that impede African access to their markets' (Diamond 2004: 284–89). These are tough and demanding recommendations which challenge both African states and societies. But they could also work to the continent's advantage, by constraining corrupt regimes and introducing some level of international trade equity. Populations may also become emboldened and more inclined to hold their governments to account. Ultimately and hopefully that could be the path towards meaningful democratic change, but caution is necessary. For some analysts, Western political 'transplants' have been 'quickly rejected by virtually all African societies', including some political dispensations such as 'the modern state, liberal constitutionalism or representative government' (Carbone 2007: 1). And, as much as it might disturb donor agencies, the real world of African politics is less about democratic accountability and rather more concerned with the appropriation of power by elites. Equally, there is a growing tendency among voters to equate democracy with socio-economic gain rather than political rights. In South Africa, for example, voters often highlight jobs, houses, water and electricity as desirable outcomes of democracy, which often leads to a 'yawning gap between declaration and performance' (Friedman 2004: 237; cf. Deegan 1998, 2001). Bratton and Mattes also remind us that, although economic reform is vital, attitudinal surveys reveal a deep antipathy to 'market liberalization' on the grounds that it fails to 'provide employment and development services with the same effectiveness and equity as even corrupt and hollowed-out states' (Bratton *et al.* 2005: 94).

Electoral politics and Africa

Any analysis of elections in Africa over recent periods has to be placed within the wider debate about democracy and its application in Africa (Deegan 2003). Democracy may be a 'learned trade' over time, yet certain critical factors affect electoral efficacy and political reform (see Box 4.1). Over 200 elections have taken place in Africa between 1989 and 2008, in certain countries for the first time. The dynamics of these elections are important, as democracy needs to develop at a local level, particularly in authoritarian or transitional states in which the general population often has very little interaction with national political processes or leaders. Results are mixed; while South Africa has moved forward from the apartheid years, Zimbabwe, for example, has flouted electoral principles. The reported results of the election for parliament's lower house is outlined in Table 4.1 but the results of the presidential election also taking place on the same day, 30 March 2008, were not released at the same time. It is clear that elections themselves arouse contention and conflict within states. In the early 2000s Côte d'Ivoire experienced civil strife following divisive elections; more recently,

Box 4.1 Critical areas for electoral reform

- Reform of political parties necessary
- Need for cohesion of opposition groups
- Better checks on the abuse of incumbency
- Improved management of elections
- Widen voter education and registration
- Extend period for international monitoring/better post–election follow–up
- A precise meaning of 'free and fair' elections needs to be universally understood
- Poorly organized elections can create tension and division
- Ruling parties often do not wish to lose power

Table 4.1 Zimbabwe elections: Parliament lower house, 30 March 2008

Party	Seats*
Zanu PF (ruling party)	96
MDC (opposition)	99
MDC (breakaway faction)	11

Source: EISA (2008a).

* These figures are contested.

Kenya in 2007/2008 experienced upheaval in the wake of contested elections. Even South Africa, widely celebrated for its transition to democracy, now has to consider where a new president will take the country and the extent to which meaningful change has taken place at grassroots level. The number of those in poverty rose from 1.9 million in 1996 to 4.2 million in 2005, based on the number of people who live on less than $1 per day (South African Institute of Race Relations 2007).

The role of international observers is an important component in the scrutiny of the conduct of elections but their stay in a country is often limited to short periods. The concentration on observation can be a problem, and international observers do sometimes prematurely declare an election to be 'free and fair'. Local monitors from civil society and NGOs could be encouraged, thus building much-needed electoral capacity within a country. Yet the term 'free and fair' is often interpreted differently in various circumstances, so observer missions, e.g. international and regional ones, make assorted assessments of election processes. Moreover, events can change very quickly in a post-election environment, for instance the aftermath of Kenya's 2007 elections, especially if the domestic political climate is fluid and the elections contested. Invariably, quite apart from considerable uncertainty about how the international community should react, it is extremely difficult to remedy the impact of a flawed election in countries divided by violence and religious/ethnic division.

Given the debacle of Zimbabwe's 2008 elections it is interesting to record the findings of the various observers of the country's 2002 elections. Although those elections were presented as multi-party, which offered choice on the ballot, in reality, 'force, coercion, legal, regulatory and ideological manipulation and control' operated at every level and conditioned the 'environment in which voting took place and the freedom of voters to cast their votes' (Booysen 2002: 9). Yet the various Observer Missions had mixed and contradictory reports, as outlined in Table 4.2. Some critiques are measured and serious whereas others seem to be perverse. Can elections really be 'legitimate' and reflective of the will of the people when operating under such conditions? Certain missions operate under a brief of reporting only that which is directly observed, as in the case of the South African Observer Mission, whose spokesperson commented on the 2002 Zimbabwe elections: 'We are very satisfied with what we saw . . . What you don't see, you can't describe as bad' (ibid.: 6). This approach was also adopted by a Nigerian observer of the São Tomé and Príncipe legislative elections also in 2002: 'My job involved going around the polling booths seeing . . . how they were opened' (Pawson 2003).[1] Of course, such attitudes make a mockery of electoral scrutiny and even when serious concerns are expressed, as was the case with the Commonwealth Observer Group's assessment, if no action is taken by either regional or continent-wide organizations such as SADC or the African Union, venal political systems corrupt the whole democratic framework, which further degenerates into autocracy. As Box 4.2 indicates, the African Union can articulate fine sentiments but they are inadequate if not supported by censure.

Table 4.2 Zimbabwe elections 2002: observer mission reports

Observer mission	*Observation*	*Bottom-line verdict*
Commonwealth Observer Group (COG)	• Legislative framework manipulated • Disenfranchisement of large numbers through voters' roll • Voter education inadequate • Security forces reluctant to intervene • Paramilitary, militia use systematic intimidation • Preponderance of violence on opposition • ZANU–PF exploitation of state resources • Local observers marginalized • MDC campaign restricted • Rule of law inadequately upheld • Intimidation of opposition media and public media biased • Election structures not independent *Praised: Determination of people to vote* *Polling and counting were peaceful*	• Determination to vote • Election marred by climate of fear and suspicion • Conditions not adequate for free expression of will of electors

Table 4.2 Zimbabwe elections 2002: observer mission reports (continued)

Observer mission	Observation	Bottom-line verdict
SADC Parliamentary Forum	• Voters' roll unacceptably delayed, not verifiable, unfair • Registration unevenly applied • Reduction of polling stations results in slow processes and causes disenfranchisement • Police partisan • Opposition campaigns interrupted • Free movement of party agents compromised • Constraints on dissemination of information • State-sponsored violence against opposition • Lack of access to media by all except ZANU–PF • Lack of independence of Independent Electoral Commission *Praised: Increased number of voting stations in rural areas* *Evidence of tolerance amongst voters* *Voting peaceful*	• Elections in climate of insecurity which began in 2000 • Massive turnout demonstrates commitment to multi-party democracy • Election process cannot be said to adequately comply with the norms and standards for elections in SADC region
South African Observer Mission	• Legislative environment uncertain • Uncertainty about numbers disenfranchised • Voters' roll and reduction in voting stations problematic • Monitoring opportunities inadequate • Absence of election time-table • Election structures should be reviewed • Violence on both sides • Intimidation of opposition • All media partisan *Praised: Security forces cooperative* *Actual election orderly and peaceful* *Polling staff professional* *High turnout*	• Large majority showed belief in credibility of their electoral system • Not adequately free and fair, but should be considered legitimate
Electoral Commissions Forum of SADC	• Violence and intimidation in pre-elections period • Omissions on voters' roll • Low levels of voter education *Praised: Good administration and logistics* *High number of candidates* *Professional counting processes* *Effective security at polling stations*	• Result legitimate and reflects the will of the people • Environment has bearing on the process, but not primary focus of the mission

continued overleaf

Table 4.2 Zimbabwe elections 2002: observer mission reports (continued)

Observer mission	Observation	Bottom-line verdict
South African Parliamentary Observer Mission	• Identified 12 core areas that were found wanting, including the legal-constitutional framework; abductions, beatings, torture and arrests • Voters' roll not available for inspection • Militarization of the election • Displacement of voters • Extraordinary presidential powers • Candidates have unequal access to electorate • Police involvement in screening of voters *Praised: High turnout* *No disturbances during counting* *Agreement (albeit late) on electoral code of conduct*	• Majority Report: Credible expression of the will of the people • Minority Report: People would be betrayed without report of injustices, inequities

Additional, summarized verdicts

Organisation of African Unity/ African Union	'Transparent, credible, free and fair'
SADC Council of Ministers	'In general the elections were transparent, credible, free and fair'
Namibian Government	'Elections were watertight, with no room for rigging'
Nigerian Government	'Peaceful poll'; 'Nothing noticed that tarnished integrity and outcome of the poll'
Norwegian Government	'Major flaws in conduct of election'; 'Failed to meet key, broadly accepted criteria'
United States Government	'Flawed 2002 election'; 'Aggressive strategy to cripple opposition'

Source: Booysen (2002).

Box 4.2 African Union electoral declaration and guidelines

Essential elements of representative democracy include respect for human rights and fundamental freedoms, access to and the exercise of power in accordance with the rule of law, the holding of periodic, free and fair elections based on secret balloting and universal franchise as an expression of the sovereignty of the people, the pluralistic system of political parties and organisations, and the separation of powers and independence of the branches of government.

African Union Declaration on Elections, Democracy and Governance, Article 3, 2003

Electoral observation and monitoring has become an integral part of the democratic and electoral processes in Africa. International, regional and national observers have come to play important roles in enhancing the transparency and credibility of elections and democratic governance in Africa and the acceptance of elections results throughout the continent. Election observation and monitoring issues can also play key roles in diminishing conflicts before, during and after elections.

The African Union, Guidelines for African Electoral Observation and Monitoring Missions, 2002

Source: Principles for Election Management, Monitoring and Observation in the SADC Region, Electoral Institute of Southern Africa, Electoral Commissions Forum 2003.

The relationship between South Africa's African National Congress and Zimbabwe's President Mugabe has long been connected by the liberation struggle and the fight against apartheid. But it has also been affected by the nature of the socio-economic aspirations of South Africa after 1994, that is, a country committed to liberalized, business-led, laissez-faire economic growth. Although the South African Communist Party and Congress of South African Trade Unions are still influential, if Zimbabwe's trade union-backed Movement for Democratic Change were supported by the South African government it would send out the wrong message about labourism and the future of the economy. Equally, South Africa knows that a worsening situation in Zimbabwe will only increase the already considerable immigration into the country. So elections become caught as pawns in the wider game of regional national interest.

The list of unsatisfactory elections is lengthy and one concern has been the extent to which opposition groups and parties are cohesive and well organized. For example, there were 125 registered political parties in Angola in 2003 who complained they were 'hindered' by a 'lack of power' and government funding, which resulted in 'the two old liberation movements (UNITA and MPLA) remaining politically dominant' (All Party Parliamentary Group for Angola 2003: 20). Even without resources the existence of so many parties indicated the opposition was likely to be fragmented. In fact, the role of the political party is seen as the weakest link in African democratization. Often parties have no constituencies or are ethnically based, lack political programmes and interaction with the populace, and have non-existent financial transparency. Internal party democracy is unknown and many opposition parties actually disband between elections. Parties desperately need reform and renewal but often the international donor community is fearful of directly involving itself in party development, preferring instead to fund NGOs which do not arouse accusations of political interference. However, wider democratic reform is unlikely to take place without changes to the structures and practices of political parties.

Closely connected to this issue is the question of party–state relations. In many countries the state is subsumed by the dominant party and elections simply become a focus for misuse of government expenditure. In some African states there are no rules on expenditure at all. This anomalous situation can result in the 'abuse of incumbency', whereby dominant parties attempt to change constitutional terms of office, control the media or outlaw political activity, and engage in coercive or violent electoral campaigns. In 2008 Cameroon's parliament adopted a constitutional bill removing a presidential two-term limit which allows President Paul Biya to extend his 25-year-rule and possibly rule for life. Although opposition groups stormed out of the chamber and riots had previously taken place, the dominant Cameroon People's Democratic Movement had a huge majority, controlling 153 out of 180 parliamentary seats. Problems are supposed to be addressed by the African Union and regional organizations. The Southern African Development Community (SADC), for example, has agreed codes of conduct and set out political norms and standards. It asserts that the following 'principles must lie at the heart' of the any electoral system:

- Broad representation of diverse political interests and population groups
- Inclusiveness and the political participation of key actors
- Political accountability of Members of Parliament to the voters
- A transparent and legitimate elections process and outcome
- The entrenchment of a culture of intra-party democracy that ensures the credibility and legitimacy of the nomination process within political parties.

(EISA 2004: 9–10)

Unfortunately as stated above not all SADC member states abide by these principles and even when acting in unison SADC proposals are largely ignored. Zimbabwe's opposition party, the Movement for Democratic Change (MDC), complained of the 'deafening silence' emanating from SADC in the weeks following the country's disputed 2008 elections. When finally SADC did convene, Zimbabwe's President Robert Mugabe refused to attend the meeting.

Accepting the legitimate outcomes of elections is critical in democratizing states but on occasion political leaders and parties enter the electoral process with the expectation that they alone will win. Such an attitude creates conditions of low participation and competition often resulting in a popular or opposition boycott of the whole electoral process.[2] Inevitably, the 'winner takes all' approach to elections excludes many and has given rise to calls for a greater emphasis to be placed on negotiation with other political groups, NGOs and stakeholders, as well as respect for and appropriate engagement with voters. However, such an approach is likely to be adopted only if there is a good level of democratization within a country anyway. In the context of David Held's notion of democratic autonomy: is there political activity beyond electoral periods? Is criticism of the government possible? How independent are the media? Can civil society operate openly and freely? In short, the character of the wider political environment is critical when analysing elections.

The 2006 Afrobarometer surveys looked closely at the perceptions of elections by Africans across the continent. As Table 4.3 demonstrates the responses to certain questions are negative and appear in countries that like to celebrate their democracy, such as South Africa. It is interesting that election outcomes have been contested in a range of countries, as documented in Table 4.4. Fifty-one per cent of respondents from Malawi, 61 per cent from Nigeria, 56 per cent from Zambia and 58 per cent from Zimbabwe regarded their elections as not free and fair. The vast majority of respondents from 18 states, ranging from 73 per cent in Mozambique to 96 per cent in Benin and Zambia, felt that politicians 'make promises to get elected' (Afrobarometer 2006: 14).

A crucial factor in African states is the great disparity between poverty for the many and the extreme wealth of a few. Although there is no direct correlation between an increase in a country's GNP and growing political reform there is widespread acknowledgement that the social impacts of extreme poverty – namely, poor education, disease and illiteracy – combine to hinder the process of democratization. Also, such negative factors prevent the emergence of an enlarging middle class who could be instrumental in underpinning democratic trends. Yet one significant study suggested that poverty has become 'a contested political concept'. South Africa, for example, 'does not have an official definition of poverty' despite the production of numerous reports (Magasela 2006: 48). Yet in 2004 President Mbeki itemized a number of services that needed to be improved: housing, water provision, basic sanitation, access to electricity, child support, reduction in HIV/AIDS and malaria, education and support for the security, police and legal process. Inevitably the setting of targets raises the prospect of how they are to be met, although David Hemson and Michael O'Donovan point out that now 'targets . . .

Table 4.3 Negative responses to elections (%)

	How well do elections:			
	Ensure that the members of Parliament reflect the views of voters		*Enable voters to remove from office leaders who do not do what the people want*	
	Well/very well	*Not very well/ not at all well*	*Well/very well*	*Not very well/ not at all well*
Kenya	43	45	39	49
Madagascar	41	48	54	35
Malawi	30	63	56	37
Mali	50	41	45	47
Nigeria	30	64	26	68
South Africa	49	36	39	46
Zambia	29	60	29	61
Zimbabwe	31	67	33	65

Source: Afrobarometer (2006).

Table 4.4 Selection of contested, violent or undisclosed election results

Country	Year	Nature of outcome
São Tomé and Príncipe	Presidential 2001; National Assembly 2002	Since the introduction of multi-party elections vote-buying has occurred but the 20 foreign observers declared the elections free and fair[a]
Côte d'Ivoire	Presidential 2000; Parliamentary 2001; prospective presidential elections delayed until November 2008	Both elections boycotted by opposition parties followed by civil war
Central African Republic	Parliamentary 1998	Lapsed into civil war by 2003
Comoros	Presidential 2002	Partial boycott and irregularities affected outcome
Equatorial Guinea	Presidential 2002	Boycott and isolated violent incidents
Gambia	Parliamentary 2002	Partial boycott and irregularities affected outcome
Guinea	Parliamentary 2002; Presidential 2003	Partial boycott and violent incidences followed by military intervention to resolve the crisis of political legitimacy
Madagascar	Parliamentary 2002	Partial boycott
Seychelles	Parliamentary 2002	Some isolated violent incidents
Sierra Leone	Parliamentary 2002	Some isolated violent incidents

Togo	Parliamentary 2002; Parliamentary 2007	Partial boycott and isolated violent incidents. Opposition claim 2007 elections flawed: 'ballot boxes were tampered with, fake election cards distributed and voting paper had been destroyed.' ECOWAS[b] monitors declare the elections 'free, fair and transparent'
Uganda	Parliamentary 2002	Some isolated violent incidents
Cameroon	Parliamentary 2007	Opposition called elections a 'sham' because of bribery and intimidation of voters
Mali	Presidential 2007	Opposition claimed election results should be null and void because of multiple voting and intimidation but observers from the ECOWAS[b] and France declare the election to be 'fair and clean despite isolated incidents of concern'
Nigeria	2007 Presidential and Parliamentary elections	Election results contested claims of violence and irregularities
Kenya	2007/8 Presidential and Parliamentary elections	Opposition party claimed election was rigged followed by conflict resulting in c. 1000 deaths and 300,000 displaced from their homes in post-electoral violence
Zimbabwe	2008 Presidential and Parliamentary elections	Undisclosed presidential election results; contested parliamentary elections and accusations of vote-rigging

a The foreign observers were from Angola, Nigeria, China, USA, Cape Verde, Portugal, Côte d'Ivoire and Gabon.

b ECOWAS: Economic Community of West African States.

are measured in terms of inputs rather than results . . . (and) the emphasis is on departmental objectives rather than on final outcomes in human development' (Hemson and O'Donovan 2006: 38).

Electoral systems have also been identified as affecting the outcomes of elections as described in Table 4.5. The Mixed Member Proportionality (MMP) system is one of overall proportional representation, established through the use of a separate national ballot paper and a number of 'compensatory seats', and has been considered in South Africa, Kenya, Zimbabwe and Tanzania. Its attraction for incumbent parties is that the constituency system is retained, thus ensuring local patronage, while at the same time allowing for a fair reflection of party strength among the electorate. The MMP system was suggested as a solution to the political and constitutional crisis in Lesotho after the 1998 parliamentary elections, when the clear win of the major party was challenged by opposition parties on the grounds of electoral mismanagement (Table 4.6). That example underlined the difficulties created by a 'winner takes all' structure that can act as a catalyst for conflict as there is so much at stake. However, the 2007 elections in Kenya have demonstrated that systems are not foolproof.

Table 4.5 Types of electoral systems and representation

Electoral system	Constituency representation	Party representation
Single-Member Plurality (includes First Past the Post system)	• Maintains traditional link between representative and constituents • Representatives often elected on a minority of total votes leading to criticism of 'wasted' votes	• Distortion of votes:seats ratio • Minor parties disadvantaged unless support is regionally concentrated • Discourages multiplication of parties; tendency for dominant party to rule
Single-Member Majoritarian (a) Alternative Vote (b) Second Ballot	• Maintains traditional link between representative and constituents • In both cases representatives usually elected by a majority	• Distortion of votes:seats ratio • No 'wasted' votes as small parties survive even if unsuccessful • Tendency toward multi-party system
Proportional Representation (a) Party List (b) Single Transferable Vote	• Individual representatives usually owe election more to party than to voters • Representatives forced to compete for 'first preference' votes	• Approximate ratio between vote shares and seat allocations • Minor parties usually gain representation; easy entry for new parties • Tendency toward multi-party systems
Mixed Plurality/ Proportional Representation = Mixed Member Proportionality	• Maintains traditional link between representative and constituency	• Approximate ratio between vote shares and seat allocation • Minor parties gain fair representation

Source: Matlosa (2003).

Table 4.6 Electoral system, size of legislature and nature of representation

Country	Electoral system	Size of legislature	Number of seats currently held by ruling party
Angola	PR	220	129
Botswana	FPTP	47	33
Lesotho	MMP	120	79
Malawi	FPTP	192	93
Mauritius	Mixed	66	54
Mozambique	PR	250	133
Namibia	PR	104	55
South Africa	PR	400	266
Tanzania	FPTP	274	244
Zambia	FPTP	158	69

Source: Adapted from interviews at the Independent Electoral Commission in Botswana and South Africa.

FPTP: First Past the Post; MMP: Mixed Member Proportionality; PR: Proportional Representation.

Ideally, electoral administration and management should ensure the legitimacy and impartiality of the electoral process. Issues such as the selection of candidates, primary elections, the level of technical assistance and voter identification are all crucial to 'electoral governance'.[3] However, it must be remembered that elections are not simply a matter of management; politics and culture are equally significant in determining a country's electoral environment. Two factors are critically important for electoral outcomes: voter registration and voter education. People need to be registered to vote because in a number of African elections unregistered voters are not included when turnout rates are calculated. In Lesotho, for example, only around 70 per cent of potential voters registered to vote. Countries with sophisticated systems, such as South Africa, do offer technical assistance to less efficient states, although even in South Africa 4 million people have yet to register to vote. If voter registration does not operate properly, the whole point of holding elections is undermined.

Yet non-registration is not only a result of system incapacity; it also reflects unwillingness on the part of the voter. This raises the related issue of voter education, which is essential in nurturing and motivating the electorate. However, it needs to be more than simply informing voters where and when to register. Voters require greater information on the consequences of not registering and the possibilities for change which the ballot implies. But sometimes weaknesses within Electoral Commissions, inefficiency or inadequacy of administrative personnel, or just plain overall incompetence mean that voter education can be poor and largely ineffective. It is clear that voter education and registration will continue to be of concern not only in electoral management but also in the wider public's experience of democracy. South Africa and Botswana have made attempts to engage in civic and voter education programmes (Figure 4.1).[4]

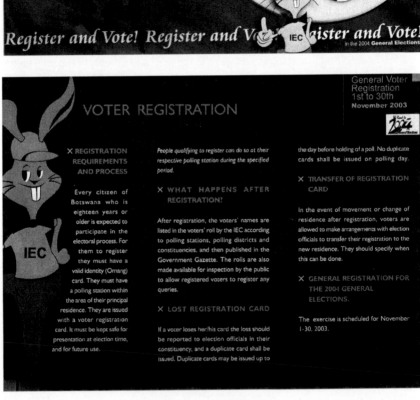

Figure 4.1 Botswana's voter registration pamphlet.

Botswana has taken the issue of voter education very seriously because of its concern about electoral apathy particularly among the young aged between 18 and 21 years. Table 4.7 outlines the low level of registration for that age group. These figures are concerning as Botswana is a very youthful nation. The last census in 1991 revealed that 60 per cent of the population is less than 30 years of age (Seleetso interview 2004). One reason identified as a possible reason for such levels of indifference is that the ruling dominant Botswana Democratic Party has been in office since 1965: 'if no realistic opportunity for change is offered to the people, elections will remain dull and the outcomes unaltered' (Good interview 2003).

It is clear that, as much as democracy is encouraged by groups within Africa, by the international community, by NGOs working on the ground and by political practitioners, there are pernicious elements within states that can undermine the process. Elections, a milestone on the road to democracy, are problematic for a number of reasons, one of which is the nature of political parties. Political parties are critical to the electoral process but it is clear that concerns about funding, policy formation, programme development, support, religious/ethnic rivalry, corruption and the lack of internal democracy have an impact on elections in a number of countries. Artificially created parties, with no constituency of support, are deleterious to the conduct of elections. The role and function of the political party in African elections needs to be addressed because weakness, malfunction and corruption within the party system leech into the wider political environment. It has been acknowledged that many African parties remain organizationally underdeveloped.[5]

The related issue of opposition cohesion is particularly important during elections because a fragmented opposition with little or no direction can undermine an electoral process and may give rise to boycotts. When opposition groups do unite, provide a purposeful approach and attract electoral support, they can campaign effectively and also may win the election. This, of course, occurred in Kenya in 2002 although it did not stop the outcome of the 2007 elections being contested. In most African states the opposition is destined to be simply that: eternally the opposition, never in power. It is here that abuse of incumbency can emerge. When political leaders form cliques, apportion power and appropriate political authority, bribery and corruption can soon become part of the political terrain. In these circumstances, better management of elections may be a means of delivering accurate election results. National Electoral Commissions within countries can be weakened by poor structures, inadequate training of personnel, administrative

Table 4.7 Registration of voters in Botswana

Age range	% registered to vote
< 21	4.6
21–40	46.7
41–64	34.3
65–70	5.5
71 <	9.0

Source: Independent Electoral Commission, Botswana (2002).

inadequacy or, as in the case of Zimbabwe, an unhealthy relationship with the ruling party.

Whatever the experience of African states, the efficiency of electoral institutions is essential to the conduct of elections. Yet improved voter education and registration is also paramount. In countries where disillusioning experiences of previous elections have the potential to alienate the electorate, voter education is particularly necessary to inculcate a feeling of engagement and commitment. Yet for nations with diverse and differentiated polities, voter induction may be needed to provide a means of demonstrating that elections need not always be corrupt, controlled and violent exercises. Education apart, there is no doubt that voter registration must be scrupulous and beyond manipulation. Elections are rightly regarded as critical components of the democratization process and much attention is focused upon them. International and regional observers are dispatched to cover and assess their outcomes. Yet more attention needs to be given to the wider political environment outside the election period. Although there are guidelines on what exactly 'free and fair' elections mean, in practice there appears to be considerable misunderstanding. Levels of electoral abuse exist in various guises: money for votes, distortion of electoral registers, mismanagement, intimidation and violence. At times, in certain countries, the political environment can be so debilitating the question must be asked: should elections be avoided altogether? Certainly, post-conflict Sierra Leone was urged to 'maintain a free, secure and fair environment throughout the electoral period' (International Crisis Group 2007d: 2). Yet this can be difficult to achieve. However, in terms of gender many countries in Africa have recorded relatively high levels of women in parliament, reaching 30 per cent in South Africa (see Table 4.8).

Although political pundits forecast that South Africa's second democratic elections would arouse less popular enthusiasm than those of 1994, the inauguration of President Mbeki on 16 June 1999 at the Union Buildings in Pretoria was a momentous occasion. Crowds jostled to see him declare his covenant to the country, and the South African Air Force and South African Airways staged a fly-past after the president took the oath of office. The spectacle and ceremony of the event gave rise to a sense of pride, achievement and hope that a five-year-old democracy

Table 4.8 Women in parliament

Country	Election	Seats	Women	% women
Angola	1992	224	34	15
Botswana	1999	47	8	18
Lesotho	1998	120	12	10
Malawi	1999	193	16	8
Mauritius	1995	65	5	8
Mozambique	1999	250	71	28
South Africa	1999	400	119	30
Tanzania	1995	275	45	16

Source: research conducted at EISA, Johannesburg, 2003.

was maturing. Journalists spoke of how 'good' it felt to be a South African as people of all races danced, sang and partied late into the night. Yet many were in no doubt that the hard work was just about to begin. A decade later with the prospect of an embattled new President Jacob Zuma in post, the challenges remain and no-one is taking democracy for granted, not even in South Africa. A high-ranking think tank, the Institute for Justice and Reconciliation, has warned that a further drop in public confidence in the country's institutions and leaders could threaten democracy. The overall confidence in South Africa's leaders had dropped from 64.5 per cent in 2006 to 57 per cent a year later: 'If the economy fails to deliver change and if delivery happens but social justice is not seen to be done, people will become indifferent to democracy' (Mathekga 2008: 4).

Countries in Africa have been encouraged to help each other but sometimes states seek political guidance from what might be regarded as unlikely nations. For example, Professor John Atta-Mills, a former vice-president of Ghana, has requested assistance from Nigeria, rather than South Africa, in making the December 2008 election in his country free, fair and transparent. It seems an odd choice especially as Nigeria itself is struggling to achieve free and fair elections and continuing complaints surface about violence, mismanagement and the absence of secret ballots (EISA 2008c). Of course, politics in Africa can be neither predicted nor pre-judged but its peoples and politicians should be mindful of the supposedly 'unspoken thoughts' of one commentator on Kenya's 2008 post-electoral events: 'here we go again, yet another African country descending into tribal violence' (Kiai 2008: 2).

5 Gender

The word 'gender' is now a ubiquitous term used by all agencies within the international community to discuss issues of concern to women. Yet for some it is a euphemism for 'women' that has been adopted as a 'neutral, apolitical' term which is not as 'threatening or divisive as "woman"' (Khan 2000: 8). Whichever way the term is used, however, there is deep concern about the situation of women in Africa. In many spheres, economic, social, political and sexual, women have been 'placed in an inferior role to men' (Masite interview 1996). It was this inequality that the former president of South Africa, Nelson Mandela, was determined to combat. South Africa, he believed, could not go forward unless 'we see in visible and practical terms that the condition of the women of our country has radically changed for the better and that they have been empowered to intervene in all aspects of life as equals with any other member of society' (RDP News 1995a). In terms of the then legal status of women, the Common Law rule, whereby a husband obtained marital power over his wife and her property, was repealed by the General Law Fourth Amendment Act in 1993. Also, the Guardianship Act of the same year gave a married couple equal guardianship rights over children. Previously, only the father had been the natural guardian of a child born within marriage. But Mandela wanted to go further especially in terms of economic gender discrimination such as employment bias in public works projects; unpaid labour; constraints in the availability of credit for women with limited collateral; and insufficient resource allocation for childcare and education. In fact, the 1996 Constitution, which contained an extensive Bill of Rights, opened the way to affirmative action not only on grounds of race but also on the basis of gender (Box 5.1).

The debate on gender issues in South Africa had been given impetus by the release of a report on the status of South African women in preparation for the United Nations World Conference on Women which was held in Beijing in 1995. The report called for the empowerment of women and highlighted key issues: the alleviation of women's poverty, improvements in health, education and job opportunities, and measures to combat violence against women (RDP News 1995b). The issue of violence against women was of concern particularly because a Commonwealth Observer Mission to South Africa had found that almost half the female population were likely to be raped at some point in their lives (according to 1991

Box 5.1 Equality clause in South Africa's Bill of Rights 1996

- Everyone is equal before the law and has the right to equal protection and benefit of the law
- Equality includes the full and equal enjoyment of all rights and freedoms. To promote the achievement of equality, legislative and other measures designed to protect or advance persons, or categories of persons, disadvantaged by unfair discrimination may be taken
- The state may not unfairly discriminate against anyone of grounds of race, gender, sex, pregnancy, marital status, ethnic or social origin, colour, sexual orientation, age, disability, religion, conscience, belief, culture, language or birth
- No person may unfairly discriminate directly or indirectly against anyone

figures; Commonwealth Observer Mission to South Africa 1993). Rape, however, did not disappear after the end of apartheid in 1994, as Table 5.1 indicates.

The Crime Information Management Centre (CIMC), which was established by the South African Police Service (SAPS) in 1996, instigated research into the nature and incidence of rape and conducted an operational analysis in three provinces: Western Cape, Northern Cape and the Free State. Although these regions had different incidences of rape and could not be regarded as fully representative of all regions, the findings revealed some similarities. In the Western Cape, over one-quarter of all the suspects involved had been under the influence of alcohol or drugs at the time the rape occurred. Also, 61 per cent of those suspected of carrying out the rapes were known to the complainant before the act occurred. In the Northern Cape, alcohol played a role in 36 per cent of all the rape cases analysed,

Table 5.1 Reported cases of rape in South Africa

Region	*1994*	*1995*	*1996*	*1997*
Eastern Cape	1258	1405	1569	1722
Free State	880	958	1038	1015
Gauteng*	2382	3006	3339	3204
KwaZulu Natal	1681	1854	2131	2292
Mpumalanga	596	682	773	820
North West	841	1001	1106	1223
Northern Cape	292	324	436	428
Northern Province	588	713	833	966
Western Cape	1327	1420	1837	1744

Source: SAPS (2001) Quarterly Report 1998.

* Gauteng included Johannesburg.

and again in two-thirds of cases the suspect was known to the victim. In the Free State, 56 per cent of rapes took place in the victims' homes, and 43 per cent of the cases involved people previously known to one another. Based on these findings, the CIMC felt the occurrence of rape in many instances was related to 'date rape' or 'acquaintance rape' rather than to the actions of strangers (SAPS 2001). It is interesting to note that in 2006 more than 50,000 rape cases were reported, which represented almost 150 per day (*Business Day* 2007).

The Beijing conference laid down a marker about violence against women, which it defined as 'any act based on gender which results in physical, sexual, and psychological harm to women' (cited in Deegan 1998). Violence against women embraces a wide variety of acts:

- Physical, sexual and psychological violence in the family, including battering, sexual abuse of female children in the family, marital rape, female genital mutilation and violence related to exploitation.
- Physical, sexual and psychological violence occurring with the general community. This includes rape, sexual harassment and intimidation at work, in educational institutions and elsewhere, trafficking in women and forced prostitution.
- Physical, sexual and psychological violence condoned by the state, wherever it occurs.

Yet women often lack access to legal information, aid or protection. The South African organization People Opposing Women Abuse found that what they called 'intimate femicide' was the main cause of violent deaths among women. These deaths were brought about by their partners (White interview 1996).

Women and society

The strategic objective of gender and women's struggle is the complete eradication of all forms of oppressive gender relations and equal roles in all spheres of life, including family roles. Yet the traditional aspects of African society have intruded into the political debate about the rights of women. Chiefdoms have assumed a patriarchal hereditary form whereby power is transferred through the male line. Rural women, as a consequence, often find their societies restrictive and controlling. States may pass legislation protecting women's rights but, if traditional leaders view this as undermining customary law and eroding the foundation of African culture, the impact will be minimal. Gender-based violence can range from rape to such traditional practices as female genital cutting, which have been viewed as physically and psychologically damaging and as human rights violations. Many victims are never seen by a medical professional to address their abuse (UNFPA 2004: 31). Female genital mutilation is a long practised, painful and invasive process which still affects 60 per cent of females in Chad despite being deemed illegal since 1995 (Drummond-Thomson 2005). Often, it is the silence surrounding African women's experiences that is of concern together with the consequent difficulty of improving their conditions. 'Hierarchies of domination are constructed and experienced simultaneously, their dynamics permeating one another' (Lentin 2000: 93; see also Tripp 2000). These 'hierarchies of domination' may be political, religious, customary, traditional, cultural or familial. More recently, however, attention has focused on the relationship between religion and women, and more specifically on the impact Islam has on women's lives.

In parts of Africa where *shari'a* law is in operation, women can find themselves in demanding situations where their assumed human rights are undermined. Incidents have occurred in northern Nigeria and Sudan in which women have been flogged and beaten for indiscretions, but how far are these punishments driven by religion and how far by culture? It has been argued that one of the receptive features of Islam in the past has been its ability to integrate with traditional African society and to adopt some beliefs and practices: 'Belief in supernatural forces, the wearing of charms, polygamous marriages became part of the way of life' of converted African Muslims. In this way converts did not find it 'too strange' to belong to Islam (Omari 1984: 25–27). In Malawi, the case of the Yao people tends to support the view that Islam adapted itself to local African culture: 'While the *shari'a* law remains important to the Yao as Muslims, in matters concerning marriage, divorce and inheritance, they prefer traditional law and custom' (Mandivenga 1991: 24). Yet the experience of Islam may be different when a state or region has declared itself to be theocratic. Islamization, argues Mervat Hatem, has been used by political conservatives to pass laws which are not directly related to the religion. One example is in the area of attempted adultery: 'While Islamic law had purposely required very difficult conditions to prove adultery' different laws can make the 'presence of any woman with a man to whom she is not married in a public place an indication of attempted adultery and grounds for incarceration' (Hatem 1993: 32).

Much of Africa's cultural activity centres on the family and ethnic group, and families play an important role in Muslim society: 'It is like a rose in which all the petals are healthy and united, extending their support to each other' (Surty 1995: 20). Yet in order to analyse contemporary family norms within a framework of Islam it is necessary to differentiate between *shari'a* and those schools of thought that have historically interpreted the Qur'an. In Islam the family is presumed to be the basic institution of moral values, but Mohamed Haddad asserts 'There is no family in Islam . . . the term family is not part of the original vocabulary of Islam.' He explains: 'Family in Arabic language is referred to by *'usra,* meaning imprisoning or protecting, or *a'ila,* which means maintaining and supplying the necessities of other persons . . . However, what is surprising is that the *Qur'an* does not contain either of these two terms!' What appears in the Qur'an is the term *'ahl,* which is quoted over 120 times in varied contexts. 'The term *'ahl* means becoming familiar or feeling at ease in a relation. It does not contain any connotation of domination, in fact quite the contrary.' Therefore, the Qur'anic concept of the family is an open entity (Haddad 2006: 60).

Yet, according to other interpretations, specific guidelines are provided within the Qur'an particularly regarding the authority of a husband to physically discipline his wife if she is regarded as disobedient, as described in Box 5.2. Again the Arabic verse used in the Qur'an, *idribu hunna* (from the root *daraba*) has a

Box 5.2 Islam and husbands and wives

If the husband senses that feelings of disobedience and rebelliousness are rising against him in his wife, he should try his best to rectify her attitude by kind words, gentle persuasion and reasoning with her. If this is not helpful, he should sleep apart from her, trying to awaken her agreeable feminine nature so that serenity may be restored, and she may respond to him in a harmonious fashion. If this approach fails, it is permissible for him to beat her lightly with his hands, avoiding her face and other sensitive parts. In no case should he resort to using a stick or any other instrument that might cause pain and injury.

According to Sheikh Yusuf al-Qaradawi, Head of the European Council for Fatwa and Research, cited in www.wikiislam.com

Box 5.3 Punishments authorized by the Qur'an and *hadith* in respect of certain crimes

The woman and the man guilty of adultery or fornication - flog each of them with hundred stripes: Let no compassion move you in their case, in a matter prescribed by God, if ye believe in God and the last day.

Qur'an 24:2

Nor come nigh to adultery: for it is a shameful (deed) and an evil, opening the road (to other evils).

Qur'an 17:32

A woman came to the prophet and asked for purification by seeking punishment. He told her to go away and seek God's forgiveness. She persisted four times and admitted she was pregnant. He told her to wait until she had given birth. Then he said that the Muslim community should wait until she had weaned her child. When the day arrived for the child to take solid food, Muhammad handed the child over to the community. And when he had given the command over her and she was put in a hole up to her breast, he ordered the people to stone her. Khalid b. al-Walid came forward with a stone which he threw at her head, and when blood spurted on her face he cursed her.

Sahi Muslim No. 4206
Cited in www.islam/sharia/

meaning of 'beat, hit, scourge or strike' although it could also be rendered as 'to cover, to separate, or to go abroad' (http://en.islam.org/sharia). Clearly, there are real difficulties in fully comprehending the nuances of interpretation. However, there seems to be authorization for punishments contained in other passages in the Qur'an and *hadith* for certain crimes, such as extra-marital sex and adultery (see Box 5.3). In northern Nigeria, the Islamic practice of speedy divorce has left some young women, subsequently rejected by their families, to become destitute and vulnerable to prostitution (confidential interview, Kano, 2005). (See Boxes 5.4 and 5.5.)

These different interpretations of Islam have been reflected in practices within parts of Africa. A comparative study of women in northern Nigeria and Senegal revealed that in Senegal 'Islam had not removed women's freedom of movement, their ability to participate in the market, their right to control what they earned and their readiness to speak out for what they wanted.' Women could work in the fields unveiled, whereas, in Islamic northern Nigeria, wife seclusion is traditional and women are largely absent from the markets (Callaway and Creevey 1994: 27). In the 1990s, certain Islamic organizations, for example the International Islamic Relief Organisation, funded by Saudi Arabia, concerned itself with women's issues emphasizing the 'special status given to women in Islam, especially in regard to their dignity and protection: sexual assault on women is regarded as a major crime.' Sudan's International Muslim Women Union also stressed the extreme importance of child care in Islam (Albadawe interview, 1997) but after 9/11 these groups were revealed as 'front' organizations propagandizing a radical agenda rather than concerned with genuine women's issues. Militant Islamists do not simply refer to a traditional set of values and beliefs; rather they largely improvise a 'novel religio-political body' of views, based on specific readings and interpretations of the Qur'an (Ayubi 1991: 119). So what does this mean for Muslim African women? The answer seems clear: a varied exposure to the vagaries of

---

Box 5.4 *Shari'a* law for matrimonial relationships

Shari'a Law for the matrimonial relationship constructs in Qur'anic terms a fortified castle of justice, peace, chastity, piety, mutual love, mercy and affection between the two spouses. The Qur'an strictly forbids sex outside marriage and leaves no room for sexual promiscuity and homosexual relations.

Source: Surty (1996: 47)

Box 5.5 Islam and men and women

Men are the protectors and maintainers of women, because Allah has given the one more (strength) than the other, and because they support them from their means. Therefore, the righteous women are devoutly obedient, and guard in (the husband's) absence what Allah would have them guard. As to those women on whose part ye fear disloyalty and ill-conduct, admonish them (first), (Next) refuse to share their beds, (And last) beat them (lightly).

Qur'an 4:34 cited in www.wikiislam.com

religious interpretation and constraint, imposed by men in positions of authority and power. In a sense, the cultural connection between Africa and Islam is only one side of the coin, the other being the way in which religious cultural practices are used as forms of oppression by dominant authorities. The central concern is that too many African women live in patriarchal societies appropriated by either religion or political elites.

Women and conflict

In 2000 the United Nations Security Council adopted Resolution 1325, which was concerned with the impact of armed conflict on women and girls (see Box 5.6). It was officially recognized that conflicts can 'privatise violence' as they engage an array of state and non-state actors; consequently more civilians are affected. Sexual violence against women is often the gendered outcome of conflict (Turshen and Twagiramariya 1998: 13). However, 'sexual violence' refers to many different crimes including 'rape, sexual mutilation, sexual humiliation, forced prostitution, and forced pregnancy' (UN Division for the Advancement of Women 2008). Box 5.7 outlines the possible reasons for these atrocities. In 1994 during the genocidal conflict in Rwanda, the Human Rights Commission's Special Rapporteur reported: 'Rape was systematic and used as a "weapon" by the perpetrators of the massacres' (Degni-Segui 1996). Box 5.8 outlines the abuses that were conducted.

In many African countries there has been an increase in militarization and the inward flow of weapons.[1] Interestingly, these guns and light weaponry have a greater 'impact on the security and daily lives of civilians, especially women, than tanks and combat aircraft' (Giles and Hyndman 2004: 32). An environment of violence becomes the norm as the theatre of conflict moves into the domestic arena. Equally, there is sometimes no cut-off line between different manifestations of conflict, just pauses before fighting begins again, for example in Darfur, Sudan. Women are often corralled in refugee camps, too frightened to return home: 'Some of those displaced in armed conflict or political terror are obliged to resettle in distant countries' (ibid.: 39).[2] The experience for women with dependent children is particularly daunting: female bodily processes – menstruation, pregnancy, giving birth, breast-feeding – 'become more burdensome, uncomfortable, and dangerous. Women and girls are vulnerable to molestation and rape from male police, local men, and even other refugees' (Nordstrom 1998: 57). One way out of this cycle of degradation is through the empowerment of women. One of the Millennium Development Goals seeks to 'promote gender equality and empower women' and Project Task Force 3 assesses women's empowerment against certain criteria based on:

1   Human capabilities as measured through education, health and nutrition
2   Access to resources and opportunities, that is, economic assets and political participation
3   Security in terms of vulnerability to violence.

(UNFPA 2004: 33)

Box 5.6 United Nations Resolution 1325: the impact of armed conflict on women and girls

- Member states should ensure increased representation women at all decision-making levels in national, regional and international institutions and mechanisms for the prevention, management, and resolution of conflict
- There should be an increase in the participation of women at decision-making levels in conflict resolutions and peace processes
- The role and contribution of women in UN field-based operations should be increased, and especially among military observers, civilian police, human rights and humanitarian personnel
- Member states should be provided with guidelines and materials on the protection, rights and the particular needs of women
- Calls on all actors involved, when negotiating and implementing peace agreements, to adopt a gender perspective, including:

    1   The special needs of women and girls during repatriation and resettlement and for rehabilitation, reintegration and post-conflict reconstruction
    2   Measures that support local women's peace initiatives and indigenous processes for conflict resolution, and that involve women in all the implementation mechanisms or the peace agreements
    3   Measures that ensure the protection of and respect for human rights of women and girls, particularly as they relate to the constitution, the electoral system, the police and the judiciary

- All parties to armed conflict should take special measures to protect women and girls from gender-based violence, particularly rape and other forms of sexual abuse, and all other forms of violence in situations of armed conflict
- It is the responsibility of all States to put an end to impunity and to prosecute those responsible for genocide, crimes against humanity, and war crimes including those relating to sexual and other violence against women and girls

Source: United Nations Security Council Resolution 1325 (2000).

In 2007 the United Nations Trust Fund to End Violence against Women provided US$1.3 million in grants to nine organizations working in 12 countries targeting the links between HIV and AIDS and violence against women. The countries in

Box 5.7 Reasons for sexual violence during armed conflict

The crimes of sexual violence are motivated by a myriad of factors. For example, a commonly held view throughout history has been that women are part of the 'spoils' of war to which soldiers are entitled. Deeply entrenched in this notion is the idea that women are property, chattels available to victorious warriors. Sexual violence may also be looked upon as a means of troop mollification. This is particularly the case where women are forced into military sexual slavery. Another reason that sexual violence occurs is to destroy male, and thereby community, pride. Men who have failed to 'protect their women' are considered to be humiliated and weak. It can also be used as a form of punishment, particularly where women are politically active, or are associated with others who are politically active. Sexual violence can be used as a means of inflicting terror upon the population at large. It can shatter communities and drive people out of their homes. Sexual violence can also be part of a genocidal strategy.

Source: UN Division for the Advancement of Women (2008).

Box 5.8 Sexual violence in Rwanda 1994

Under-age children and elderly women were not spared. Other testimonies mention cases of girls aged between 10 and 12 years. Pregnant women were not spared. Women about to give birth or who had just given birth were also the victims of rape in hospitals. Their situation was all the more alarming in that they were raped by members of the militias some of whom were AIDS virus carriers. Women who were 'untouchable' according to custom (e.g. nuns) were also involved and even corpses, in the case of women who were raped just after being killed.

Source: Degni-Segui (1996: para. 17).

Africa include the Republic of Congo, Ethiopia, Ghana, Mozambique, Guinea and Cote d'Ivoire. Table 5.2 outlines the initiatives.

> Sexual violence is a weapon of war, an instrument of terror that hurts and punishes women and men on the other side, fractures communities and forces women to flee their homes. Silence and shame shroud the survivors of rape or other forms of sexual violence. Many become infected with HIV and AIDS, and face disease, stigma and social rejection.
>
> (UNIFEM Goodwill Ambassador Nicole Kidman at
> www.unifem.org)[3]

Table 5.2 Initiatives to target links between HIV/AIDS and violence against women

Country	Initiative
Republic of Congo	Women infected or affected by HIV/AIDS in seven rural settings with a high prevalence of gender-based violence will benefit from medical care, psycho-social support houses and micro-finance initiatives to improve their economic security, health and well-being
Ethiopia	To foster a law enforcement environment responsive to the concerns of women victims of violence, a project will build the capacity of para-legal organizations, police representatives, judges and prosecutors in three areas of Ethiopia afflicted with a high rate of HIV/AIDS
Ghana	To help women living with HIV to access their rights, the project will provide them with legal assistance, build their capacity to mobilize resources, and engage students in efforts to transform behaviour to end violence against women
Mozambique	The project will help to open doors to essential services for survivors of gender-based violence. As part of a dialogue with community leaders about traditional beliefs and practices that increase women's exposure to HIV infection, a nation-wide 'men-to-men' campaign will be launched
Guinea	To reduce sexual violence and unsafe sex in the country's mining zones, a project will help establish peer support groups to raise women's rights awareness and advocate for state protection
Côte d'Ivoire	To reduce the stigma and discrimination faced by HIV-positive women in the post-conflict country, public authorities and traditional leaders will be trained on women's rights, and women will receive counselling support

Source: www.unifem.org/news_events/story.

Gender equality and women's empowerment

The 2006 World Development Report (World Bank 2006) called the differential access to resources, assets and opportunities between men and women the 'inequality trap' out of which further negative aspects developed. Ultimately, these inequalities had detrimental consequences not only for women, but also for their families and communities. A framework for gender equality was devised, as outlined in Figure 5.1, which connects the domestic arena (household) to the wider economic environment and political arena (society). The framework connects the key areas of gender equality: 'Gender inequality in rights, resources, and voice can surface in three domains: in the household, in the economy and markets, and in society' (World Bank 2007: 106). Box 5.9 outlines the connections between these three elements.

With regard to sub-Saharan Africa, the report held that gender equality and women's empowerment 'consistently lags behind in most areas.' The inequality starts early, as Table 5.3 indicates, with differences in primary education completion rates between boys and girls. The worst performing countries in terms of primary completion rates and under-5 mortality rates are Burkino Faso, Sudan and Malawi.

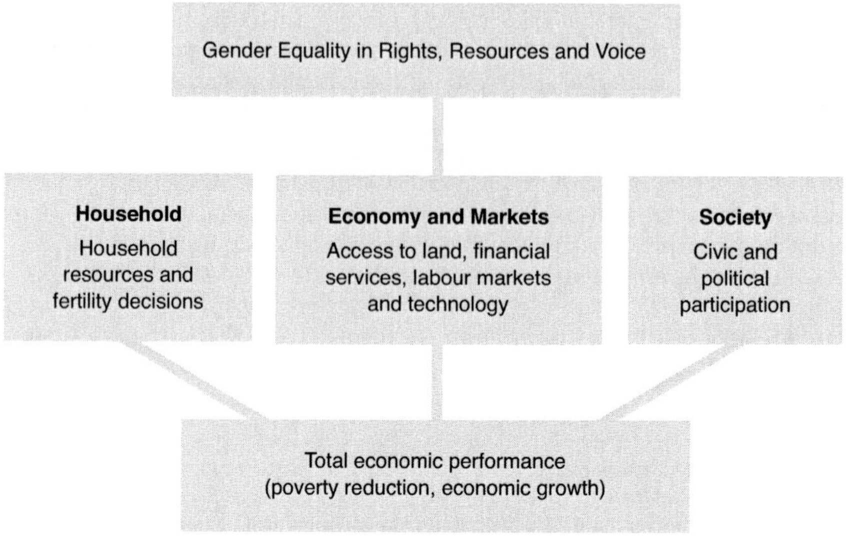

Figure 5.1 Gender equality: a framework. Source: World Bank (2007: 107)

Box 5.9 Linkages between gender inequalities

- In the household, increased gender equality between men and women changes the allocation of household expenditures, resulting in a larger share of resources devoted to children's education and health.
- Gender inequalities influence the distribution of household tasks, limiting women's ability to work outside the home, as well as women's control over fertility decisions.
- In the market, gender inequality is reflected in unequal access to land, credit, and labour markets, and in less access to new production technologies.
- In society, gender inequality is expressed as restrictions to women's participation in civic and political life
- In addition to improving individuals' lives, increased gender equality can contribute to better overall economic performance.

Source: World Bank (2007: 106).

One of the reasons for the disparity in the numbers of girls and boys being educated at secondary level is adolescent motherhood, which is associated with 'early departure from school, lower human capital accumulation, lower earnings, and a higher probability of living in poverty' (World Bank 2007: 126). Even in relatively prosperous South Africa, 49 per cent of pregnancies among African

Table 5.3 Girls' and boys' primary school completion rates (%)

Region	Girls		Boys	
	1991	*2004*	*1991*	*2004*
Sub-Saharan Africa	47.1	56.9	62.3	67.3
East Asia and Pacific	92.3	96.3	92.3	95.8
Middle East and North Africa	73.3	89.0	87.8	92.9
South Asia	68.3	83.0	90.4	90.2

Source: World Bank (2006).

women occur before they are 20 years old, which limits their educational, training and employment opportunities.[4] In fact, the high incidence of teenage births and their health, social and economic costs have led the Global Monitoring Report to call for countries to monitor the percentage of women aged between 15 and 19 years who are mothers or are pregnant, as an additional indicator of gender equality and women's economic empowerment. Figure 5.2 outlines the extent of the incidence across some African states. In traditional cultures girls may be married at the age of 11 or 12 years often for economic gain through dowry transfer.

In terms of political participation, a key indicator of women's advancement, Namibia adopted quota laws for parliamentary and municipal elections in the mid-1990s and women's representation in parliament rose to 28 per cent during 1990–2003. Similarly, in South Africa, when the country's first democratic elections were held in 1994, one-third of all names on each party's national and provincial electoral lists had to be women, and they had to be distributed on the lists in such a way that a third of them would be elected. For the first time black

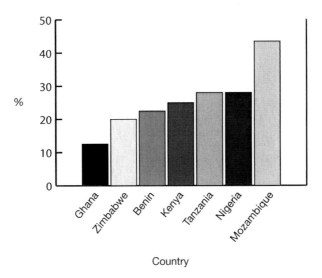

Country

Figure 5.2 Adolescent motherhood: percentage of girls aged 15–19 years (2000–2004).

women were political representatives. Also the local elections in 1995 resulted in a number of women from all walks of life becoming councillors and mayors. One woman, the daughter of a shepherd, cleaned the toilets at the neighbourhood school but she was elected mayor of her local town (Masite interview 1996). Certainly, black women in South Africa brought a new dimension to local politics:

> The hard jobs are done by women. They must keep their kids safe and protected. Men look after their own needs first, not looking to the children, the community. Single-parent families are many and are headed by women. Some can't afford services. A woman councillor would understand their problems.
>
> (Sibisi 1996: 11)

Female political representatives also tackled issues that had not been considered before: help and protection for battered women, homelessness and squatter camps.

The plight of women in rural Africa is especially concerning as they often live in areas without electricity or infrastructure. Equally, nearly half of the households are headed by women. It has been estimated that rural women spend between 90 minutes and three hours per day collecting wood for fuel. Women also travel long distances on foot to fetch clean water (White interview 1996; Haines interview 1996). Often rural women find themselves at the bottom of the heap on grounds of class and gender and many have the least access to processes of decision making unless they take up the challenge themselves. Interestingly, yet perhaps not surprisingly, the Afrobarometer found that rural women in Lesotho, who were excluded from formal education and confined to their areas, tended to be largely apathetic about politics, a sphere they felt had little impact on their lives or life-chances (Brattone *et al*. 2005: 165). Yet, in low-level economies, rural women are able to save, establish loan clubs and engage in income-generating activities. A study of the saving and lending habits of women in the community of Rhini, in South Africa's Eastern Cape region, revealed that women began trading as hawkers and started a money-lending club which made small loans at a standard interest rate of 40 per cent. The majority of credit association members used their funds not only for personal or domestic purchases, but also 'to support business ventures' (Buijs 1995: 9). Equally, Muslim women living in seclusion (purdah) in Sokoto, northern Nigeria, also engaged in informal economic activities. One study revealed that 88 per cent of respondents had 'participated in one form of income-generating activity or another' (Baba and Umaru 2001: 13). Table 5.4 outlines the varied nature of those activities. In order to sell their wares outside the seclusion compound, women often rely on children to hawk their products. Handcrafts usually involve cap weaving and cloth embroidery. Hair plaiting was conducted only in Sokoto South and the medium of exchange was usually on the basis of bartering other goods, such as toilet soap or household necessities. In Botswana, hairdressing has proved to be a popular activity for women, who often conduct their trade from a stationary van.[5]

Table 5.4 Distribution of women's informal economic activities (%)

Activity	Sokoto North	Sokoto South
Selling water/soft drinks	3.3	7.5
Processing and selling food	21.7	45.0
Hair plaiting	0.0	14.2
Handcrafts	62.5	15.0

Source: Baba and Umaru (2001: 13).

Notes: The figures do not add up to 100. The food items processed include *fura*, a porridge made by cooking and pounding millet grains. The resultant paste is rolled into balls and sold.

Ninety-four per cent of women in Sokoto state participated in saving associations or networks, with most favouring the rotating savings associations (*adashi*) or the reciprocal gift network (*biki*) otherwise known as 'bartering'. Participation in an *adashi* group allows a woman to raise lump sums of money at short intervals through her savings. This is especially important for the 'secluded Hausa women who are often by-passed by other sources of finance'. But the *adashi* makes no loans, probably reflecting the restriction on interest (*riba*) which is observed in Islam. In terms of membership, the *adasha* groups are 'open' and 'cut across age, occupation, ethnic group and place of residence' (Baba and Umaru 2001: 14–16). The women use the *adashi* funds in a variety of ways, for example in the traditional areas of female responsibility – cosmetics, toiletries, room decoration – but also on food items and the purchase of clothing, which are core male responsibilities. This is an indication of the transfer of male responsibilities on to women at times of economic pressure (ibid.: 19).

Credit associations operate rather differently and demand weekly contributions from members. There are also restrictions on membership. For example, in southeast Nigeria membership was open only to married women in each community. Unmarried women were not admitted on the grounds that they were not regarded as belonging to the community because they will leave after marriage (Nwajiuba 2000: 7). Yet, despite the restrictions, these associations were of particular benefit to women because they operated a policy of not requiring collateral before granting credit to borrowers. Traditional collateral and security is often land, which is not usually controlled by women. Again rural women use the credit predominantly to maintain their farming livelihoods – crop production and livestock rearing – as well as hospital bills and other social needs. Although credit associations are both useful and necessary they operate at a very low level of finance and the volume of credit which women obtain is 'inadequate relative to their needs' (ibid.: 15).

It is clear that capacity building is essential and UNIFEM has called for governments, NGOs and donors to focus more directly on women and poverty-reduction strategies (UNIFEM 2007). The World Bank acknowledges that gender disparities at the micro level not only disadvantage women but also reduce the growth potential of regions as a whole: 'The existence of gender-related barriers can thwart the economic potential of women as entrepreneurs and workers, and such barriers have an adverse impact on enterprise development' (World Bank 2007: 69). It has also drawn up data on the nature and size of female-owned enterprises, as outlined in Table 5.5.

However, most of women's economic activities take place in the informal sector, which is difficult to monitor and assess. Equally, the informal sector is not an ideal form of enterprise for a country's development as neither taxes nor regulation may be imposed. This is one reason why South Africa has tried to target and organize the informal sector. As part of metropolitan initiatives, partly funded by the corporate sector, arts and craft markets have been established with the aim of 'getting people off the street'. Traders then pay rent for each market stall. This has occurred in Johannesburg and Tshwane (formerly Pretoria) and is a marked improvement from the dreadful conditions of informal female street traders who were often accompanied by their babies. By using tourism as the 'engine of

Table 5.5 Percentage of female-owned enterprises, by sector and size

Country	Textile	Afro-food	Other manufacture	Services	Micro (1–9 employees)	Small (10–49 employees)
Angola		40	10	29	25	25
Benin		13	8	n/a	10	7
Botswana			58	56	56	54
Burundi			21	32	31	42
Ethiopia	14	11	10	n/a	11	12
Gambia	24		11	36	27	18
Malawi		23	15	n/a		15
Mali		30	3	n/a	19	11
Mozambique		46	42	n/a		43
Namibia			17	45	41	32
South Africa	15	3	10			12
Tanzania		9	6	n/a	3	10
Uganda		38	16	41	31	30
Zambia		15	13			8

Source: Adapted from World Bank Enterprise Surveys, 2002–2006 (http://web.worldbank.org/wbsite/external/countries).

Table 5.6 Percentage of household spending on utilities

Expenditure	September 1999	May 2000	May 2001
Council Service payments	51.0	72.0	68.0
Electricity cards	0.0	97.0	97.0

Source: Interview with the Community Agency for Social Enquiry, Johannesburg, 2002.

growth' local women in rural areas started to provide bed and breakfast facilities (Sithole interview 2002). There has also been an upgrading of the informal settlements in the Gauteng region (including Johannesburg and the former Pretoria) with the provision of electricity. In Albertina, a small settlement of 493 residents, predominantly female, almost all households spend at least some money on electricity cards and council services (see Table 5.6). Although the improvement of the locality is beneficial and to be welcomed, the question of 'affordability' is a serious concern. Community-based organizations assert that 'one of the most important policy issues demanding attention are the needs of women and children'. Essentially, there must be sustainable ways in which female households can meet their 'social, economic and material' requirements.[6] If charges that poverty 'wears a female face' and that an overwhelming majority of 'the poor and marginalized are women' are to be combated, African states together with international agencies, must make gender equality an absolute priority.

6 Corruption

One of the key tasks of the Afrobarometer survey in African countries has been to adequately define what is meant by the term 'corruption'. To some this may seem a strange quest, surely the answer is obvious: 'over-billing, bribes, kickbacks, "ghost" employees, retainers for relatives, excessive overtime claims, personal use of pension schemes and state vehicles, misappropriation of state and donor funds, extravagant travel abroad for suspect state purposes, the falsification of public documents and records' etc. (Gundy 2000: 46). Others put it more pithily: corruption is 'the unsanctioned or unscheduled use of public resources for private ends' (Lodge 1997: 10), or more succinctly 'the abuse of entrusted power for private gain' (Transparency International 2007). So why bother interviewing and asking questions when the answers are widely known and acknowledged? Well, one reason is because a debate has developed regarding the possible cultural causes of corruption. That is, societies who see a cultural obligation to give gifts or who place familial loyalty over the demands of office may not fully identify corrupt practices: 'from an African perspective it is perfectly in order to exchange gifts' (Ouma 2005: 473–90). So gift-giving may be carried from the private to the public sphere with no acknowledgement that the environment may be different (Robertson-Snape 2006: 589–602). The Afrobarometer study wished to establish if corruption really did have a cultural base and whether the concept was perceived differently in varied communities. Essentially, it asserted: is it accurate that the 'international community may be defining as corrupt actions that merely reflect normal cultural practices of "gift giving" in Africa?' (Afrobarometer 2005: 32).

Table 6.1 outlines the questions that were posed in the context of defining corruption and charts the averaged percentages of all respondents. It is clear that respondents recognized corruption, which led Afrobarometer to conclude: 'traditional cultural practices, whether of gift giving or other varieties, do not, in the eyes of the public, entitle government officials to take advantage of them' (ibid.). However, the aggregated responses do not always reflect the attitudes of individual countries, which deviate quite considerably from those figures. Table 6.2 considers specific states – Uganda, Zambia, Nigeria, Namibia and Madagascar – all of which define, explain or excuse aspects of corrupt practices. Madagascar makes

Table 6.1 Defining corruption in Africa

Questions posed in survey to Africans	Selection of responses in categories	% of total respondents
1. A public official decides to locate a development project in an area where his friends and supporters live	Not wrong at all	13
	Wrong but understandable	24
	Wrong and punishable	61
	Don't know	3
2. A government official gives a job to someone from his family who does not have adequate qualifications	Not wrong at all	5
	Wrong but understandable	18
	Wrong and punishable	75
	Don't know	2
3. A government official demands a favour or an additional payment for some service that is part of his job	Not wrong at all	5
	Wrong but understandable	16
	Wrong and punishable	77
	Don't know	3

Source: Afrobarometer (2005).

an interesting study because around one-third to two-fifths of respondents did not condemn outright the corrupt acts of officials in allocating development projects. Equally, one-quarter to one-third of Nigerian respondents partly accepted corruption whereas, in a Transparency International public opinion survey on whether or not corruption affected people's lives, more than '70 per cent' of Nigerian respondents indicated that 'corruption affected their personal and family lives to a large extent' (Transparency International 2006). This suggests that if communities do not lay down firm rules for public and bureaucratic officials on what is and is not acceptable behaviour the effects of corruption will seep into their own lives. Sending out mixed messages about corrupt practices in the public domain simply encourages more corruption at grassroots level, which infiltrates people's daily lives and quickly has a corrosive effect on wider society.

Bureaucracies have long been seen as susceptible to corruption because they are employed by the state and are often paid very little. Consequently, they resort to corrupt practices in order to augment their incomes:

> the pocketing of a proportion of the money handed over in payment for government services, such as, export licences, legal fines, passports or even the simple registration of births and deaths. Indeed, anything that needs an official stamp or signature.
>
> (Thomson 2000: 84)

Certainly, Transparency International reports:

> Bribery for access to services is most common in Africa. Registrations and permits command the biggest bribes, on average more than $50. Bribes to

Table 6.2 Certain countries' responses to corrupt practices

Questions posed as in Table 6.1	Categories of responses	Madagascar	Uganda	Nigeria	Namibia	Zambia
1. A public official decides to locate a development project in an area where his friends and supporters live	Not wrong at all	38	31	13	13	13
	Wrong but understandable	35	35	30	30	33
	Wrong and punishable	23	34	51	52	54
2. A government official gives a job to someone from his family who does not have adequate qualifications	Not wrong at all	9	7	6	6	3
	Wrong but understandable	34	29	25	20	26
	Wrong and punishable	53	63	68	73	71
3. A government official demands a favour or an additional payment to some service that is part of his job	Not wrong at all	9	8	7	9	8
	Wrong but understandable	30	29	25	30	22
	Wrong and punishable	58	62	66	58	29

Source: Afrobarometer (2005).

Note: Don't Know is excluded from this table but included in the original.

utility companies average $6 but are still large enough to place electricity and other vital services out of the reach of the Continent's desperately poor citizens.

(Transparency International 2006)

African respondents to the Global Corruption Barometer revealed they had, on average, paid more than two bribes each for access to services that should be their right. Ultimately, it is the public who is 'the victim in this vicious corruption cycle' (ibid.).

Judicial corruption

> Equal treatment before the law is a pillar of democratic societies. When courts are corrupted by greed or political expediency, the scales of justice are tipped, and ordinary people suffer. Judicial corruption means the voice of the innocent goes unheard, while the guilty act with impunity.
>
> (Huguette Labelle, Chair of Transparency International)

> If money and influence are the basis of justice, the poor cannot compete. Bribery not only makes justice unaffordable; it ruins the capacity of the justice system to fight against corruption and to serve as a beacon of independence and accountability.
>
> (Akere Muna, President of the Pan African Lawyers' Union)

Institutions that are intended to provide checks and balances within political systems are generally under-resourced and lack independence. The UK's Commission for Africa viewed corruption as a 'by-product' of weak governance that manifests itself in a variety of ways: judicial, political and economic. The role of the justice system, including judges and lawyers, police and prison officers, is to guarantee rights and uphold the law equally for all sections of society. If this is lacking, ordinary people suffer violence, crime and insecurity. In order to fulfil their role, 'all sections of the justice system need to be impartial, adequately funded and independent of government' (Commission for Africa 2005: 149). The Commission found, however, that this is often not the case: 'too little money and too few professionally trained people continue to hamper performance, as does political intimidation and corruption.' It cites the example of Sierra Leone, which has a population of nearly 6 million yet has only 125 lawyers, 95 of whom are based in the capital, Freetown, with cases taking three or four years to come to court (ibid.: 144). For Transparency International judicial corruption includes any inappropriate influence on the impartiality of the judicial process by any actor within the court system. 'Judicial systems debased by bribery undermine confidence in governance by facilitating corruption across all sectors of government ... they send a blunt message to the people: in this country corruption is tolerated' (Transparency International 2007). For some examples of judicial corruption see Box 6.1.

Box 6.1 Examples of judicial corruption

- A judge may allow or exclude evidence with the aim of justifying the acquittal of a guilty defendant of high political or social status
- Judges or court staff may manipulate court dates to favour one party or another
- In countries where there are no verbatim transcripts, judges may inaccurately summarise court proceedings or distort witness testimony before delivering a verdict that has been purchased by one of the parties in the case
- Junior court personnel may 'lose' a file – for a price.
- Judges may hire family members to staff their courts or offices

Source: Transparency International (2007).

Generally, there are two types of corruption that most affect judiciaries:

1 political interference in judicial processes by either the executive or legislative branches of government;
2 bribery.

One example of political interference in Zimbabwe over the critical issue of land rights is cited in Box 6.2. A pliable judiciary provides 'legal' protection to those in power and encourages an environment in which the rule of law is meaningless. In states where the political elite is so powerful, laws become arbitrary and distorted. Equally, bribery can take place at every level of the legal process, as outlined in Box 6.3. Opaque court processes that foster bribery can also prevent the media and civil society from monitoring court activity and exposing judicial corruption. That is why corruption in the judiciary is a 'central focus' of global

Box 6.2 Corrupt judges and land rights in Zimbabwe

In 2000 the Zimbabwean government began a purge that resulted in most independent judges being replaced by judges known to owe allegiance to the ruling party, Zanu PF. Corruption has played a role in compromising judicial independence because the allocation of expropriated farms to several judges has made them beholden to the executive. The failure of the courts to uphold the rule of law in land cases has created the impression that the security of property rights is no longer guaranteed. With few exceptions, judges are seen to have collaborated with a government that has violated many of the rights of its citizens, including freedom of expression, freedom of the press, freedom of assembly and the right to free and fair elections.

Source: Moyo and Ashurst (2007).

Box 6.3 Examples of bribery within the judicial system

- Court officials may extort money for work they should do anyway
- Lawyers may charge additional 'fees' to expedite or delay cases
- Lawyers may direct clients to judges known to take bribes for favourable decisions
- Judges may accept bribes to delay or accelerate cases
- Judges may accept bribes to accept or deny appeals, or to influence other judges

Source: Transparency International (2007).

anti-corruption efforts. A corrupt judiciary has a 'powerful and corrosive' influence over society as a whole (Transparency International 2007). Box 6.4 outlines the problems confronting some African states.

If judicial corruption is to be undermined it needs to be tackled head on. Transparency International has found that certain commonalities can be identified which may point the way towards reform. The problems included:

- Judicial appointments – The failure to appoint judges on merit can lead to the selection of pliant, corruptible judges
- Terms and conditions – Poor salaries and insecure working conditions, unfair processes for promotion, lack of training leads to court personnel being vulnerable to corruption
- Accountability and discipline – Unfair or ineffective processes for the discipline and removal of corrupt judges
- Transparency – Opaque court processes prevent the media and civil society from monitoring court activity and exposing corruption

(Transparency International 2007)

One of the interesting findings in the Transparency International Global Corruption survey is that a majority of people in six of the seven sub-Saharan African countries polled perceived their legal system/judiciary to be corrupt. These were Cameroon, Congo-Brazzaville, Gabon, Kenya, Nigeria and Senegal. Only South Africa disagreed with this view. Yet in the Afrobarometer, when respondents in Kenya and Nigeria were asked whether judges and magistrates were corrupt, a minority thought they were (see Table 6.3). There was consistency only in South Africa, which suggests that perceptions of corruption may alter dependent upon the type of question asked. What is revealed in both the Transparency International findings and the Afrobarometer is that the police are considered to be the most corrupt. Fifty-five percent of African respondents in the Global Corruption survey had paid a bribe to the police and the majority of respondents in the Afrobarometer considered the police to be corrupt (see Table 6.4) The police force is the organization to which bribes are most commonly paid.

Box 6.4 Persistent judicial problems in Africa

- Nigeria, Niger, Zambia, Zimbabwe: Political influence over the selection of judges is especially serious
- Niger: Less than 200 judges and law officers for a population of 11 million. The excessive workload on the lower courts slows down proceedings, allowing corruption to flourish
- South Africa: Few courts are computerized and many transactions are not properly recorded. An audit of magistrate offices uncovered significant misappropriation of funds with regard to maintenance, bail money and deposits
- Zambia: Lack of training and shortage of magistrates
- Kenya: The saying 'why hire a lawyer, if you can buy a judge' is common. Widespread loss of public trust in the justice system

Source: Transparency International (2007).

Table 6.3 Perceptions of corruption among judges and magistrates (%)

How many judges and magistrates do you think are involved in corruption?	*South Africa*	*Kenya*	*Nigeria*
None/Some of them	62	57	56
Most/All of them	22	28	41

Source: Afrobarometer (2005).

Table 6.4 Perceptions of corruption among the police (%)

How many police are involved in corruption?	*Total respondents*
None/Some of them	40
Most/All of them	45

Source: Afrobarometer (2005).

Political corruption

The political environment in many African states has been fraught with difficulties, not least within the sphere of corrupt practices:

> Africa has suffered from governments that have looted the resources of the state; that could not or would not deliver services to their people; that in many cases were predatory, corruptly extracting their countries' resources; that maintained control through violence and bribery; and that squandered and stolen aid.
>
> (Commission for Africa 2005: 106)

This damning indictment of Africa's political history was made by the UK's Commission for Africa, which, under the direction of the UK's then Prime Minister, Tony Blair, was intended to focus attention on the continent. But do Africans regard their politicians as corrupt? Table 6.5 indicates that at an aggregate level a majority do not. However, at individual country level this perception changes. For example, in Nigeria, 54 per cent consider their president and his entourage to be corrupt and a massive 59 per cent regard members of parliament as corrupt. These were the highest percentages of perceived political corruption across the whole Afrobarometer survey of this area.

Improved governance lies at the heart of combating corruption in Africa and the UN has outlined the central tenets of good governance (see Box 6.5). Yet, although two-thirds of African countries have had multi-party elections within the recent past, not all elections have involved the transfer of power from one party or president to another. As elections have become increasingly recognized as necessary political events, when they are badly or corruptly managed, popular frustration emerges. Contested, violent and corrupt electoral behaviour have been apparent in a range of countries: Zimbabwe, São Tomé and Príncipe, Togo, Equatorial Guinea, Côte d'Ivoire and Mauritania, with Côte d'Ivoire lapsing into civil conflict following disputed polling. The role of political parties can also be problematic with many lacking any financial transparency or internal democracy. If one-quarter of respondents believe their members of parliament are mostly corrupt, as Table 6.5 indicates, then political parties are also implicated: 'looting is carried out by political actors dipping straight into state funds' (Williamson 2005). In 2008 a prominent cabinet minister in Tanzania resigned following allegations that he had 'stashed away $1 million in an offshore account' (EISA 2008d).

If members of parliament are not trusted to carry out their duties appropriately and honestly they can provide no oversight or guidance in regard to curbing corruption. Transparency International staff are involved directly with members of parliament through the African Parliamentarians' Network against Corruption (APNAC). There is also the African Union Convention on Combating Corruption and Related Offences, which some countries have signed. Interestingly, the AU Convention does not define the term 'corruption'; rather it defines acts of corruption, providing comprehensive guidelines to what is not acceptable behaviour (see Box 6.6). Yet according to the African Human Security Initiative (AHSI) 'the

Table 6.5 Perceptions of corruption among politicians

Question	*Mean of respondents (%)*
Are the president and his officials corrupt?	
None/Some of them	54
Most/All of them	22
Are members of parliament corrupt?	
None/Some of them	52
Most/All of them	25

Source: Afrobarometer (2005).

Box 6.5 The UN's Commission on Human Rights

The UN Commission on Human Rights has identified eight major characteristics of good governance:

1 Participation: good governance needs organized and informed participation in public affairs by both men and women. Such participation could either be direct or through legitimate intermediate institutions or representatives;
2 Rule of law: there should be a fair legal framework that is enforced impartially. Furthermore, there should be protection of human rights and an impartial enforcement of laws. This would require an independent judiciary and an impartial and incorruptible police force;
3 Transparency: decisions taken by public bodies must be taken and their enforcement carried out in a manner that follows rules and regulations. In addition, information should be freely available and directly accessible to those who will be affected by the decisions of the public authorities;
4 Responsiveness: institutions and processes should try to serve all stakeholders within a reasonable timeframe;
5 Consensus: in view of the fact that there are several actors and as many viewpoints in a given society, good governance requires mediation of the different interests in society to reach a broad consensus on what is in the best interest of the whole community and how this can be achieved;
6 Equity and inclusiveness: all members of a society need to feel that they have a stake in it and do not feel excluded from the mainstream of society. This is important particularly to the most vulnerable members of the society;
7 Effectiveness and efficiency: processes and institutions should produce results that meet the needs of society while making the best use of resources at their disposal; and
8 Accountability: governmental institutions, private sector and civil society organisations must be accountable to the public and to their institutional stakeholders.

Source: Resolution 2000/64. United Nations Commission on Human Rights

Box 6.6 Definitions of acts of corruption by the African Union Convention on Combating Corruption and Related Offences

a The solicitation or acceptance, directly or indirectly, by a public official or any other person, of any goods of monetary value, or other benefit, such as a gift, favour, promise or advantage for himself or herself or for another person or entity, in exchange for any act or omission in the performance of his or her public functions

b The offering or granting, directly or indirectly, to a public official or any other person, of any goods of monetary value, or other benefit, such as a gift, favour, promise or advantage for himself or herself or for another person or entity, in exchange for any act or omission in the performance of his or her public functions

c Any act or omission in the discharge of his or her duties by a public official or any other person for the purpose of illicitly obtaining benefits for himself or herself or for a third party

d The diversion by a public official or any other person, for purposes unrelated to those for which they were intended, for his or her own benefit or that of a third party, of any property belonging to the state or its agencies, to an independent agency, or to an individual, that such official has received by virtue of his or her position

e The offering or giving, promising, solicitation or acceptances, directly or indirectly, or any undue advantage to or by any person who directs or works for, in any capacity, a private sector entity for himself or herself or for anyone else, for him or her to act, or refrain from acting, in breach of his or her duties

f The offering, giving, solicitation or acceptance directly or indirectly, or promising of any undue advantage to or by any person who asserts or confirms that he or she is able to exert any improper influence over the decision making of any person performing functions in the public or private sector in consideration thereof, whether the undue advantage is for himself or for anyone else, as well as the request, receipt or the acceptance of the offer or the promise of such an advantage, in consideration of that influence, whether or not the influence is exerted or whether or not the supposed influence leads to the intended result

g The significant increase in the assets of a public official or any other person that he or she cannot reasonably explain

h The use or concealment of proceeds derived from any of the acts referred to in this article, and

i Participation as a principal, co-principal, agent, instigator, accomplice after the fact, or in any other manner in the commission or attempted commission of, in any collaboration or conspiracy to commit any of the acts referred to in this article.

Source: Article 4. African Union Convention on Combating Corruption and Related Offences.

characteristics of good governance complement those that seek to measure the levels of corruption'. A country lacking any of the UN's essential characteristics of good governance means that it 'offers a permissive environment for corruption' (Kututwa 2005: 3).

Certainly, if corruption is to be eradicated, societies, states and grassroots organizations must be pro-active, yet this raises the question of how far people actually feel empowered. The issue of empowerment concerned Afrobarometer, which wanted to understand 'how African citizens will respond when they encounter situations of incompetence or abuse of power on the part of the state'. Would they fight back or would they 'acquiesce, letting the state continue to get away with mismanagement and abuse of public trust?' There was also a political dimension to this issue: were they 'active and watchful' citizens or 'passive subjects of an all powerful state'? The results, when averaged, seem to indicate that the majority of respondents would act as pro-active citizens and lodge complaints (see Table 6.6). Yet when individual countries are considered the responses vary considerably. As Table 6.7 demonstrates, the negative or passive replies from respondents in Zimbabwe, Lesotho, Nigeria and Zambia to being left off the electoral roll were far higher than the mean figure of 25 per cent. In Zimbabwe, a total of 35 per cent of respondents felt they should wait or do nothing as it was of no use. The responses

Table 6.6 Would people fight against corruption?

Question	Mean response (%)
What would you do if election officials left your name off the voters' roll?	
Don't worry, wait	7
Nothing, no use	18
Offer tip or bribe	1
Use connections	7
Lodge complaint	55
What would you do if you suspected a school or clinic official of stealing?	
Don't worry, wait	4
Nothing, no use	11
Offer tip or bribe	1
Use connections	7
Lodge complaint	64
What would you do if the police wrongly arrested someone in your family?	
Don't worry, wait	3
Nothing, no use	7
Offer tip or bribe	4
Use connections	10
Lodge complaint	67

Source: Afrobarometer (2006: 39).

Table 6.7 Country responses to corruption (%)

What would you do if election officials left your name off the voters' roll?	Zimbabwe	Lesotho	Nigeria	Zambia
Don't worry, wait	3	6	6	5
Nothing, no use	32	28	25	27
Offer tip or bribe	1	1	2	1
Use connections	4	2	8	4
Lodge complaint	57	56	49	58

Source: Afrobarometer (2006: 39).

to this issue are much the same in Lesotho (34 per cent) and just marginally lower in Zambia (32 per cent) and Nigeria (31 per cent). Even though more respondents would take some type of formal action, around one-third would not, which is an extremely large percentage. Equally, these figures suggest that significant minorities feel disempowered and unable to do anything when confronted by the state. The Afrobarometer aggregates all responses other than in the category 'lodge complaint' as indicators of 'acquiescence' because 'in one way or another, they all accept the failures of the state system to function as it should, and either give-up, or try to circumvent the system' (Afrobarometer 2006: 38).

Economic corruption

It has been estimated that around 42 per cent of Kenya's gross national product goes to bribes (Kodi interview 2004). Corruption, of course, can be broken down into different levels of abuse. Petty corruption operating at low levels of society affects primarily poor people, whereas grand corruption is more prevalent in the procurement areas and relates to 'kickbacks' so that a contract can continue. The 'legendary 20% on top' has serious macroeconomic impacts (Williamson 2005). The drive of the 'publish what you pay' campaign that was directed at the relationship and exchange of monies between political elites and the corporate sector has been strong and supported by Human Rights Watch and Transparency International (see www.publishwhatyoupay.org). Of course, many countries in Africa have abundant natural resources which can be beneficial yet at the same time problematic. Although they may bring considerable income to the respective country they have also been identified as 'vulnerable' areas, especially in the sphere of natural resource extraction, where 'corruption can lead to conflict, or political and social unrest' (Eigen 2006). The Extractive Industries Transparency Initiative (EITI) introduced in 2002 was designed to increase transparency in revenue flows between oil, gas and mining companies and their host governments. The objectives of the Initiative are to monitor and publicize these revenues so that 'citizens can hold their governments to account for their use of the money' (ibid.). An agreement is made under which oil, gas and mining companies agree publicly to disclose all payments they make to developing countries and the governments agree to publish what they receive. Four African states, Nigeria, Ghana, Republic of Congo and São Tomé and Príncipe, have decided to participate in the Initiative. This is an important move because it is often resource-dependent countries that have poor levels of human development, which are, in part, linked to the 'mismanagement and misappropriation of revenues and corruption'. For example, revenues resulting from oil exports often increase the wealth of the ruling elite alone (Commission for Africa 2005: 145). Table 6.8 indicates the UNDP Human Development Index in relation to the countries' dependence on natural resources. See Box 6.7 for the Nigerian profile.

The corporate environment has also needed to address the issue of complicity in corruption, both within the business community as well within relations between business and the public sector. It has been recognized that the 'willingness of some businesses to engage in bribery may create a more permissive climate in which public officials feel that they have *carte blanche* to seek to extort payments' (Business Action for Africa 2006: 37). Another area, procurement, that is, the way in which governments buy in goods and services, is causing concern. Abuse of this system takes many forms. The Commission for Africa were most concerned that, although public sector contracts were put out to tender, 'bribes – known by euphemisms such as "signature bonuses" – can be requested or offered which result in the accepted bid not being the best available.' But politicians and public officials are not the only actors involved in this corrupt practice; so too are 'the bankers, the lawyers, the accountants and the engineers working on public contracts' (Commission for Africa 2005: 150). So in terms of international trade, procurement, extraction of natural resources and professional engagement with Africa the developed world is also culpable. One member of the Commission for Africa asserted: 'It's not enough to say Africans are corrupt, you have to ask who is corrupting them? It's not enough to say Africans are stealing money, you have to ask who is banking that money for them?' (Ms Anna Tibaijuka cited in Bunting 2005: 6). These are hard issues to confront but if corruption is to be tackled it has to be fully acknowledged that, whereas natural resources, such as oil and

Table 6.8 Natural resources and HDI ranking

Country	% share of primary commodities in exports (2000)	HDI ranking (2002) (out of 177)
Equatorial Guinea	91.8	109
Angola	92.6	166
Congo	97.5	168
Gabon	86.6	122
Guinea-Bissau	99.7	172
Nigeria	98.1	151

Sources: UNCTAD Commodity Yearbook 2003 (www.unctad.org/inforcomm/yearbook); UNDP Human Development Report 2003 (http://hdr.undp.org/en/reports/global/hdr2003).

HDI ranking includes life expectancy, education as measured by literacy and school enrolment rates, and standard of living as measured by per capita gross domestic product and purchasing power.

Box 6.7 Nigeria's profile

Nigeria is the largest oil and gas producer in Africa. Petroleum accounts for over 70% of the country's revenues at all levels of government, 40% of Gross Domestic Product, and more than 85% of foreign exchange earnings. Improving transparency in this sector offers great benefits not only to the industry but also to the country as a whole. Mrs Obiageli Ezekwesili, Chair of the Nigerian Extractive Industries Transparency Initiative, is interviewed by Transparency Watch.

Q. What challenges face the Initiative?

A. The volume of crude oil that is unaccounted for. Nigeria's measurements are of oil that reaches export terminals, rather than oil pumped directly from oilfields. What is currently in place does not follow the oil through the pipeline.

Q. Has the Initiative changed Nigeria's relationship with oil and gas companies?

A. Because Nigeria has made the publication of payments and revenues compulsory the companies know the government is not fooling around.

Q. How many Nigerians are aware of this Initiative?

A. About 45% and growing

Q. How can civil society strengthen this Initiative?

A. This Initiative should be spread across a wide range of sectors. Civil society should benefit from the power of the internet to spread information and share experiences.

Source: www.transparency.org/publications/newsletter/2006/July_2006/interview.

diamonds, have generated conflict within Africa, much of the wealth they have generated has ended up in Western bank accounts. That is why it is important that the Business Action for Africa network includes companies such as De Beers, Shell, Rio Tinto and Anglo American, as well as banks: Standard Chartered and Citigroup. These are relatively new initiatives but they have not come a moment too soon in highlighting the complex international dimensions of economic corruption.

Under the AU/UK's New Partnership for Africa's Development (Nepad), the African Peer Review Mechanism was introduced, to which 24 countries, including Ghana and Kenya, have signed up. Central to tackling corruption and a key part of wider moves to enhance governance is to have greater levels of transparency. It is hoped APRM will provide an African approach to improving good governance and accountability as well as providing a means to curb corrupt practices. Countries will essentially assess each other and potentially it is a strong measure because it involves a number of key areas:

- political issues, democracy and governance and the rule of law;
- economic governance and long-term poverty reduction;
- socio-economic governance including evaluation of policies on such issues as health, education, water and sanitation;
- corporate governance – looking at the health of the private sector.

Some sceptics have judged the APRM initiative as simply a means of letting 'the bad boys review themselves.' Yet its report on Kenya's post-2007 electoral conflict did raise the issue of corrupt practices and pointed to the fact that members of the ruling party and high-ranking government officials had been neither 'investigated nor prosecuted' and were still in post. The inability or unwillingness to act against them 'underlined the general public perception of impunity' and further exacerbated feelings of injustice within the country. In fact, the report was seen as 'remarkably frank' as it 'did not shy away from highlighting issues of corruption, especially in land allocation' (APRM Eminent Persons' Report on Kenya 2008 and B. Manby, both cited in EISA 2008b). This may be a positive sign that the APRM will actually lead to a greater sense of responsibility and accountability within the continent.

Anti-corruption measures

For the African Human Security Initiative (AHSI) the legislative framework is the starting point in the fight against corruption. All states should have anti-corruption laws in place that lay out a clear and unambiguous process:

1 the enactment and enforcement of criminal laws that effectively deal with corruption;
2 the adoption of legislative mechanisms and procedures for the public to submit complaints related to corruption, including the protection of witnesses and whistle-blowers (Kututwa 2005: 3–4).

A number of countries have introduced anti-corruption laws. In 2001 Ethiopia introduced new legislation, an Anti-Corruption and Economic Crimes Act was enacted in Kenya in 2003, South Africa passed the Prevention and Combating of Corrupt Activities Act no. 12 in 2004 and Nigeria has promulgated the Independent Corrupt Practices and Other Related Offences Act, which criminalized corruption. However, the fight against corruption needs more than legislation; it needs 'strong political will on the part of the government to ensure no offender escapes the law – regardless of position or status in society' (ibid.: 4). There are even problems in those countries that have introduced legislation: in Kenya, for example, people who have been accused of corruption are still in government. Equally, the African Human Security Initiative doubts there is adequate political will in Ethiopia or Senegal to confront corruption. The anti-corruption campaign in Ethiopia seems more interested in settling 'political scores' rather than seriously attacking corrupt practices (ibid.).

Concerns have also been expressed about Nigeria and its decision to change its anti-corruption apparatus and introduce a new anti-graft body, the Special Legal Unit. This unit is intended to be distinct from the Economic Financial Crimes Commission, a body which had gained national and international respect for Nigerian law enforcement, which loses key powers. Following the difficult elections of 2007 it is feared that organizations with overlapping powers will simply compete with each other rather than deliver efficient and effective oversight (Africa Programme, Chatham House, 29 October 2007). Oversight institutions include all bodies that are specifically charged to investigate and prosecute those found guilty of committing acts of corruption. The AU's Convention on Corruption provides states with guidelines on the competence of these agencies. States must ensure that:

1 anti-corruption agencies are autonomous, independent and governed by laws that are effective;
2 other oversight institutions are introduced, e.g. Inspector-General/Auditor-General;
3 the independence of the judiciary is safeguarded and there is effective parliamentary oversight.

One of the central requirements of oversight institutions is highly qualified, professional staff. But these skills can be lacking in personnel who have not been trained adequately or educated appropriately. Even in Botswana there is recognition of the need for capacity building in the form of legal and management training in public institutions (Kututwa 2005; Seleetso interview 2004).

The World Bank has begun a process of enforcement monitoring of the performances of certain countries with regard to anti-corruption measures. It focuses on primary government corruption enforcement institutions: anti-corruption agencies, prosecution services and the courts. In order to carry out this analysis, the bank has framed a number of questions. To what degree are these institutions investigating and prosecuting allegations of corruption? What percentage of complaints is investigated? How many investigations mature into prosecutions? How many result in convictions? And within this, are anti-corruption institutions monitoring these questions? In the case of Nigeria, the government initiated 209 investigations in 2005. That same year prosecutions were started in 14 cases and one court case ended with an acquittal (Mennen *et al.* 2007). Although this is not perfect information, as the prosecution office in Nigeria does no reporting, any information is regarded as better than none. That is why Transparency International (TI) has begun to monitor civil and criminal proceedings. In Ghana, for example, it has promoted court monitoring by raising awareness, offering training and preparing a Judiciary Watch manual. TI's offices in Madagascar have distributed brochures that describe court procedures in different languages. The main objective of this action is to 'promote transparency in the Ministry of Justice and reduce petty corruption by informing users about court procedures' (Transparency

International 2006). It is clear, then, that monitoring anti-corruption measures operates at both high and low levels within society.

Can corruption be overcome?

There is no doubt that corruption is many-faceted and can be deeply rooted within countries. Consequently, no one-dimensional measure will fully tackle the problem. Certainly, the political will and determination of leaders is essential but it may not be sufficient. There must be institutional reform and increased accountability of the judiciary, legislature, security services and other institutions of government. But again, without adequately trained, educated and rigorous personnel these institutions may be weak and ineffective. Legal systems must focus attention on procurement processes and not be afraid or uncertain of prosecuting powerful and important people if they are suspected of engaging in corrupt practices. A free media and active, sophisticated civil society both play an important role in shining a light on corruption. The international community's emphasis on anti-corruption is useful but should not lead to purely cosmetic organizations being set up in states that are keen to tick the boxes of multilateral donors. Any anti-corruption institution set up simply to meet the requirements of international agencies will be neither effective nor efficient. Equally, the business practices of the developed world must not exacerbate or be complicit in corrupt arrangements with governments of developing countries. Grand corruption and looting cannot be addressed without the skilled assistance of countries in the West, especially when monies have been spirited away to Western banks. Asset recovery is now gaining far greater attention. The United Nations also has an important role to play in both alerting the global environment to the menace of corruption and providing a framework for tackling the issue. Although it has tended to concentrate on advocacy, it has become pro-active on certain occasions. For example, the UN held a panel on the illegal exploitation of the mineral resources of the Democratic Republic of Congo (see www.un.org/apps). If corrupt practices are viewed as a part of everyday life about which little or nothing can be done, a deep malaise spreads over the whole of society with pernicious effects on all sectors: political, economic, legal and business. In short, every aspect of a nation becomes tainted with corruption. Although Transparency International found there were some grounds for optimism in Africa's anti-corruption measures, there was a considerable 'gap between commitments and actions'. Ultimately, it concluded 'greater political commitment is required if African governments are to be effective in combating corruption' (Transparency International 2006).

7   Disease and human security

Important health issues

The health problems confronting Africa are numerous and varied but, perhaps most worryingly, many are preventable through either treatment or improved sanitary conditions. According to reports from the African Red Cross and Red Crescent Health Initiative (ARCHI), 70 per cent of all childhood mortality is the result of five major conditions: diarrhoeal diseases, acute lower respiratory tract infections (ARI), malnutrition, malaria and measles. Often children suffer multiple conditions simultaneously so managing just one condition would not necessarily prevent death from other underlying illnesses. Even mild malnutrition increases the risk of death from other preventable diseases, as immunity and resistance are low. Consequently, ARCHI recommends that programmes need to focus on all five conditions at the same time (African Red Cross and Red Crescent Societies 2007). Figure 7.1 provides a collective indication of common diseases in the continent; Box 7.1 gives a more detailed breakdown of the illnesses which are challenging communities and governments.

The Health Initiative, running between the years 2000 and 2010, coordinates the work of the 53 Red Cross/Red Crescent (RC/RC) groups operating in Africa into a process which aims to be more effective at the grassroots level. Sometimes just a lack of a particular vitamin can have a major impact on a young child's survival chances. For example, Vitamin A deficiency (VAD) in children under the age of five years can dramatically increase their risk of early death. Africa has the highest prevalence of clinical VAD, which causes blindness and debilitation (see Box 7.2). Yet this deficiency can be easily remedied, as the vitamin can be administered with the oral polio vaccine and measles vaccines from six months of age. In fact, immunization programmes could successfully prevent a range of diseases that are unnecessarily affecting young Africans but sometimes, although an effective vaccine may exist, it is not widely used. One example of this is the high incidence of yellow fever in 34 African countries despite the fact that a vaccine could be used (see Box 7.3). Because immunization rates are poor, epidemics continue to occur. The disease is found in tropical forest areas where the virus survives in monkeys. Humans contract the disease via mosquitoes, which spread it

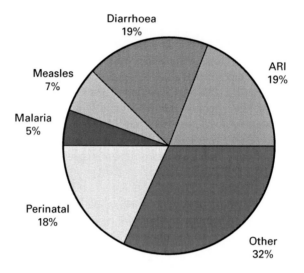

Figure 7.1 Major health problems in Africa. ARI – acute respiratory illness.

Box 7.1 Common diseases in Africa

- Diarrhoeal – various diseases carried by waterborne viruses, bacteria and parasites, e.g. cholera, dysentery, *E. coli*
- Tuberculosis – bacterial infection transmitted by coughs and sneezes
- Malaria – parasites transmitted by mosquito
- Hepatitis B – virus transmitted through blood, causing liver diseases
- Tetanus – bacterial infection affecting babies and mothers during birth due to insanitary conditions
- Pertussis – bacterial infection of the lungs
- Sleeping sickness – infection by the parasite *Trypanosoma gambiense*
- Meningitis – bacterial infection transmitted by human contact
- AIDS – caused by virus transmitted in bodily fluids

Box 7.2 Countries with known Vitamin A deficiency

Countries with population suffering clinical symptoms of Vitamin A deficiency

Angola, Benin, Burkina Faso, Cameroon, Chad, Ethiopia, Ghana, Kenya, Malawi, Mali, Mauritania, Mozambique, Niger, Nigeria, Rwanda, Togo, Uganda, Tanzania, Zambia, Zimbabwe

Source: www.ifrc.org.

Box 7.3 Countries at risk for yellow fever outbreaks

Countries at risk for yellow fever: 34 countries, all in Africa

Angola, Benin, Burkino Faso, Burundi, Cameroon, Cape Verde, Central African Republic, Chad, Congo, Côte d'Ivoire, Democratic Republic of Congo, Equatorial Guinea, Eritrea, Ethiopia, Gabon, Gambia, Ghana, Guinea, Guinea-Bissau, Kenya, Liberia, Mali, Mauritania, Niger, Nigeria, Rwanda, São Tomé and Príncipe, Senegal, Sierra Leone, Somalia, Sudan, Togo, Uganda, Tanzania.

Source: Strategic Plan 1998–2001, Global Programme for Vaccines and Immunization, World Health Organisation, Geneva, cited in http://ifrc.org/WHAT/health.archi/fact/Fyelfev.

throughout villages. Routine childhood immunization programmes could prevent the incidence of this disease.

Despite a World Health Organisation (WHO) campaign to eliminate leprosy by 2000 there are still incidences of the disease across Africa, as Table 7.1 demonstrates. Elimination of leprosy in WHO terms was defined as bringing the prevalence to below one case per 10,000 of population but, as Table 7.1 indicates, this has not occurred and in countries such as Mozambique, Madagascar and Guinea cases are more than six per 10,000 of population. Certainly, from the writer's experience in Kano, northern Nigeria, leprosy sufferers begged in the streets and endured advanced symptoms of the disease, including the loss of hands and limbs and disfigurement.[1] During the past 10 years another disease, malaria, has seen a series of epidemics in sub-Saharan Africa. An estimated 300–500 million cases each year cause '1.5 to 2.7 million deaths' and more than '90% of those deaths are in children under 5 years of age in Africa' (www.ifrc.org/WHAT/health/archi/fact/fmalar). Factors favouring the spread of malaria include:

- the resistance of the mosquito to drugs;
- conflicts that have forced mass migration of people to or from infected areas;
- migration of non-immune people to infected areas for agricultural reasons;

Table 7.1 Leprosy – the most endemically affected countries in Africa

Country	Incidence	Prevalence per 10,000
Nigeria	12,878	1.06
Mozambique	11,072	6.24
DR Congo	4,863	1.01
Ethiopia	8,104	1.35
Madagascar	11,005	6.78
Sudan	4,065	1.34
Guinea	4,805	6.56
Niger	2,738	2.71

Source: WHO Weekly Epidemiological Redord 2001, cited in www.ifrc.org/WHAT/health/archi/fact/Fleprsy.

• changing rainfall patterns that favour mosquito breeding sites;
• adverse socio-economic conditions, which lead to inadequate health budgets for fighting the disease (Thomas C. Nchinda, cited ibid.).

The control of malaria, therefore, concerns everyone and requires the partnership of community members and local development agencies. Insecticide-impregnated mosquito nets have been introduced with some success but real eradication of the disease means tackling the areas in which mosquitoes dwell: stagnant water and poorly drained land.

Taken together, inadequate water, sanitation and hygiene are among the leading causes of disease, especially in rural areas, as Table 7.2 indicates. Yet RC/RC groups alone cannot resolve these enormous infrastructural problems. Although it is recognized that community-based health care cannot be fully considered with-

Table 7.2 Percentage of rural communites with access to safe water in African countries

Less than 25%	26–50%	51–75%	Over 76%
Angola	Burkino Faso	Benin	Botswana
Chad	Burundi	Ghana	Equatorial Guinea
Congo	Cameroon	Lesotho	Rwanda
Eritrea	Côte d'Ivoire	Mali	
Ethiopia	Gabon	South Africa	
Liberia	Guinea	Zimbabwe	
Sierra Leone	Kenya		
Somalia	Malawi		
Zambia	Namibia		
	Niger		
	Nigeria		
	Senegal		
	Swaziland		
	Tanzania		

Source: African Red Cross and Red Crescent Societies (2007).

out addressing the issue of safe water, local populations as well as governments need to address the problems. ARCHI has established Water and Sanitation (Wat-San) activities which forge links with communities, local and central government and other international humanitarian agencies. The provision and use of latrines (see Table 7.3) is vitally important in improving sanitation and personal hygiene. Even in urban areas of some African states it is not unusual to see men defecating in back streets or in railway sidings.[2] Red Cross and Red Crescent organizations outline essential points in the delivery of hygiene education and practice:

- People need to be able to clean themselves after defecating, and in a hygienic manner. Appropriate cleansing materials (sticks, paper, water), depending on cultural practices, need to be made available at the latrines, preferably with soap.
- Handwashing, particularly after defecating and before preparing food, has been shown to be protective against fecal–oral illnesses. Any efforts to promote handwashing should have a simple monitoring component to ensure that increased handwashing is actually occurring.
- Soap provides protection from diarrhoeal illness independent of any education programme which may accompany it. Thus, the availability and use of soap should be seen as important to good health.
- Educational messages should be short and focused. All messages in an education campaign should promote measures known to prevent the specific health threats in the community and should focus on behaviors which are not presently practiced by a significant portion of the population.

> (*The Johns Hopkins RC/RC Health Emergency Reference Manual*
> 1999, cited in www.ifrc.org/WHAT/health/archi/fact/FWATSANI)

Encouragingly, the US Carter Center Health Program has helped construct 300,000 latrines in Ethiopia during the past three years (www.cartercenter.org/health).

Table 7.3 Percentage of rural communites with access to sanitary latrines in African countries

Less than 25%	26–50%	51–75%	Over 76%
Benin	Angola	Uganda	Kenya
Cape Verde	Botswana	Zambia	Rwanda
Chad	Burkino Faso		South Africa
Côte d'Ivoire	Burundi		Tanzania
DR Congo	Cameroon		Togo
Eritrea	Ghana		
Ethiopia	Equatorial Guinea		
Gambia	Lesotho		
Guinea	Nigeria		
	Zimbabwe		

Source: African Red Cross and Red Crescent Societies (2007).

HIV/AIDS

AIDS has captured global attention in recent years with UNAIDS and the World Health Organisation estimating that 39.5 million people worldwide are infected with HIV and of this figure 24.7 million HIV-positive people live in sub-Saharan Africa (UNAIDS and World Health Organisation 2006). The comparative regional statistics of HIV/AIDS appear in Table 7.4 and demonstrate that two-thirds of all people with HIV live in this region. Equally, almost three-quarters of all adult and child deaths due to AIDS occur in sub-Saharan Africa, 2.1 million of the global 2.9 million deaths. As UNAIDS asserts: 'Africa remains the global epicentre of the AIDS pandemic' (ibid.: 6). Southern African states have some of the highest infection rates in the world, as Table 7.5 indicates.

Recently, however, HIV infection has been viewed in the context of the wider environment in which diseases exist. In South African communities already profoundly affected by HIV a new and more virulent strain of tuberculosis (TB), called XDR-TB, emerged in 2006. This particularly aggressive strain of TB, apparently resistant to available antibiotics, may in fact have been encouraged by the general poor and irregular treatment of tuberculosis itself and deficiencies in general health systems. In countries where TB treatment is poorly handled and few sufferers complete their antibiotic therapy, risks of failed therapy multiply difficulties. The failed therapy of mainstream TB, that is, 'poorly handled treatment and incomplete antibiotic courses, often promotes the emergence of drug-resistant strains' (Garrett 2007: 10). Badly monitored or administered treatment of TB exacerbates and increases the risk of those falling victim to specific illnesses.

Table 7.4 Regional statistics of HIV/AIDS

Region	People living with HIV	New infections 2006	AIDS deaths 2006	Adult prevalence (%)
Sub-Saharan Africa	24.7 million	2.8 million	2.1 million	5.9
South and Southeast Asia	7.8 million	860,000	590,000	0.6
East Asia	750,000	100,000	43,000	0.1
Latin America	1.7 million	140,000	65,000	0.5
North America	1.4 million	43,000	18,000	0.8
Western and Central Europe	740,000	22,000	12,000	0.3
Eastern Europe and Central Asia	1.7 million	270,000	84,000	0.9
Middle East and North Africa	460,000	68,000	36,000	0.2
Caribbean	250,000	27,000	19,000	1.2
Oceania	81,000	7,100	4,000	0.4
Total	39.5 million	4.3 million	2.9 million	1.0

Source: UNAIDS and WHO (2006).

Table 7.5 HIV-positive figures in certain Southern African states

Country	% of population
Botswana	24.10
Swaziland	33.40
Zimbabwe	25.06
Lesotho	23.20
South Africa	19.95
Namibia	19.94
Mozambique	16.10

Source: UNAIDS and WHO (2006).

Other diseases have also been linked to HIV; for example, it is claimed that an 'intimate relationship' exists between HIV and malaria, especially for pregnant women when 'being infected with one exacerbates cases of the other' (ibid.).

It has been acknowledged for some time that the AIDS pandemic directly threatens African states from a variety of angles: social, economic and political. The illness 'kills farmers, prevents adults from passing down knowledge on food production to future generations, and leaves families without labour, seeds or savings which will carry them through periods of drought' (Patterson 2005: 4). Equally dramatic are the changes in life expectancy, especially if the disease is considered from a long-term perspective: 'in many southern African countries, AIDS has wiped out all the progress that states have made toward increasing life expectancy' (Youde 2005: 198). Many countries now have life expectancy rates lower than those in the 1960s. In Botswana, for example, the 'average life expectancy for a child born today is around 38 years – a full 30 years less than would be predicted without AIDS' (ibid.: 198). (See Table 7.6.)

The human costs are enormous with children orphaned, mothers infected and societies decimated. Patterson considers how certain countries within the continent – Uganda, Ghana, South Africa, Swaziland and Zimbabwe – are responding to the crisis. Some states are accused of being 'weak and ineffective' and at times in denial about the severity of the disease. Often a combination of poverty, lack of development, institutional weaknesses and the absence of political will undermine efforts to tackle the problem at national level. In fact, these difficulties are highlighted: 'might programmatic aid for HIV/AIDS simply become another means by which African state officials gain resources for patronage? . . . the AIDS issue may be ripe for political manipulation by some African state leaders' (ibid.: 188). If political elites are seen to be culpable then health care processes have also been criticized. A 2006 World Bank report estimated that around half of all funds donated for health efforts in sub-Saharan Africa 'never reach the clinics and hospitals at the end of the line.' Why? Because 'money leaks out in the form of payments to ghost employees, padded prices for transport and warehousing, the siphoning off of drugs to the black market, and the sale of counterfeit – often dangerous – medications.' In Ghana, for example, '80 per cent of donor funds were diverted from their intended purposes' (Garrett 2007: 4). Certainly, the World

Table 7.6 Life expectancy rates affected by AIDS

Country	Life expectancy in 2002 (years)	Non-AIDS life expectancy in 1960s (years)
Botswana	38	68
Zimbabwe	36	70
South Africa	50	65

Source: UNAIDS and WHO (2002).

Health Organisation has condemned countries for misappropriating funds given for immunization programmes. In one West African country, the political elite used the monies for holidays in Portugal (author's confidential interview). Yet according to the Afrobarometer, which recorded public opinion findings from 18 African countries between 2005 and 2006, overall, 'health workers are regarded as relatively honest by much of the public.' Sixty-four per cent believe that 'none or only some health workers are involved in corruption, compared to 20 per cent who think most or all of them are' (Afrobarometer 2006). Even in Ghana 69 per cent of the respondents believed there was little or no corruption against only 17 per cent who believed there was much. Nevertheless, when individual countries are examined the differences are greater, as shown in Table 7.7.

If health workers are not perceived to be corrupt, there are real problems with the delivery of medicines or other supplies, indicating that serious obstacles exist. Table 7.8 illustrates the worrying responses of people who seem to rarely have access to the medicines they require, with Zimbabwe recording the worst figures: 79 per cent of respondents not receiving medicines almost on a regular basis. Of course, Zimbabwe has been much criticized and grim accounts have appeared of President Mugabe and his silence about the rate of HIV infections until they 'skyrocketed' to the degree that 'more than 1,200 Zimbabweans were dying each week from the disease' (Batsell 2005: 69). Although Mugabe has acknowledged the presence of the disease since 2000, some international AIDS NGOs complain that the problem still remains on the 'periphery of the political landscape' (Patterson 2005: 8). Neither ZANU-PF nor the opposition MDC placed the disease centre-stage during parliamentary or presidential elections. Yet, encouragingly, the latest UNAIDS report reveals declines in the national HIV prevalence rates in Zimbabwe and Kenya largely thanks to behavioural change, that is, 'increased condom use, few partners and delayed sexual debut' (UNAIDS and WHO 2006: 6).

More generally, the Afrobarometer observed that in many states there was a 'disconnect between highly positive ratings of government performance and frequent reports of problems encountered in the health care system.' For example, respondents in Uganda, where nearly two-thirds in the survey regularly have little access to medicines, actually gave their country 75 per cent, the highest rating, for its handling of health care services. Equally, the government of Kenya, a country that also has difficulty in distributing medicines, was given a rating of 69 per cent by respondents who believed it was improving basic health services. In

Table 7.7 How many health workers are involved in corruption (%)?

	Malawi	Nigeria	Namibia	Mozambique
None/some of them	53	65	60	56
Most/all of them	24	32	32	27

Source: Afrobarometer (2006).

Table 7.8 Lack of medicines or other supplies (%)

Is there a lack of medicines and other supplies?	Kenya	Malawi	Senegal	Uganda	Zambia	Zimbabwe
Never	14	18	27	15	6	5
Once or twice	20	8	10	13	20	10
A few times/often	51	62	57	61	42	79

Source: Afrobarometer (2006).

fact, respondents in only two countries believed their governments were handling medical services badly: Nigeria with 58 per cent and Zimbabwe with 67 per cent, against 42 per cent and 32 per cent, respectively, who believed their governments were doing well (Afrobarometer 2006: 21). Yet overall figures present a more worrying picture about the quality of health care, as Table 7.9 indicates. Expensive services, long waiting times, absent doctors and lack of necessary attention are features of health care provision which must be addressed.

In South Africa, President Thabo Mbeki also adopted a controversial stance on HIV/AIDS. In 1999 he questioned the scientific evidence that HIV was the sole cause of AIDS. However, responding to criticism from civil society, Mbeki shifted position and by 2002 he expanded the AIDS budget to 1 billion Rand. Certainly, there have been efforts to combat the spread of the disease but as of 2006 there had been 'no evidence of a decline' (UNAIDS and WHO 2006: 6). Ghana, a country with relatively low HIV prevalence rates, has been trying to tackle AIDS yet even its response is not without difficulties: 'Though Ghana's political environment has become more open, with free media, opportunities for civil society activism, and competitive elections, state officials have done little more than what is required by international donors to address AIDS' (Patterson and Haven 2005: 92; see also Whiteside 2008). However, more people are receiving antiretroviral (ARV) therapy within the region, as outlined in Table 7.10.

There is, of course, a strong international dimension to the issue. The United Nations, the World Health Organisation, numerous charities and NGOs, as well as the funding priorities of developed nations, have all adopted HIV/AIDS as a major project to be tackled. Now the business and corporate sectors are involved in many African countries especially in relation to the health of their workforces. Anglo-American, for example, has been pro-active for a number of years in providing assistance to its workers suffering from the disease. In most states in-

Table 7.9 Experiences of health care (%)

	Never	Once or twice	A few times/often
Long waiting times	23	14	47
Absent doctors	38	15	30
Lack of attention or respect from staff	39	15	30
Services are too expensive/ unable to pay	41	14	29

Source: Afrobarometer (2006).

Table 7.10 Antiretroviral (ARV) treatment, June 2006

Geographical region	Estimated number of people receiving ARV therapy	Estimated number of people needing ARV therapy	ARV therapy coverage (%)
Sub-Saharan Africa	1,040,000	4,600,000	23
East, South and Southeast Asia	235,000	1,440,000	16
Latin America and Caribbean	345,000	460,000	75

Source: UNAIDS and WHO (2006).

ternational donors have concentrated on prevention by focusing on behavioural attitudes. In Botswana, for example, the notion of one partner was promoted during the 2004 election campaign (see Figure 7.2), while in South Africa the National Youth Commission (NYC) advanced calls for fidelity and carefulness in sexual relationships. The NYC introduced 'Young Positive Living Ambassadors' to 'encourage young HIV positive men and women to send out a message of warning to the wider population.' Essentially, three main points were promoted aimed at changing sexual behaviour. The slogan used was 'ABC', meaning: Abstinence, Be Faithful and Use Condom.[3] This strategy was also adopted in Uganda, where the United Nations Population Fund (UNFPA) reported 'dramatic' changes in condom use, particularly among unmarried men and women.

> Condom use by sexually active women aged 15–17 increased from 6% to 25% and by those aged 18–19 from 3% to 12%. For men aged 15–17, condom use rose from 16% to 55% and in those aged 18–19, from 20% to 33%.
> (UNFPA 2004: 69)

However, with the disease becoming more prevalent among women – on average there are '13 infected women for every 10 infected men' – there is also a clear gender dimension to HIV/AIDS. There is no question that the disease affects women disproportionately. UNFPA estimates that in sub-Saharan Africa 60 per cent of persons infected by HIV/AIDS are female, and it has referred to the 'femi-

Figure 7.2 Botswana links HIV to election campaign.

nization of the pandemic' (ibid.). Forty-two per cent of the adult population in Swaziland is positive, yet among 25- to 29-year-old women, the infection figure is as high as 56 per cent (www.avert.org/aids-swaziland). Rising rates of infection among women and adolescent girls reflect what the organization regards as their 'greater vulnerability' within society. 'Gender inequalities and male domination in relationships can increase women's risk of infection and limit their ability to negotiate condom use. Poverty leads many women and girls into unsafe sexual relations, often with older partners' (UNFPA 2004: 65). This tendency reflects the patriarchal nature of African societies which 'rob women of their power to make decisions regarding sexuality.' Ultimately, women become vulnerable and their life choices are constrained by men who dictate the practices: 'a wife who asks her husband to use a condom may be subject to physical violence and charges of unfaithfulness' (ibid.: 23). The feminization of the epidemic is further exacerbated by women's roles within the family, where they act as managers and caregivers for family members also infected with HIV. The inequality confronting women in a range of important spheres – legal, economic and social – further compounds the situation. The UNFPA sets down a series of action plans designed to confront inequality as outlined in Box 7.4.

As a majority of HIV transmission takes place through sexual contact, reproductive and sexual health information and services provide a critically important means of inhibiting HIV/AIDS infection. Such services can help prevent transmission by providing education on risks to influence sexual behaviour, detecting and managing sexually transmitted infections (STIs), and promoting the correct

Box 7.4 Confronting inequality

- Ensure that adolescent girls and women have the knowledge and means to prevent HIV infection through advocacy campaigns that convey basic facts about women's heightened physiological vulnerability and dispel harmful myths and stereotypical notions of masculinity and femininity, warn that marriage does not necessarily offer protection from HIV transmission, and involve both young men and women in promoting sexual and reproductive health.
- Promote equal and universal access to treatment by ensuring that women make up 50% of the people able to access expanded treatment interventions.
- Promote girls' primary and secondary education and women's literacy by eliminating school fees, promoting zero tolerance for gender-based violence and sexual harassment, offering literacy classes for women that focus on HIV/AIDS, providing life skills education both in and out of school, and creating curricula that challenge gender stereotypes and promote girls' self-esteem.
- Relieve the unequal domestic workload and caring responsibilities of women and girls for sick family members and orphans by providing support for caregivers.
- End all forms of violence against women and girls by undertaking media campaigns on zero tolerance for violence, male responsibility and respect for women and dangerous behaviour norms.
- Promote and protect the human rights of women and girls by enacting, strengthening and enforcing laws protecting the rights, reporting violations to the UN Committee on the Elimination of Discrimination Against Women, protecting women's property and inheritance rights, and supporting free or affordable legal services for women affected by HIV/AIDS.

Source: UNFPA (2004: 64).

and consistent use of condoms. Although these policies are well-intentioned they can be difficult to implement in certain societies. In Tanzania, for example, 'the prevalence of the disease is greater among married, monogamous young women than among sexually active unmarried women' because they 'cannot negotiate condom use even if they know their husband now has or previously had multiple partners' (ibid.: 67). Yet it would be misleading to suggest that no improvements have taken place. Six of the eleven African countries studied in the 2006 UNAIDS report indicated a 'decline of 25% or more in HIV prevalence among 15–24 year olds in capital cities.' And in some countries the percentage of 'young people having sex before the age of 15 declined and condom use increased' (UNAIDS and

WHO 2006: 4). These positive moves are in large part a result of the pro-active campaign to target young people. The African Youth Alliance, for example, has attempted to spearhead information for young people, primarily those aged between 10 and 19 years, with the aim of reducing the incidence of HIV/AIDS and other STIs in Botswana, Uganda and Tanzania (UNFPA 2004: 82).

Other factors such as poverty and lack of education can also play a part in increasing the likelihood of acquiring the disease. Reports from Uganda indicated that a child who drops out of school is 'three times more likely to be HIV positive in his or her twenties than a child who completes basic education' (UNAIDS and WHO 2006: 15). Consequently, widening opportunities for education is a priority that UNAIDS recognizes. In 2006, it reported that 21 of 25 countries in sub-Saharan Africa had 'reduced or eliminated school fees for vulnerable children and implemented community-based programmes to support orphans' (ibid.). Also linking HIV awareness with general reproductive health and family planning has helped extend the reach of health services. The International Conference on Population and Development defines reproductive health as a state of 'complete physical, mental and social well-being.' It provides for the 'right of men and women to be informed and to have access to safe, effective, affordable and acceptable methods of family planning of their choice' (UNFPA 2004: 37). Such health provision can provide practical, economic gains at many levels:

- Gains to individuals: improved maternal and infant health; expanded opportunities for women's education, employment and social participation; reduced exposure to health risks;
- Gains to families: reduced competition and dilution of resources; reductions in household poverty; and more possibility for shared decision-making;
- To society: accelerated demographic transition; increasing economic development.

(ibid.: 39)

Box 7.5 The Millennium Development Goals

The Millennium Development Goals commit the international community to achieving the following by 2015:
1. Eradicate extreme poverty and hunger
2. Achieve universal primary education
3. Promote gender equality and empower women
4. Reduce child mortality
5. Improve maternal health
6. Combat HIV/AIDS, malaria and other diseases
7. Ensure environmental sustainability
8. Develop a global partnership for development

Certainly, sub-Saharan maternal mortality rates are disturbingly high with a one in twenty risk of pregnant women facing such a death. There is, of course, no single answer to the wider health issues confronting African nations as well as the HIV/AIDS challenge. At base level, societal structures will have to change and governance capacities of states and civil societies will need to improve. But equally, the international community will be required to continue to play an important role at the same time as African states will be encouraged to take responsibility for strategic priorities based on their specific national contexts. There will, however, be neither quick nor easy solutions as countries most affected by HIV and AIDS will 'fail to achieve Millennium Development Goals to reduce poverty, hunger and childhood mortality, and countries whose development is already flagging will continue to weaken, potentially threatening social stability and national security' (UNAIDS 2006: 6).

Human security

There has been an increasing acknowledgment that conflicts and disasters render communities and populations more vulnerable to disease and degradation and it is within this context that the term 'human security' has been framed. The UN Commission on Human Security defined the term:

> Human security means protecting people from critical and pervasive threats and situations, building on their strengths and aspirations. It also means creating systems that give people the building blocks of survival, dignity and livelihood. Human security connects different types of freedoms – freedom from want, freedom from fear and freedom to take action on one's own behalf. To do this, it offers two general strategies: protection and empowerment. Protection shields people from dangers. It requires concerted effort to develop norms, processes and institutions that systematically address insecurities. Empowerment enables people to develop their potential and become full participants in decision making . . . human security complements state security, furthers human development and enhances human rights. . . . respecting human rights is as the core of protecting human security.
> (UN Commission on Human Security 2003, cited in Hough 2004: 15)

It is, perhaps, not surprising that the HIV/AIDS pandemic and associated health problems have raised the issue of human security: 'rapid negative change in the health status of a population and pathogen-induced demographic collapse may . . . figure in the destabilisation of states' (Upton 2004: 73). In other words, virulent diseases not only decimate populations but in so doing also damage the very fabric of the state. Human security, then, is not just concerned with state and government structures, it embraces the society as a whole. The high level of attention given to health by the international community results from the recognition that a strong relationship exists between health and development, which can be a crucial determinant of economic development, peace and security.

In 2000 the United Nations passed Resolution 1308, stressing that the HIV/ AIDS pandemic, if left unchecked, 'may pose a risk to stability and security' and that its spread was 'exacerbated by conditions of violence and insecurity' (UNSC Resolution 1308, July 2000, www.un.org/Docs/SC/UNSC_resolutions). Certainly, UNAIDS acknowledges the 'potential for conflicts and disasters to increase vulnerability and contribute to the spread of HIV.' As a consequence, it calls on countries to integrate their HIV policies into action plans for emergency situations and to invest in HIV awareness and training to be incorporated into operations of 'national uniformed services and international peacekeepers' (UN-AIDS and WHO 2006: 16). Infection rates among some African military forces have reportedly been high: in Malawi '75% of its military personnel infected with HIV, Uganda . . . has a 66% infection rate in its military . . . In Zimbabwe, estimates show than 80% of the military personnel are HIV positive' (Ostergard 2002: 343). Yet the assumption that a higher prevalence of HIV exists in military than in civilian populations has been questioned (see Whiteside *et al.* 2006: 201). However, within conflict situations, for example in Sierra Leone, Rwanda and the Democratic Republic of Congo, reports have surfaced of infected troops raping women with the intention of spreading the virus (Youde 2005: 200). Rape and gender-based violence occur more often during war, and victims of this abuse are more likely to contract a sexually transmitted disease, including HIV/AIDS. Equally, conflict always creates societal dislocation and separation. UNFPA as-serts that until recently there were few attempts to prevent sexual and gender-based violence in times of conflict or displacement. Now various initiatives are targeting conflict-affected populations:

- Raising awareness about and condemning sexual violence as violations of human rights and a threat to public health;
- Supporting education and information campaigns;
- Promoting safety measures for women in displacement camps, includ-ing adequate lighting, security patrols, the safe location of services and facilities, and ensure that water, fuel, food and other provisions can be obtained without having to venture too far;
- Advocating for the enactment and enforcement of laws and policies against sexual and gender-based violence, and providing training for police and judges;
- Involving men to promote behaviour change.

(UNFPA 2004: 83–84)

Refugees and internally displaced persons (IDPs)

Two of the most critical consequences of conflict have been the increases in the numbers of refugees and internally displaced persons. Technically the term 'refugees' refers to those who have been displaced across the border of their home states, whereas 'internally displaced persons' means those who have been displaced within their country of origin. Both categories, however, have a significant impact on human security. According to the 1951 Convention Relating to the Status of Refugees, a refugee is a person who,

> owing to a well-founded fear of being persecuted for reasons of race, religion, nationality, membership in a particular social group, or political opinion, is outside the country of his/her nationality, and is unable to or, owing to such fear, is unwilling to avail himself of the protection of that country.
>
> (cited in Clover 2002)

Internally displaced people are

> persons or groups of persons who have been forced or obliged to flee or to leave their homes or places of habitual residence, in particular as a result of or in order to avoid the effects of armed conflict, situations of generalised violence, violations of human rights or natural or human-made disasters, and who have not crossed an internationally recognized state border.

This is the definition given in the 'Guiding Principles on Internal Displacement' drawn up by the United Nations Office for the Coordination of Humanitarian Affairs in 1998 (cited ibid.). Table 7.11 outlines the nature of the problem in 2001 but, worryingly, refugee children under the age of 18 years constitute 56 per cent of all refugees in Africa as a whole. However, in countries of asylum – Angola, Togo, Guinea, Burundi, Rwanda, and the Democratic Republic of Congo – that figure increases to over 60 per cent (Clover 2002: 2; see Table 7.12).

Incidences of conflict, sporadic violence, droughts, famines, floods and general attrition between communities and ethnic or religious groups have been features of the African landscape for many years. Recently, one of the most desperate situations has been in the Darfur region of Sudan, where the UNHCR had to create a separate unit, called Sudan/Chad Special Operations, dedicated to these two countries only. The agency set up 26 offices in both states with 868 posts in the field and operated on several humanitarian fronts:

Table 7.11 Refugees, internally displaced persons and asylum seekers in Africa 2001

Region	Refugees	Asylum seekers	Internally displaced	Returned IDPs	Returned refugees
Central and West Africa	851,540	12,800	410,686	213,361	86,539
East and the Horn of Africa	2,261,319	45,464	443,834	n/a	183,892
Southern Africa	308,540	19,788	257,508	n/a	8,930
Total	3,421,399	78,052	1,112,028	213,361	279,361

Source: Clover (2002).

Table 7.12 Countries with the most internally displaced persons, November 2000–March 2001

Country	Number of IDPs
Sudan	4,000,000
Angola	3,800,000
Democratic Republic of Congo	1,800,000
Sierra Leone	1,300,000
Uganda	610,000
Rwanda	600,000
Burundi	580,000
Somalia	350,000
Ethiopia	350,000
Eritrea	208,000

Source: Clover (2002).

- Eastern Sudan, which hosts 120,000 Eritrean refugees
- The Darfur region where 207,000 refugees have moved to Eastern Chad; 1.8 million Internally Displaced People and 700,000 persons in West Darfur
- South Chad which hosts 48,000 refugees from the Central African Republic
- Southern Sudan where it is hoped refugees and Internally Displaced People will return.

(*Africa Newsletter* 2006: 5)

The decision to create this special unit for Chad and Sudan was prompted 'by the complexity and scale of the humanitarian crisis in Darfur' as well as the 'prospect for peace in Southern Sudan and the expected challenges of preparing for the repatriation of half a million Sudanese refugees from seven neighbouring countries' (ibid.). However, as the Darfur crisis widened, Chad and Sudan were reintegrated into the Africa Bureau of UNHCR in May 2006. One of the central concerns has been to strike a balance between the need to keep the momentum of repatriation and the necessity of ensuring that the rights of refugees and their basic needs are met. The concern, then, is not only with people being forced from their homes, but also with how they might return. In a sense, this debilitating population movement is at the core of much instability within the continent. In fact, on 28 June 2006 a special open session of the UN Security Council was held to discuss the protection of civilians in armed conflict situations. Justifiable fears existed that displaced populations could be harassed and attacked, and camps were vulnerable to infiltration by armed elements. The council believed such situations not only potentially constituted a threat to human security but could develop into a menace to international peace. UN Resolution 1674 reaffirmed that it was the responsibility of the international community to protect civilians from genocide, war crimes and crimes against humanity. The resolution also highlighted the importance of peacekeeping operations in relation to the situation of the displaced; peacekeepers were called on to take 'all feasible measures to ensure security in and around camps' (UN Security Council Resolution 1674, www.un.org/Docs/ SC/UNSC_resolutions). It also wished peacekeepers to create conditions for safe and dignified return together with helping the displaced resolve conflicts and rebuild their societies.

Although it is commendable that the UN Security Council has taken such an interest in displaced people, the actual work on the ground is exceptionally demanding. In fact, according to the US Committee for Refugees and Immigrants' assessment, refugee rights protection has deteriorated in 19 African countries (cited in International Refugee Rights Initiative 2006: 3). Particularly negative were the connected issues of physical protection of refugees, the processes of repatriation and the forced return of asylum seekers. In Uganda, for example, 'changes in the tax system apparently no longer allowed refugees to use receipt of tax payment as identification, thus limiting freedom of movement for some' (ibid.). Yet, the International Refugee Rights Initiative (IRRI) regards refugees in Africa as quite fortunate in that the 'African regional refugee convention offers additional protection beyond those found in international law' (ibid.).

Certainly, the African Commission on Human and People's Rights has been established and Article 12 of the African Charter states that:

> Every individual shall have the right to freedom of movement and residence within the border of a state provided he abides by the law.
>
> (Paragraph 1)

> Every individual shall have the right, when persecuted, to seek and obtain asylum in other countries in accordance with the laws of those countries and international conventions.
>
> (Paragraph 3)

These precepts are premised on the existence of conditions of peace, law and order. Yet internal displacement itself is often created by chaotic and lawless situations. So, in a sense, these factors undermine the African Charter. That is why theoretically the rights of IDPs in Africa are supported whereas in reality they are very difficult to meet. The IRRI readily recognizes that refugees in the region still suffer human rights violations in exile: 'Refugees are subjected to continuing insecurity in host countries. Often their freedom of movement is restricted and access to economic and social rights limited.' The central difficulty is one of enforcement. Governments are often unable or unwilling to implement commitments and the UNHCR does not have a 'comprehensive enforcement role due to its delicate relationship with the states within which it operates' (IRRI 2006). For the Special Rapporteur on Refugees, IDPs and Asylum Seekers in Africa, Bahame Tom Nyanduga, who was appointed by the African Commission, the situation is clear:

Despite the clear guarantees, rights and freedom provided for under the African Charter and within the constitutions and laws of all African countries, the prevailing political and socio-economic conditions in many African countries militate against the enjoyment of these rights and freedoms.

(Nyanduga 2006)

Also conflicts are extremely difficult to resolve and, even when peace agreements are signed, IDPs may not agree with them. For example, the Darfur Peace Agreement, signed in May 2006, was rejected by groups of internally displaced persons who demonstrated against the agreement.

At base level it is generally violence that creates the substantial movement of peoples, and an NGO, Africa Internally Displaced Persons Voice (www.africaidp. org), based in Zambia, has called for the root causes of conflict to be addressed. This is not easy in a continent that has witnessed a considerable level of armed combat and brutality. Civilian populations have been subjected to 'torture, rape, sexual and gender-based violence, destruction of property, households, farms and crops and other abuses' (ibid.). Nevertheless, in order to find real and lasting solutions to the protracted problems of IDPs, there has to be some understanding of the following key points:

- Their peaceful co-existence with resident populations
- Their voluntary repatriation and return or,
- Their local integration.
  (www.refugee-rights.org/NGODirectory/AfricaIDPVoice-Zambia.htlm)

These aspects require considerable negotiation between different groups and involvement of local authorities and host populations. But when economic resources are stretched and governance is poor it is not difficult to see how tensions can arise between local populations and IDPs, especially if the numbers are large. Ultimately, the challenge of preventing internal displacement can be addressed only by requiring states to educate their people at all levels about the sanctity of human life and respect for human rights. In terms of human security, the objectives are clear: peace, repatriation and the prevention and sustainable resolution of conflicts. For African communities, already challenged by considerable health issues, many of which are exacerbated by shifting populations and weak governments, the demands may seem insuperable.

8 Conflict, arms and reconstruction

One of the most disturbing reports to emerge in 2007 was a study produced by Oxfam, Saferworld and Iansa that analysed the economic cost of armed conflict to Africa's development. In a study of 23 African countries, including Angola, Burundi, the Central African Republic, Chad, DRC, Republic of Congo, Côte d'Ivoire, Djibouti, Eritrea, Ethiopia, Ghana, Guinea, Guinea-Bissau, Liberia, Niger, Nigeria, Rwanda, Senegal, Sierra Leone, South Africa, Sudan and Uganda, the report maintained the total cost of conflict was US$284 billion between the years 1990 and 2005. This figure represented an annual loss of 15 per cent of gross domestic product amounting to an average sum of US$18 billion per year lost by Africa on account of armed conflict. The average annual loss of 15 per cent is an 'enormous economic burden' which represents 'one and a half times average African spending on health and education combined' (Oxfam 2007). The cost of these conflicts is equivalent to the foreign aid Africa has received over the same period (EISA 2007a). Thirty-eight per cent of the world's armed conflicts are being fought in Africa and in 2006 nearly 50 per cent of all 'high-intensity' conflicts were in Africa. Almost half of the countries on the continent have been involved in some form of conflict since 1990. Table 8.1 outlines the cost of conflict for selected countries. The Democratic Republic of Congo (DRC) suffered more than a decade of foreign invasion and civil war that caused the deaths of around 4 million people and has lost the country 29 per cent of its gross domestic product. At one stage it was 'occupied by six foreign armies – Angola, Zimbabwe, Namibia, Uganda, Burundi, Rwanda and remnants of the predominantly Hutu rebel forces – is tormented by militias and is unable to meet the most basic needs of its people' (International Crisis Group Africa 2001: i). For the damage caused by Uganda's activities in the northeastern part of the DRC, the International Court of Justice ruled that Uganda should pay reparations.

One of the most distressing and debilitating features of states in sub-Saharan Africa, and one that has profoundly affected the lives and life-chances of many people, has been the seemingly endless capacity for violent struggle. Wars, ethnic hatred, civil disorder and spiralling military expenditure have been characteristics of the region for many years. Some wars have lasted almost a generation. In Angola, for example, a civil war continued for 19 years between the National Union

Table 8.1 Selected country results for the cost of conflict

Country	Conflict years	Number of years	Projected growth (%)[a]	Actual growth (%)	Loss (% of GDP)[b]
Burundi	1993–2005	13	5.5	−1.1	37
Rwanda	1990–2001	12	4.5	2.8	32
DRC	1996–2005	10	5.4	0.10	29
Eritrea	1998–2005	3	4.8	−3.8	11
Republic of Congo	1997–99	3	3.3	0.03	7.1

Source: Oxfam (2007).

a Average of annual growth during war years.
b Average of annual loss as a percentage of gross domestic product.

for the Total Independence of Angola (UNITA) and the Popular Movement for the Liberation of Angola (MPLA). Also military government has been prominent in states within the region since independence from colonial rule. A so-called People's Army ruled under Jerry Rawlings in Ghana and the military governed in Nigeria until very recently. In these instances, the military saw itself as saving a country from corrupt civilian government as in Nigeria in 1966, Ghana in 1972 and Sierra Leone in 1968 (Deegan 1996: 188).

Populations tended not to have much to say about such changes, for often the distinction between civilian and military regimes was more apparent than real, with very little to choose between two essentially authoritarian forms of government (Luckham 1991: 367). Samuel Finer, in his seminal work on the military, *The Man on Horseback*, argued that there was 'a distinct class of countries where governments have been repeatedly subjected to the interference of their armed forces.' Neither liberal democratic nor totalitarian societies, these states fall somewhere on the margins of political efficacy and often have continual military engagement. Finer saw military interference not as a 'mere set of ephemeral, exceptional and isolated adventures' but as a political phenomenon far more profound; one that was 'abiding, deep seated and distinctive.' In part, he saw the prevalence of the military as a reflection of societies at a low level of political culture in which legitimacy and consensus were largely irrelevant and, perhaps more significantly, ones that were 'deeply divided by culture and ethnic pluralism' (Finer 1962: 129). It was not necessarily the case that the peoples of those states had no political ideas or were unable to act from political conviction; rather there was little cohesion within the population. When issues arose they were often decided by force or the threat of it and in countries divided by tribalism or ethnicity this could involve whole masses in bitter internecine conflict. Militias would emerge and, through violence and indiscriminate killings, dominate the environment. Finer's interpretation carries a resonance in contemporary Africa and partly explains the ease with which armies and militias operate almost uncontrollably in some countries. For example, militias armed with an array of weaponry hunted both ethnic groups, the Hutus and the Tutsis, in Rwanda 'with diabolical frenzy.' According to one refugee everyone was under threat: 'they kill you just for looking at them' (Dowden 1994).

Whereas the end of the Cold War led to many of its proxy wars in Africa coming to an end, the security vacuum left in its wake was filled with a new phenomenon of civil conflicts that have caused 'more people to die in Africa over the last two decades than anywhere else on earth.' It is estimated that '3.3 million people' died in the Congo, 800,000 lives were claimed in the Rwandan genocide in 1994 and 'over 250,000 people have died in Burundi since 1993' as a result of civil war (Nepad Secretariat 2005: 2). But these deaths do not all occur in combat. In fact, 'indirect' deaths are 14 times higher than those due to fighting: 'the greater part of the human cost results not from deaths and injuries due to combat but indirectly from the loss of health and livelihoods caused by the disruption of economy and society.'

Compared with peaceful countries, African countries in conflict have, on average:

- 50% more infant deaths
- 15% more undernourished people
- Life expectancy reduced by five years
- 20% more adult illiteracy
- 2.5 time fewer doctors per patient
- 12.4% less food per person.

(Oxfam 2007: 6)

The impact of conflict on women and displaced peoples are discussed in other chapters but it is apparent that conflict can maim a society and sow the seeds of future hate and division in the process. An arena has been termed 'military when the expectation of violence is high' (Lasswell and Kaplan 1950: 252) and various forms of military organization have been prominent in Africa's history (cf. Thomson 2000; Zack-Williams *et al.* 2002; Clapham 1998). It is clear that in the past incidents in which violence was used to overthrow and replace governments became 'a common if not normal pattern of political change . . . [the] frequency and persistence of military violence provides *prima facie* evidence that large numbers of people continue to think that military power is useful, perhaps even an indispensable, instrument of policy' (Garnett 1991: 81). Violence, however, can be organized and deliberate or a 'spontaneous and sporadic' outcome of a crisis. Laurie Nathan (1998: 5) outlined four reasons why he believes violence may manifest itself:

1. If groups are marginalised because of their race, ethnicity or religion, and if citizens are subject to oppression and repression
2. If people are hungry and have no access to resources and economic opportunity, some may turn to banditry as a means of subsistence. They may also initiate riots in protest against corruption and the accumulation of wealth by the ruling elite
3. If the state is too weak to maintain law and order, communities, and in some cases, the state itself, will privatise security

4. If the state does not have the legitimacy and institutional capacity to resolve low-level political and social conflict, some individuals and groups will attempt to protect their interests and settle their disputes through violence.

Yet, equally, violence has also been viewed as irrational, arbitrary and indiscriminate with a 'root cause' that may be ambivalent and unfocused.[1]

Military Marxism

In the past, recourse to violence may have been a reflection of a political problem of self-styled leaders, accountable to no-one and largely ignoring the welfare of their peoples. It arose during the Cold War period because of ideological currents running through the continent after the colonial period. Chinese socialist ideas of people's armies and the stress on the inequity of capitalism led to an intellectualization about the role and influence of militias in the developing world. Even in 1983, writers were imagining the existence of a 'block of revolutionary nation-states in Southern Africa' which would maximize the possibility of socialist construction within Africa and elsewhere in the world system (Bush 1983: 11). Militias were examined in terms of their relationship to capital and class division. Robin Luckham looked at military rule from a Marxist perspective, questioning 'to what extent do those who control the superstructure rely on repressive rather than ideological mechanisms to establish their hegemony?' (Luckham 1991: 366). It was possible for militias to have a revolutionary function – to represent excluded classes and groups in times of crisis and to harness anti-imperialist, anti-capitalist sentiment. Some viewed militias as desirable features of Africa's political terrain in that the process of proletarianization could be combined with the struggle for national liberation (cf. Magubane 1983: 19; Nzongola-Ntalaja 1983). In certain countries, Angola for example, the Soviet Union and China competed with each other in their support of the 'armed struggle'. Initial tensions between militias regarding the direction 'national liberation' should take ultimately led to killings and a civil war. Such conflicts were a consequence of international spheres of interest and competition between different manifestations of the socialist world. Yet societies were pitched against societies on the basis that the black bourgeoisie were 'couriers of imperialism'. The further advancement of the national liberation struggle, therefore, required that 'African people settle matters with their own bourgeoisie' who had become reformist rather than revolutionary (Magubane 1983). Class struggle connected politicized movements with active militancy and contributed to a 'heightened collective revolutionary consciousness' (Wallerstein 1983: 168). An intellectual climate existed which both legitimized and defended violence: 'Military action which toppled a civilian regime must be seen in the context of wider societal class contradictions' (Aidoo 1983: 152). Struggles would inevitably take place depending on the 'correlation of class forces, the degree of organisation of the working class and its enemies' (ibid.).

To an extent, 'scientific socialism' – based on the principles of Marx and Lenin – came to be seen in some quarters as the answer to Africa's problems. 'Two parallel routes to what was asserted to be a more orthodox Marxism in Africa emerged by the mid-1970s but in their origins they both differed significantly from the classical Marxist path to power' (Hughes 1992: 10). These movements were referred to as 'Afro-Marxist' or 'Afro-Communist' (Ottaway and Ottaway 1986; Young 1980). One important feature of these movements was the fact they were invariably led by disaffected soldiers. Country followed country – Somalia, Benin, Ethiopia, Madagascar, Ghana and Burkino Faso – in their eagerness to pronounce People's Republics led by radical, revolutionary, Marxist military groups. More recently, these groups have been called 'second liberation movements' in that they waged a liberation struggle against earlier post-colonial authoritarian regimes (Clapham 1998). In the case of the African National Congress's military campaign against South Africa, in part funded by the Soviet Union, the objective was the destruction of the apartheid system (Deegan 2001). Yet it would be wrong to idealize many second liberation movement leaders: 'their persistent politicking under the banner of liberation, with all its military and violent connotations, speaks loudly of a leadership mindset that found it difficult to turn its back on the revolutionary methods that brought them to power' (Salih 2007: 673). Although some highlight ideological justification –

> In situations of acute material deprivation, political oppression and social conflict, its Marxism–Leninism appeal rested on the promise of rapid development, social justice and popular sovereignty. The radical soldiers shared the illusion that socialism could be attained speedily and by decree
>
> (Markakis cited in Hughes 1992: 14)

– others have no doubt the adoption of Marxist terminology was simply a means of gaining control over the state. In countries such as Ethiopia and Madagascar, military leaders often lacked 'ideological convictions' and simply pursued pragmatic and parochial political courses (Decalo interview 1995). Equally, even by 1991, a military presence within government could be identified in a range of countries, as Table 8.2 indicates.

The flow of arms into Africa

The question is, however, does this ideological and military background of many African states have any bearing on recent conflicts? Certainly, it could be argued that one reason why militias, arms trading, immediate recourse to violence and, at times, indiscriminate killing continue is the widespread acceptance of military-political solutions to problems. Marxism as an ideology may have gone but as a method of military struggle it seems to have remained. For, although the end of the Cold War led to many of its proxy wars in Africa coming to an end, the security vacuum left in its wake was filled with a new phenomenon of venal civil con-

Table 8.2 General features of Marxist–Leninist dominant parties in 1991

Country	Party name in 1990	Year founded	Origins	No. of name changes prior to 1991	Military men in government in 1991 (% and number/total)	Factionalism
Angola	MPLA	1956	Anti-colonial	0	9.5% (2/21)	Some internal dissent
Benin	PRPB	1975	Founded by military	1	27.3% (3/11)	Some internal dissent
Congo	PCT	1964	Founded by military	1	86.9 (20/23)	Severe
Ethiopia	WPE	1984	Founded by military	0	76.5% (13/17)	Severe
Mozambique	Frelimo	1962	Anti-colonial	0	16.7% (2/12)	Some internal dissent

Source: Yearbook of International Communist Affairs, cited in Hughes (1992).

Frelimo: The Front for the Liberation of Mozambique

MPLA: The Popular Movement for the Liberation of Angola

PCT: The Congolese Labour Party

PRPB: The People's Revolutionary Party of Benin

WPE: Workers' Party of Ethiopia

flicts. Clearly, then, ideology and Cold War rivalry are not the only causes of war in the continent. Is there, then, something terribly wrong with Africa as a whole? Well, there are some deeply pessimistic views of the continent:

> the African state . . . [is] becoming increasingly divisible internally, over-whelmed by the centrifugal forces of ethnicity, regionalism, and competing claims for authority. Civil wars, decaying economies, and political instability . . . [are] just some of the monuments to the unpreparedness of most African states to issue legitimate power and authority across geographic reaches.
>
> (Khadiagala 1996)

Certainly, Diamond, Linz and Lipset (1989) also point to ethnic division, weak political structures, lack of legitimacy, undermined and distorted local institutions, state monopoly over economic development and weak private sectors as factors contributing towards conflict and instability. But to this list it is possible to add other causes: competing religious agendas, the rise and virulence of non-state actors and the increasing availability of and access to weaponry of one form or another (Deegan 1996; UN Security Council 2003). Writing in the late 1980s of civil–military relations in Uganda, Kokole and Mazrui (1988) referred to the 'sheer availability of arms and ammunition' within the country and in the 1990s it was possible to buy an assault weapon in South Africa for less than US$10 (interview with representative of the South African Police, Johannesburg 2000). This chimes with the 2003 United Nations Security Council report on Liberia, the Commission for Africa's report in 2005 and the 2007 report on Africa's Missing Billions. See Boxes 8.1, 8.2 and 8.3. A most critical issue confronting Africa today is that of the flow of arms into the continent. As the scale of the production of arms in sub-Saharan Africa is small and restricted to a few countries – 22 companies in South Africa, one in Nigeria and a reconditioning arms capability in Uganda – much is imported. The Africa's Missing Billions study analysed the United Nations Commodity Trade Statistics Database information for 2005: of US$59.2 million-worth of small arms imports to African countries, US$58.5 million came from outside Africa. This suggests 99 per cent of arms are imported from outside the continent and only 1 per cent originate from African countries. With regard to the importation of ammunition, Spain is the 'biggest supplier' to sub-Saharan Africa although in East Africa, Kenyan, Ugandan and Sudanese manufactured ammunition was found in the hands of non-state armed groups in several countries (Oxfam 2007: 20).

Although it is acknowledged that 'the problem of armed violence in Africa is a complex one, requiring solutions at local, national, regional and global levels, from conflict prevention to enforcement of national gun laws, to disarmament, demobilisation and reintegration (DDR), to effective peace-building strategies' (ibid.: 22), it has also been suggested that 'poverty, inequality and ambitions to power' are the principal causes of conflict in the continent. In that context, arms transfers are 'not a cause of conflict' but a consequence (Hiltermann 1998: 119). However, once a conflict escalates into, within or across borders, 'arms begin to play an important role, as they are the primary tools by which the various

Box 8.1 Report of the UN Security Council Panel on Liberia 2003

1   Liberia's conflict is once more no longer isolated and its refugees and armed fighters have spilled over into its neighbours. Armed youths from Liberia, Sierra Leone, Guinea and Cote d'Ivoire who have become accustomed to a life of conflict, banditry and lawlessness have joined armed groups in Liberia and western Cote d'Ivoire

2   The region is awash with weapons and several companies have been involved in sanctions-busting by providing arms to Liberia and to Cote d'Ivoire

3   Weapons have been obtained in Serbia in 2002 from the arms manufacturer, Zastava, using a false Nigerian end-user certificate. The Panel suspects that preparations are ongoing for trans-shipments of 50 tons of Serbian military equipment from Belgrade to Liberia via Kinshasa, using an end-user certificate from the Democratic Republic of Congo.

Source: UN Security Council (2003).

Box 8.2 Report of the Commission for Africa

There is evidence that the transport of illicit weapons to and within Africa continues by sea, air and land. An Arms Trade Treaty would establish an unequivocal international legal mechanism to prevent arms transfers when they are likely to be used in violent conflict, human rights abuses, terrorism or for other serious abuses contrary to international law.

Source: Commission for Africa (2005).

sides seek to settle their differences.' Sometimes, perhaps just as worryingly, the exchange of arms becomes almost a way or life and a means of livelihood. As Box 8.4 demonstrates, the acquisitions of small arms and light weapons among pastoral groups in the Kenya–Uganda border area has become normal trade.

Resources can be shifted to enable the purchase of weapons and, on the supply side, arms traders start offering their wares in what is a highly competitive trade (ibid.). The position of arms brokers was also flagged up by the Commission for Africa (2005: 164), which found they played 'a major role in supplying weapons to African conflict zones.' Although some arms brokers 'learnt the tricks of the trade' during the years of the Cold War when gun-running was widespread among the client states of the West, China and the Soviet Union, now many are from new states such as Azerbaijan, Belarus, Ukraine and Turkmenistan (Human Rights Watch 1998: 7).

However, some countries in Africa have made efforts to prevent the irresponsible transfer of weapons by agreeing to regional initiatives: the 2004 Nairobi

Box 8.3 International arms flow into Africa

- 95% of Africa's most commonly used conflict weapons come from outside the continent.
- The most common weapon is the Kalashnikov assault rifle, the most well-known type being the AK-47, almost none of which are made in Africa.
- Military ammunition is also imported from outside Africa
- Government forces are not the only users of weapons
- Rebel army groups and bandits typically obtain their arms and ammunition by seizing them from police and army stockpiles. This was illustrated during the 1990s in conflicts in:
  - Republic of Congo
  - Ethiopia
  - Guinea-Bissau,
  - Liberia
  - Sierra Leone
  - Somalia
- While the Lord's Resistance Army in Uganda has stockpiles of weapons obtained many years ago, it continually acquires weapons by capturing them from Ugandan defence forces
- African governments distribute arms to non-state forces
- The recipients of these arms might be militias in-country, militias in other countries, or 'local defence groups'
- The governments generally do not have adequate 'command and control' over the groups using these weapons
- Consequently, there is an increased risk of diversion of these weapons to illicit trade.
- Africa desperately needs to stop the flow of arms to those who abuse human rights and ignore the rule of war.

Source: Oxfam (2007).

Protocol for the Prevention, Control and Reduction of Small Arms and Light Weapons, which applies to the Horn of Africa and Great Lakes region. Equally, the Economic Community of West African States (ECOWAS) Convention on Small Arms and Light Weapons, their Ammunition and other Related Materials (Oxfam 2007: 22). In a sense, these initiatives are building on the 2000 Bamako Declaration on an African Common Position on the Illicit Proliferation, Circulation and Trafficking of Small Arms and Light Weapons (Sabala 2004: 3; see Box 8.5) Certainly, more recently there have been moves to institute 'tough international controls on arms transfers' and, in 2006, 153 countries agreed to start developing an Arms Trade Treaty (ATT). Forty-two African countries voted to start the process of negotiation in the UN General Assembly and this is an ongoing process.

Box 8.4 Trade in arms on the Kenya–Uganda border

Arms are freely available and cheap. In 2003–4 an AK47 cost 2/3 cows. Arms traders can buy highly desirable goods such as radio, mobile phones and general electronics from markets in Kampala and take them to the north for cheap guns. Bullets are convertible currency. One bullet can be used to buy a glass of beer. Often women selling beer accumulate many bullets which they barter for a cow. Bullets are even put in the offering plates in church. Guns are now an instrument of economic subsistence as well as protection.

Source: Mkutu (2007).

Box 8.5 Declaration against the spread of small arms and light weapons

The uncontrolled proliferation of small arms and light weapons in Africa:

- Sustains conflicts, exacerbates violence, contributes to the displacement of innocent people and threatens international humanitarian law, as well as fuels crime and encourages terrorism
- Promotes a culture of violence and destabilises societies by creating a propitious environment for criminal and contraband activities
- Has adverse effects on security and development especially on women refugees
- Has devastating consequences on children, a number of whom are victims of armed conflict while others are forced to become child soldiers
- Undermines good governance, peace efforts and negotiation, jeopardises the respect for fundamental human rights.

Source: Bamako Declaration (2000).

The Commission for Africa (2005: 163) called for the international community to 'adopt more effective and legally-binding agreements on arms brokering . . . and common standards of monitoring and enforcement'. Although these initiatives may not completely eliminate conflict within Africa they do acknowledge that stemming the flow of weapons may encourage non-violent ways of settling disputes and by so doing encourage a maturing of political processes. Of course, it must be remembered that private military organizations (PMOs) have long had a presence within the continent, be they the mercenaries of the past or the contemporary security organizations that protect foreign corporate personnel and property, operate as agents of governments and are utilized by political elites. Private military groups are also used in demobilization programmes and, although there are legitimate ethical concerns regarding their potential over-engagement in some states, they are unlikely to disappear in the near future.

Peace and security initiatives

Within Africa and beyond there has been a growing recognition that peace and development are interdependent. Without peace there can be no sustainable development, and without development it is impossible to establish enduring peace. Consequently, post-conflict reconstruction and peace building have become joint priorities among policy makers. African perspectives on peace and security have received attention in reports at international level, e.g. the Report of the Group of Eminent Persons on Civil Society and UN Relationships, the report of a High Level Panel and the UN Secretary-General's report 'In Larger Freedom: Towards Development, Security and Human Rights for All'.[2] In 2002, UN General Assembly Resolution 57/7 endorsed Nepad as the strategic framework for cooperation of UN programmes on the continent and in 2003 an AU–Nepad Peace and Security Agenda was adopted which specified the eight priorities contained in Box 8.6.

These eight priorities demand considerable degrees of capability, resources and manpower but the newly formed African Union agreed to the principles. The African Union transformed itself from the Organisation of African Unity (OAU), in Durban in 2002, and at the first session of the assembly it adopted a protocol relating to the establishment of a Peace and Security Council (PSC). The PSC replaced the former OAU's Mechanism for Conflict Prevention, Management and Resolution. The PSC was established as a standing decision-making organ for the prevention, management and resolution of conflicts: 'it is a collective security and early warning arrangement to facilitate timely and efficient response to conflict and crisis situations in Africa' (African Union 2002b: Article 2 (1)). Besides the promotion of peace and security, the PSC also deals with preventive diplomacy, the management of disasters, humanitarian action and post-conflict reconstruction, and its existence is intended to demonstrate that member states of the AU are ready and willing to take whatever steps are necessary for the establishment of durable peace and security within the continent. Article 4 of the Protocol specifically mentions the peaceful settlement of disputes and conflicts, the sanctity of human life, respect for the rule of law and the interdependence of security and socio-economic development in line with the Charter of the United Nations and the Universal Declaration of Human Rights. Although it promises respect for the sovereignty and territorial integrity of member states and the principle of non-interference of any member state in the internal affairs of the another and the respect of existing borders, it does make clear that the AU will intervene in the affairs of member states 'in respect of grave circumstances, namely war crimes, genocide and crimes against humanity' (ibid.: Article 4). Equally, it asserts the right of member states to request intervention from the Union in order to restore peace and security.

One of the major objectives of the Peace and Security Council was to create and operate an African Standby Force (ASF), which would be composed of

Box 8.6 The eight priorities of the AU–Nepad Peace and Security Agenda

1 Developing mechanisms, institution building processes and support instruments for achieving peace and security in Africa

2 Improving capacity for, and coordination of, early action for conflict prevention, management and resolution, including the development of peace support operations capabilities

3 Improving early warning capacity in Africa through strategic analysis and support

4 Prioritising strategic security issues as follows:
   - Promoting an African definition and action on disarmament, demobilisation, rehabilitation and reconstruction (DDRR) efforts in post-conflict situations
   - Coordinating and ensuring effective implementation of African efforts aimed at preventing and combating terrorism

5 Ensuring efficient and consolidated action for the prevention, combating and eradicating the problem of the illicit proliferation, circulation and trafficking of small arms and light weapons

6 Improving the security sector and the capacity for good governance as related to peace and security

7 Generating minimum standards for application in the exploitation and management of Africa's resources (including non-renewable resources) in areas affected by conflict

8 Assisting in resource mobilisation for the African Union Peace Fund and regional initiatives aimed at preventing, managing and resolving conflicts on the continent.

Source: Nepad Secretariat (2005: 5).

'standby multidisciplinary contingents, with civilian and military components in their countries of origin and ready for rapid deployment at appropriate notice' (Box 8.7). It also requires that member states 'take steps to establish standby contingents for participation in peace support missions decided on by the Council or intervention authorised by the Assembly' (ibid.: Article 13 (1) and (2)). Standby Forces should be able to deploy rapidly in cases of grave circumstances such as genocide, war and other crimes against humanity. It is recognized that in many instances there have been long delays in the deployment of United Nations forces on African soil. Furthermore, the ASF could deal with low-intensity conflict in which the UN Security Council may not be involved. There is also the necessity for the AU to play an appropriate role in conflict situations by co-deploying a force with any UN missions in Africa. The ASF has a number of varied demanding functions including observation, monitoring, preventive deployment in trou-

Box 8.7 Objectives and principles of the African Union, Peace and Security Council

- To promote peace, security and stability in Africa
- To anticipate and prevent conflicts
- To promote and implement peace-building and post-conflict reconstruction
- To co-ordinate and harmonise continental efforts in the prevention and combating of international terrorism in all it aspects
- To develop a common defence policy for the African Union
- To promote and encourage democratic practices, good governance and the rule of law

Source: African Union (2002b: Article 2 (1)).

bled areas, peace building and humanitarian assistance. Certain scenarios were identified in which the Force could become engaged in different roles:

- AU/regional military advice to political missions;
- AU/regional observer missions co-deployed with UN missions;
- AU/regional peace-keeping force and preventive deployment missions;
- stand-alone AU/regional observer missions;
- AU intervention, for example in genocide situations when the international community does not act promptly.

The African regional economic communities as outlined in Box 8.8 have demonstrated their willingness to deal with conflicts in their regions. For example, the Economic Community of West African States (ECOWAS) has intervened in several recent regional conflicts, including Liberia, Sierra Leone and Côte d'Ivoire. Also its counterpart in Eastern Africa, the Inter-Governmental Authority for Development (IGAD), has led the mediation of conflicts in Sudan and Somalia. Equally, South Africa led regional efforts to negotiate a peace agreement in the Democratic Republic of Congo. Regional efforts, although useful in some respects, are not entirely successful as 'neighbours are often not impartial actors' and to some extent may be caught up in conflicts: 'Thus, such organisations do not provide an unqualified solution to violent conflict in Africa' (Commission for Africa 2005: 167). One concern is that the emphasis in African peace keeping has been 'placed heavily on the security side, rather than conflict prevention.' The AU has 56 staff members in its Peace and Security Division yet only 13 in its Political Division, which hampers its ability to identify early warnings of potential conflict that appear in certain political systems and to be able to conduct some form of negotiation between competing elites. In certain quarters there have been calls for greater levels of support for the AU's political division (e.g., at the conference 'Reconciliation and Reconstruction in Africa: Beyond the Peace Agreements', Wilton Park, 26–30 July 2004).

> **Box 8.8 Composition of the African Standby Force**
>
> 1 Military Staff Committee
> 2 Headquarters based in Addis Ababa with the following elements:
>   • Continental Planning Element
>   • Continental Military Logistic Depot
> 3 Regional Training Facilities
> 4 Regional Standby Brigades in five African regions: West, South, East, Central and North:
>   i FORMACBRIG: Brigade representing the Economic Community of Central African States
>   ii EASBRIG: Will be established by the Inter-Governmental Authority for Development (IGAD) of East Africa
>   iii ECOBRIG: Brigade representing the Economic Community of West African States (ECOWAS)
>   iv SADCBRIG: Representing the Southern Africa Development Community (SADC)
>   v NASBRIG: Representing the Arab Maghreb Union (AMU)

In 2003 the AU mandated its first deployment of a peace mission, the AU Mission in Burundi (AMIB), which deployed 2650 peace keepers consisting of soldiers from South Africa, Ethiopia and Mozambique together with AU observers from Burkino Faso, Gabon, Mali, Togo and Tunisia, giving a total strength of 3335 persons (Agoagye 2004). AMIB was mandated for one year's deployment pending the arrival of a UN Peacekeeping force. Its key objectives were to 'implement the Ceasefire Agreements; support disarmament, demobilisation and reintegration of combatants; create conditions favourable for a UN Peacekeeping missions and contribute to the political and economic stability' in the country (ibid.: 3). These aims were incredibly demanding of a first mission with such limited personnel and resource shortages. The total cost of the mission was US$13 million, which the AU could not raise. The European Union pledged €25 million but the funding was disbursed very slowly. Inevitably, it could never achieve its overall objectives but it did manage to 'create conditions conducive for political negotiations' and it essentially held the line until the UN Security Council authorized the deployment of the UN Mission in Burundi (ibid.).

The AU also deployed a mission to Darfur, Sudan, in 2004, which was a difficult deployment (see case study below). Despite the fact that AU missions lack large numbers of personnel and are financially challenged they have raised the profile of 'African solutions to African problems' at least superficially. But can ambitious aims be met in the medium term? Bereng Mtimkulu, head of the AU Peace Support Operations, is unequivocal:

Will the African Standby Force compete with the UN standby arrangement? The response is absolutely no . . . how much longer will the AU's poor peacekeepers be the firefighters as they enter treacherous terrain to police shaky ceasefire agreements only to hand over to the well-endowed UN to complete the task? How well can the AU salvage institutional pride when clearly it cannot stay the course in complex operations owing to fragile structures and unpredictable funding.

(Mtimkulu 2005)

These concerns have been recognized and the call has gone out to donors to fund 'at least 50% of the AU's Peace Fund' in order for it to be able 'to act quickly and effectively to prevent and resolve violent conflict.' In spite of the 'inflexibility' of EU development assistance the EU's African Peace Facility, which provides €250 million from the European Development Fund to support African-led peacekeeping operations in Africa, is a 'significant innovation.' The EU has also approved a €6.5 million support programme for the AU's Peace and Security Department (Reconciliation and Reconstruction in Africa conference, 2004).

With regard to demobilization, disarmament and re-integration (DDR) the situation is complex especially in light of the fact that 'half of all countries emerging from conflict relapse into violence within five years' (Collier and Dollar 2004: 244). That is why effective post-conflict peace building is a difficult task, requiring long-term commitment from local and international actors (Cilliers 2004). Security must be established and this requires disarming and reintegrating ex-combatants. There have been arms collection programmes, for example 891 assault rifles were collected in the 2002–3 DDR programme in the Central African Republic and 1100 weapons were taken by international peace keepers in eastern DRC (Amnesty International *et al.* 2006). But for ex-combatants, returning refugees, and internally displaced persons to be reintegrated, war economies must be dismantled. Although this is desirable it must be acknowledged that much of the DDR theory makes the assumption that there is a formal economy for demobilized fighters to be reintegrated into. In many poor economies the informal sector is dominant and on occasions the civilian population feel disadvantaged: 'the civilian population, which has struggled through war, often feels twice punished. They suffer the consequences of the fighting, and then the fighters themselves are rewarded for stopping the fighting' (Reconciliation and Reconstruction in Africa conference, 2004). These dynamics can lead to a self-defeating cycle and a war economy that is difficult to break. The brutal consequences of conflict on societies are not easily remedied and women, children and the young often suffer most, for example from sexual violence, HIV/AIDS and other health problems, the plight of child soldiers and other human rights violations (see Box 8.9). Although there is no precise format for dealing with post-conflict societies, certain phases have been identified, as outlined in Tables 8.3 and 8.4. The emergency phase follows immediately after the hostilities have ended when there is a pressing need for a safe and secure environment to be established. This is a period when many external organizations are involved, for example military units such as one of the brigades of the African Standby Force or a peace operation deployed by the AU or UN, humanitarian NGOs such as the International Committee of the Red Cross or

Box 8.9 Children in internally displaced persons' (IDP) camps

In a survey of over 300 child soldiers in Uganda, over 90 per cent had post-traumatic stress of clinical importance. In IDP camps in northern Uganda, boy and girls play games 'only about violence, about the war, abduction, and death. Not about family life – cooking, hunting, and digging – like it used to be' (Oxfam 2006).

In some countries, conflicts have raged for so long that children have grown into adults without ever knowing peace. I have spoken to a child who was raped by soldiers when she was just nine years old. I have listened to children forced to watch while their families were brutally slaughtered. I have been chilled listening to children who have been so manipulated by adults and so corrupted by their experiences of conflict that they could not recognise the evil of which they had been a part.

Source: Graca Machel, cited in UN Office on Drugs and Crime (2005).

Table 8.3 Goals within three phases of post-conflict reconstruction

Areas of concern	Emergency phase	Transition phase	Development phase
Political transition, governance and participation	Determine the governance structures, foundations for participation and process for political transition	Promote legitimate political institutions and participatory processes	Consolidate political institutions and participatory processes, e.g. elections
Human rights, justice and reconciliation	Develop mechanisms for addressing past and ongoing grievances	Build the legal system and processes for reconciliation and monitoring of human rights	Establish a functional legal system based on accepted international norms
Coordination and management	Develop consultative and coordination mechanisms for internal and external actors	Develop technical bodies to facilitate programme development	Develop internal sustainable processes and capacity for coordination

Source: Nepad (2005).

others. However, there is also a need for domestic civil society to be involved lest the process seem too alien. African institutions, such as the AU, Nepad or regional organizations, can seem remote to the lives of ordinary people and real concerns have been expressed (see Box 8.10) that often point to reasons why those countries were vulnerable in the first place. Sometimes, traditional structures, elders within the community and local organizations can play a role in mitigating tension but it

Table 8.4 Phases of activities in post-conflict reconstruction

Emergency	Transition	Development
• Humanitarian relief and food aid • Resettlement of internally displaced persons • Mine action programmes • Demobilization and reintegration of ex-combatants	• National unity and reconciliation • Rehabilitation of physical infrastructure • Rebuilding and maintaining key social infrastructure • Restoration of main productive sectors • Restoration of macroeconomic stability	• Establishment of political legitimacy • Reconstruction of framework of governance • Implementing economic reforms • Broad-based participation/consensus building

Source: Nepad (2005).

Box 8.10 Concerns about post-conflict reconstruction

Externally driven post-conflict reconstruction processes that lack sufficient local ownership and participation are unsustainable. They cause resentment. The relationship is further complicated by the unequal power balance between internal and external actors, where the latter is empowered by virtue of being the benefactor. But even when external actors have adopted policies that encourage local ownership and participation they often fail to identify credible internal partners because of conflicting claims of ownership and lack of capacity in, for example, education, language skills and institutions. Local people are often intimidated by the education, experience, organisation, scope and resources of the external actors. In many cases, the indigenous educated and experienced administrators, managers, academics and professionals have left the country, and some of those that remain may be excluded from the post-conflict reconstruction effort as they were associated with the former discredited regime.

Source: Nepad (2005).

---

must be recognized that in the immediate aftermath of conflict people are largely preoccupied with basic survival and coping mechanisms. For real construction to take place, however, local people have to be engaged in the process but many are unable to and rapidly become viewed as 'victims' who then become susceptible to the possibility of renewed conflict. In a sense, there can be an extraordinary sense of powerlessness among general populations within some African states, which is directly related to socio-economic development issues. This is why post-conflict sustainable development programmes are so important and why the phase can last anywhere from four to ten years. Nepad, however, takes a far more profound view of sustainable development in states emerging from war: 'the country is likely to continue to address conflict related consequences in its development programming for decades' (Nepad Secretariat 2005).

The cessation of hostilities is only the beginning of a long, hard process that has its own difficulties. Although, in a sense, the experiences of South Africa are atypical within the continent, that country began a policy of demilitarizing the South African state only after the political and security environment changed. With the demise of the Cold War, the end of apartheid and the introduction of democratic elections in 1994, the country could move forward. The South African White Paper on Defence motivated demilitarization: 'While the potential for instability and conflict remains in the post-apartheid era, the salient fact is that the government is no longer unrepresentative and at war with its own people and neighbouring states in Southern Africa' (Deegan 2001: 104; see also Barber 1999; Spence 1999). As Laurie Nathan (1998: 5) makes clear, dealing with the military aspects of conflict alone will not resolve issues, as they are the 'symptoms rather than the causes of intra-state crises.' It might stop the fighting for a while but the pernicious elements of society will remain and generate further crises which will be met with further military action. In short, 'the crises create a security vacuum which state and non-state actors seek to fill by violent means; demilitarisation is contingent on the filling of that vacuum by legitimate political means.' It is, of course, quite true that only with democratic and effective governance can development and human security be achieved and sustained. But realistically is that a likely scenario for the African continent now? Perhaps, in the future and in some countries and regions, Southern Africa for example, but at the moment, for some states, it is almost a miracle that conflict ends at all, and in others it has yet to. Ultimately, there should be peace and justice but these are contested arenas in war-torn countries. It may be possible to achieve some kind of peace in certain states but justice for all communities could be light years away.[3] Nevertheless, the notion of a Continental Early Warning System (CEWS) has gained attention and security institutes have called for the establishment of a 'dedicated CEWS at continental and regional levels that uses open-source information and interacts with civil society and others in the provision of conflict prevention information' (Institute for Security Studies 2004). Conflict prevention, then, is being prioritized as the way forward.

Case study: Sierra Leone

The difficulties of dealing with conflict resolution and rebuilding states following long and destructive wars can never be overestimated but the example of Sierra Leone may offer some lessons. The 11-year war in the country was formally declared to be over by the President in 2002, but at its beginning it seemed confusing to outside observers mainly because of its diffuse nature and spontaneous acts of looting and violence. Box 8.11 outlines some key facts about the country's civil war. A complicating factor in the war was the role played by diamonds: 'Dia-

Box 8.11 Key facts in Sierra Leone's 1991–2002 civil war

- The war began in 1991 when ex-army corporal Foday Sankoh and his Revolutionary United Front (RUF) took up arms against the then President Joseph Momoh, seizing towns near Liberia's border.
- Although the rebels gained some popularity at first, they quickly earned a reputation for murder, rape, mutilation and recruiting child soldiers.
- The war was funded partly by diamonds mined in southern and eastern Sierra Leone. This led to a global campaign against so-called 'blood diamonds' mined in conflict zones.
- The Armed Forces Revolutionary Council (AFRC), a group of army officers allied to the rebels, overthrew the elected President Ahmad Tejan Kabbah in 1997. A Nigerian-led regional force reinstated Kabbah within a year.
- A truce was agreed in 1999 but it fell apart in 2000 and the United Nations Mission in Sierra Leone was attacked. There was a hostage crisis and the RUF captured 500 UN peacekeepers. Britain, the former colonial power, sent troops to help the UN force.
- The rebels were driven back into the countryside and the UN was able to deploy troops. Disarmament was completed in 2002 and the war was formally declared over.
- Kabbah was re-elected in 2002. The RUF stood as a political party but won little support in the election. Sankoh died in prison in 2003 while facing a war crimes indictment.
- The death toll from the war is estimated at 50,000.
- Former Liberian President Charles Taylor, who supported the RUF, was put on trial in 2007 in the Hague on charges of war crimes and crimes against humanity in Sierra Leone's civil war.

Sources: International Crisis Group Africa (2001); Reuters (2007).

monds have been central to the conflict in Sierra Leone' (Smillie *et al.* 2002). However, the illicit market in Sierra Leonean diamonds was 'not generated by the conflict'; it had existed since the 1950s, when diamond-producing areas were 'plagued by criminal gangs' (UN Office on Drugs and Crime 2005: 21). Private military firms, such as Executive Outcomes, protected small mining companies during the 1990s and the Revolutionary United Front (RUF) became increasingly involved in organized 'crime and terrorism' (ibid.: 22).[4] Whereas the RUF had called the country's various governments corrupt and accused them of misman-agement of diamond and mineral resources, they themselves committed 'horren-dous' abuses. People were raped and had limbs amputated. Equally, the attraction of making profits from diamonds was simply too tempting to resist (Shah 2003).

The UN-brokered peace deal in 1999 was extremely fragile. Human Rights Watch criticized the UN for agreeing to a truce that ultimately would give the rebels amnesty for their human rights abuses. And in any event the abuses were continuing (Human Rights Watch 1999). In 2000 the United Nations Security Council decided to impose an 18-month ban on diamond exports from Sierra Leone, and the Kimberley Process Certification Scheme was introduced in 2002 as outlined in Box 8.12 (see Table 8.5). When Britain became engaged in 2000 its expressed aim was 'the establishment of sustainable peace and security, a stable democratic government, the reduction of poverty, respect for human rights, the establishment of accountable armed and police forces, and the enhancement of the UN's reputation in Africa more widely' (Riley 2006: 6). These were challenging objectives but the commander in charge of the mission, Major General Jonathon P. Riley, was immediately confronted with how to rebuild the country's army. He decided upon three priorities:

- The manning, training and equipping of the Sierra Leone Army, air force and navy
- The structural institutional reform of the Sierra Leone Armed Forces

---

Box 8.12 Sierra Leone, diamonds and conflict

The Kimberley Process

The Kimberley Process Certification Scheme for trade in rough diamonds was launched in 2002. Over 50 governments and the EU stated their readiness to implement the Certification Scheme with effect from January 2003. There is no common certificate so all member states print and circulate their own Kimberley-compatible certificates. The scheme is an export and import control regime. Producer countries will control the production and transport of rough diamonds. Imports of rough diamonds not accompanied by a Kimberley Process certificate will be banned. Sierra Leone has a fully functional Kimberley Process.

The Government Gold and Diamond Office estimated in 2003 that total production of diamonds is worth around US$100 million per annum. Smuggling accounts for over 50 per cent of the trade. The infrastructure in the diamond-rich areas is severely damaged and there is tension between the indigenous people and other groups. The existence of strident youth groups and predatory traders has contributed to an increase in tension.

The government has launched, with co-financing from UNDP, a Diamonds for Development initiative that is designed to set up community-based projects in diamond-producing chiefdoms.

Source: UN Security Council (2003).

Table 8.5 Sierra Leone diamond export figures per year

Year	Weight (carats)	Value (US$)
2000	77,372.39	10 million
2001	225,519.83	26 million
2002	351,859.23	41 million
2003	78,555.73	11 million

Source: Government Gold and Diamond Office, Freetown, cited in UN Security Council (2003).

- Fighting the RUF either directly, using Sierra Leone Army units with mentors, or by manoeuvre to force them to accept the UN's Demobilisation, Disarmament and Re-integration (DDR) process.

(ibid.: 3)

These essential elements had to be in place before post-conflict reconstruction could take place. Governance was vital, not just local and national government but 'the electoral process, the minimizing of corruption, the legal system – not just public order, but law and order – a working financial system with functioning banks and a code of conduct for financial business enshrined in the legal system' (ibid.). So to what extent have these aspects been achieved? Well, the civil service has been strengthened by the formation of a Senior Executive Service, which has recruited high-level staff externally. An anti-corruption commission has been set up to investigate and eradicate corruption. Some foreign judges have been appointed to preside over anti-corruption cases. Presidential and parliamentary elections took place in 2002 and 2007 and Ernest Bai Koroma, who won 54 per cent of the vote, was sworn in as Sierra Leone's new President on 17 September 2007. In his inaugural speech he promised 'zero tolerance on corruption' and on the mismanagement of state resources. Certainly, the World Bank maintains that:

more than 1 million Sierra Leoneans have benefited directly from their programmes designed to restore social stability and economic activity:

- 16 demobilisation centres and 7 interim care centres disarmed 72,000 people
- Around 50,000 ex-combatants were trained of which c50% have found employment or are self-employed
- 220,000 internally displaced people are back in their locations of choice
- 269 projects were implemented in agriculture, community infrastructure, education etc.
- 84 schools and 28 health centres are back in operation
- 200,000 people have access to portable water.

(http://web.worldbank.org/WBSITE/EXTERNAL/EXTABOUTUS/
IDA/O,,contentMDK)

The African Development Fund has provided US$12.24 million and the security sector is democratically accountable to the government in that the President is Commander-in-Chief of the armed forces and the Deputy Minister of Defence is a civilian.

There is little doubt that the country has emerged from a massively destructive and long-lasting war. The Economic Community of West African States (ECOWAS), the AU, the UN and the UK government have all played a role in this transition and helped the country move away from a war situation. There have also been considerable developments on the social and political fronts. Yet still there are concerns: Is a 7000-strong policing community able to deliver services and exert effective control over swathes of the country? What will be the continuing role of 'chiefs' in rural communities, who exercise customary rights? Has corruption been adequately eliminated? (Cf. Baker 2006; Fanthorpe 2006.) It is too early to conclude definitively what the future trajectory of Sierra Leone may be. But the caution exists: the security may be fixed but if the other essentials are not, conditions will have been created for the next military coup (Riley 2006: 4).

ANALYSIS: SUDAN: DARFUR CRISIS

The crisis in Darfur, Sudan, has raged since 2004, claimed the lives of 200,000 people and forced 2.2 million others to flee their homes. The United Nations, the African Union and the European Union together with the mediating countries of Libya and Nigeria have all attempted to resolve the conflict. Yet the crisis still persists: 'violence is increasing, access for humanitarian agencies is decreasing, international peacekeeping is not yet effective and a political settlement remains far off' (International Crisis Group 2007a). This study analyses the responses of the international community and the trajectory of this complex and unresolved problem.

Ethnicity and religion in Sudan were complicated by the introduction of *shari'a* (Islamic law) in 1983. From that time, believed the former state minister of foreign affairs, Bishop Gabriel Roric, minority rights became confused with religious rights (Roric interview 1997). Since Sudan's independence from the British in 1956 it has been difficult to create a national culture that is capable of uniting ethnic, regional and religious forms of identity. Such a culture would require political structures that are sufficiently strong to withstand parochial or primordial demands, yet flexible enough to allow for popular participation. However, the status of *shari'a* law, first introduced by the secular government of Colonel Nimeiri in 1983 as a means of quelling opposition, and further enhanced by General al-Bashir after 1989, has been one of the most contentious and divisive measures especially given the country's complex ethnic structure. The 1996 census reported a population of 27 million people; according to an earlier census conducted in 1955/56, the only one that included ethnic origin, there are 19 major ethnic groups. These groups can be further divided into 597 smaller sub-groupings, speaking over 100 different languages. Around 60 per cent of the population is Muslim and 15 per cent is Christian; the remainder adhere to traditional religions.

The Darfur crisis

The events in Darfur first hit the international media in 2003 and according to one report 'shocked the world' (Begum 2004: 48). Others interpreted the crisis as 'an integral part of Sudan's failed system of governance fostered by unwise state policy, which manipulated ethnic and tribal differences to maintain political and economic power' (Jibril 2004a: 2). The region, comprising three states, Northern, Southern and Western Darfur, and with a population of 6 million divided into nine main ethnic groups, lurched into conflict when two rebel groups, the Sudan Liberation Movement/Army (SLM/SLA) and the Justice and Equality Movement (JEM), launched attacks against 'government installations'. It might be regarded a curious move by the JEM, which was now supported by the notorious Hasan Turabi, who had previously led the radical National Islamic Front, backed the 1989 military coup by General al-Bashir and, during the 1990s, presided over a system in which 'arbitrary detention and torture leading to mutilation and death' were regular practices (Woodward 1997: 101). In fact, he declared in 1997 that, although the Sudanese model of Islam placed an emphasis on 'rights and obligation' in which there was no coercion, it did not uphold 'freedom of will' in the Western sense (Turabi interview 1997). However, issues, personalities and politics in Sudan are never straightforward. By 1999 President Bashir had dismissed Turabi as Speaker of the National Assembly and subsequently arrested him, since which time Turabi has been in and out of state custody and until recently under house arrest.

The spur for the conflict was allegedly the prospective Comprehensive Peace Agreement between the government in Khartoum and the peoples of the south. Rebel groups in Darfur believed the region to be excluded from the country's burgeoning economic benefits, particularly increasing oil wealth. The government, on the other hand, condemned the JEM and SLML/SLA for initiating and orchestrating a 'war of aggression' against the army (Mans 2004: 291). The Sudanese government sought to crush the rebellion at first through the use of conventional armed forces, including helicopter gunships, MIG jets and Antonov bombers (International Development Committee 2005: 9). It also recruited and armed local militia groups, which became known as the *Janjawiid* (meaning armed men on horseback), and the conflict rapidly turned into an humanitarian disaster. The militias mainly attacked civilians. Many people were killed and by early 2004 more than 1 million people were displaced and became refugees. According to one source, these events will never be forgotten: 'The unprecedented mass killings, pillage of resources, destruction of livelihood, as well as the abduction, gang rape of women and other crimes committed . . . have left deep scars' (Abrahamson 2004).

Although conflict in the region flared in February 2003, tensions in Darfur were of long standing and 'popular opposition against the Khartoum government no new phenomenon' (Mans 2004: 292). As far back as 1983, 'other nomadic groups, such as the *Maraheel* were accused of perpetrating violent acts . . . similar to those of which the *Janjawiid* are allegedly engaged in today' (El Talib 2004: 3). The major function of these groups was to protect the herds of nomadic tribes in western Sudan from 'looters, highway robbers and attacks from other nomadic tribes . . . on their grazing land and water.' In 1983, the Sudan People's Liberation Movement/Army (SPLM/SPLA) initiated military operations against the then government of President Jaafar Numeiri in the southern and western areas of the country. The *Maraheel* and other nomadic communities, who were potential targets of such operations, requested protection from government security forces. However, the reason why the *Janjawiid* recently found much publicity in the international media was the 'intensity of the attacks, their widespread presence and the quality of weaponry used' (ibid.). It was not to be too long before the world became aware of the violence, forced migration and human rights abuses being visited on the peoples of the region.

Unlike the civil war between north and south, which had been identified as a Muslim north threatening to impose itself on a predominantly Christian/Animist south, Darfur is religiously homogeneous, that is, Islamic. Yet the region has many ethnicities and tribes. Certainly, the government's Islamic Al Zakat Bureau made distinctions between the 'poor and indigent' and 'means of production' within the region when allocating funding, dividing the locality into Southern, Northern and Western Darfur with clearly differentiated rates of resources. Table 8.6 illustrates the considerable socio-economic differences between Southern Darfur and the Northern and Western regions.

By the 1989 military coup, the Popular Defence Forces (PDF) had emerged as an 'official army of reservists under the guidance and command of the regular army. Many nomadic tribal members enthusiastically joined the PDF' (ibid.). According to some analysts, the issue of an Arab/African divide in the region is misleading. Alex de Waal asserts:

> From the viewpoint of Southern Sudan, 'African' and 'Arab' are polar opposites. From the viewpoint of Darfur, the distinction between 'Arab' and 'African' did not arise. Darfurians had no difficulty with multiple identities and indeed would have defined their multi-ethnic kingdom as encompassing Arabs, both Bedouins and cultural Arabs.
>
> (de Waal 2005: 187)

Over the centuries 'blood lines have intermingled, laying waste to . . . polarised definitions' although people tend to classify themselves as Arab or African (Abrahamson 2004). Another study regards the perception of the conflict as 'Arabs (attacking) Africans' as a 'simplistic characterisation' (Begum 2004: 45). Abdelbagi Jibril maintains:

> The irony of the Darfur crisis is that the people of the region, both Africans and Arabs, have more common denominators than differences. Apart from a few exceptions, all the tribal groups in Darfur have developed complementary socio-cultural systems. The people of the region practice Sunni Islam and many among them use Arabic as their *lingua franca.* Yet difficulties have beset the region caused in the main by diminishing resources brought about by gradual desertification together with a drought in 1984–85 which exacerbated conditions and fanned tensions between the 'pastoralist nomad and farmer.'
>
> (Jibril 2004a)

Table 8.6 Actual payments for means of production and those of the needy

State	The poor and indigent (million Sudanese pounds)	Means of production (million Sudanese pounds)
Southern Darfur	302.0	90.6
Northern Darfur	40.3	12.1
Western Darfur	38.8	11.5

Source: Zakat (1997).

Certainly, taken as a whole, the region had poor socio-economic indicators, with some of the highest illiteracy rates and lowest school enrolment figures in the country (see Table 8.7).

International alert

By March 2004, the outgoing UN Humanitarian Coordinator for Sudan, Mukesh Kapila, called international attention to the 'the world's greatest humanitarian and human rights catastrophe', which was taking place in Darfur. The UN estimated that 700,000 people had been displaced by violence with 110,000 fleeing into neighbouring Chad. Eight months later, that figure had increased to nearly 200,000 refugees in Chad, 1.6 million internally displaced and 400,000 labelled 'conflict-affected' and in need of humanitarian aid (Abrahamson 2004: 5). UN Secretary-General Kofi Annan toured the region in June–July 2004 and through a process of diplomacy managed to get the government in Khartoum and the rebel organizations to sign a joint communiqué which called for unrestricted humanitarian access, an end to impunity, cessation of hostilities and the disarming of the *Janjawiid* and other militias. The communiqué also enabled the creation of the Joint Implementing Mechanism, headed by Annan's Special Representative to Sudan, Jan Pronk, and the Sudanese Foreign Minister, Mustafa Osman Ismail.

It was not long before the UN Security Council adopted the US-drafted Resolution 1556, on 30 July, which required the Secretary-General to report to the Council every 30 days on progress made in the region. A Plan of Action was drawn up for August, 'requiring the government to make steps to disarm and apprehend militias, end impunity, widen humanitarian space and deploy increased police troops to protect certain heavily populated camps for the internally displaced' (ibid.). The backdrop to the events in Darfur had been the ongoing negotiations surrounding a Comprehensive Peace Agreement aimed at ending the war between north and south Sudan.

Table 8.7 Illiteracy rates and school enrolment, ages 7–9 years

Region	Illiteracy rate	School enrolment (%)
Khartoum	31.8	58.7
Blue Nile	48.3	44.0
Kordofan	74.0	30.0
Dar Fur	76.4	29.5
Northern	40.6	60.0
Eastern	56.2	36.5
Red Sea	n/a	46.0
Equatoria	71.2	27.5
Bahr el Ghazal	85.9	5.3
Upper Nile	86.3	17.0

Source: Abdalla and Suliman (1995).

Some commentators have been critical: 'the response of the international community fell dramatically short of meeting the challenge posed by the crisis in Darfur . . . and is still reluctant to undertake meaningful measures to prevent the commission of these crimes or protect the people on the ground' (Jibril 2004a). Others were more scathing: 'We deliberately choose to describe Darfur as a failure of British policy because we believe the Foreign Office's record amounts to appeasement of the National Islamic Front regime in Khartoum' (Tinsley 2005). The UK Department for International Development (DfID) admitted that the early warnings, in 2003, from a range of non-governmental organizations – Amnesty International, the International Crisis Group, Justice Africa and Medicins Sans Frontieres – were 'not taken seriously.' Some NGOs were warned that 'it was not the right time to highlight Darfur for fear of jeopardizing the North–South peace process' (International Development Committee 2005: 17). Although the UN launched an appeal – the Greater Darfur Special Initiative – in September 2003 and the UN Office for the Coordination of Humanitarian Affairs cautioned that the region was heading for a humanitarian crisis, the donor response was 'insufficient'. The DfID believed that the USA, the European Commission and the UK were 'shouldering too much of the responsibility'. The UK had already donated £9.5 million for humanitarian assistance by the time the UN made its appeal for US$534 million in March 2004. On balance it was felt that other countries 'should have done more', particularly Arab countries, who donated a 'disappointing' 2.5 per cent of the total $1.3 billion that had been committed, and that was mainly dispensed through in-kind bilateral humanitarian aid (ibid.: 18). For one analyst this response from Arab quarters came as no surprise: 'some of Sudan's North African neighbours went as shamefully far as blankly supporting Khartoum in its carnage in Darfur' (Jibril 2004a).

The question of genocide

If initial responses to the crisis could have been quicker, there also seemed to be confusion among the international community about whether or not the humanitarian disaster occurring in the region was, in fact, genocide. In 2004, the US Secretary of State, Colin Powell, returned from a visit to Sudan and declared that he believed the actions taking place in Darfur could be described as genocide. In citing the State Department investigation that had been conducted in the Chad refugee camps, with the American Bar Association and the Coalition for International Justice, Powell identified 'a consistent and widespread pattern of atrocities – killings, rapes, burning of villages – committed by *Janjawiid* and government forces against non-Arab villagers'. From this evidence he concluded that 'genocide has been committed in Darfur and that the government of Sudan and the Janjawiid bear the responsibility.' He also conceded that genocide might still be occurring (http://platform.blogs.com/passionofthepresent). Powell's statements were contentious. Under Articles II and III of the 1948 Convention of the Prevention and Punishment of Genocide, two essential elements constituted genocide:

1　the mental element, meaning the 'intent to destroy, in whole or in part, a national, ethnic, racial or religious group';
2　the physical element, meaning (a) killing members of a group; (b) causing serious bodily and mental harm to members of the group; (c) deliberately inflicting on the group conditions of life calculated to bring about its physical destruction in whole or in part; (d) imposing measures intended to prevent births within the group; (e) forcibly transferring children of the group to another group.

(Tinsley 2005: 4)

The government of Sudan categorically rejected Powell's assertions, claiming that the situation in Darfur was 'not tantamount to genocide' and pointed out that neither the EU nor the AU had used 'such strong language' (http://news.bbc.co.uk/2/hi/Africa/3940547). In August 2004, the UN High Commissioner for Human Rights, Louise Arbour, and UN Special Advisor on the Prevention of Genocide Juan Mendez undertook an assessment tour of Darfur. According to Arbour, the internally displaced persons were held 'captive in prisons without walls', as they could not move outside the camps' perimeters for fear of attacks. She added:

Janjawiid attacks against villagers are still ongoing, but the type of attacks has changed to a new pattern of individual attacks on a massive scale. In all the camps where . . . women attempt to step out to collect firewood there is very widespread preying on these individual victims.

Mendez asserted that:

the vulnerability of certain ethnic groups and the instability of the situation generally are such that we have not turned the corner on preventing genocide from happening in the future in Darfur. Therefore, we need to be vigilant and to execute certain measures by which we can prevent genocide from happening.

(cited in Jibril 2004a)

By 2005, a special UN inquiry reported that the Khartoum government had not pursued a policy of genocide but had committed war crimes and crimes against humanity that 'may be no less serious and heinous than genocide' (*The Times*, 23 April 2005, cited in Tinsley 2005: 3). The European Union stated that genocide was not taking place in Darfur, as did the African Union (AU). Clearly, it was becoming apparent that the international community could not agree on the nature of the humanitarian crisis. The Nigerian President, Olusegun Obasanjo, who was chairperson of the AU and actively engaged in attempting to resolve the problem, stated at the United Nations in New York on 23 September 2004:

Before we can say that this is genocide or ethnic cleansing, we will have to have a definite decision, plan and programme of a government to wipe out a particular group of people. Then we will be talking about genocide, ethnic cleansing. What we know is not that. What we know is that there was an uprising, rebellion and the government armed another group of people to stop that rebellion. That's what we know. That does not amount to genocide from our own reckoning. It amounts to, of course, conflict. It amounts to violence.

(cited in Abrahamson 2004: 9)

These differences of interpretation only served to create further ambiguity about the nature of the crisis.

African solutions to African problems

The African Union (AU) became involved in the international community's response to the conflict in Darfur. The UK government stressed the notion of 'African led solutions for African problems' as part of its strategy for dealing with the continent within its policy of New Partnership for Africa's Development (Nepad). It should be noted, however, that the AU's presence in Sudan was possible only with the consent of the host government and Khartoum repeatedly ruled out military intervention by non-African organizations. It is interesting that, within the AU, Khartoum's position was backed by Chad, Egypt, Liberia and Nigeria in its promotion of 'African solutions for African problems'. Yet even this involvement led to criticism that it took 'more than six months to deploy a mere 2,400 AU monitors in a region the size of France', while the UN estimated that 12,000 troops were needed (Tinsley 2005: 6). Initially, only Nigeria and Rwanda sent monitors. Canada and the UK offered to send monitors but were firmly rejected by Khartoum (author's interview with a former member of the UK forces, May 2005). President Obasanjo presided over AU-sponsored peace talks between Khartoum government officials and members of the two rebel groups in Abuja in August 2004. He argued that more AU troops were needed to disarm the rebels, as Sudan's forces seemed incapable of carrying out this task without further bloodshed, while the government could disarm the *Janjawiid* militia. Obasanjo emphasized the need for unity of purpose among Africans to end the crisis without the intervention of foreign forces: 'Africa cannot continue to be the problem child of the world known for the pitiable pictures of miserable looking children and women dying of malnutrition and diseases as a result of wars and internal crises' (http://platform.blogs.com/passionofthepresent). The talks were praised as a breakthrough, with an agreement reached that the Sudanese government would accept a larger AU peacekeeping force in Darfur.

Nigeria's then president was consistently regarded as the driver of strong action by the AU but South Africa also claimed it was committed to helping ensure peace and stability in Darfur. However, South Africa would not act unilaterally in Sudan; the then Deputy President, Jacob Zuma, asserted that his country's efforts would be in conjunction with the AU's Peace and Security Council. Some critics claimed that South Africa failed to demonstrate a firm determination to deal with the issue but, in fairness, if the AU was to act effectively it had to be united. Certainly, some progress seemed to be apparent during continuing rounds of peace talks and by November 2004 two protocols were signed between the government of Sudan and the rebel groups, the SLM/SLA and JEM, on humanitarian issues and security. The Humanitarian Protocol included commitments on free movement and access for humanitarian agencies; the protection of civilians; the role to be played by the international community; and an implementation mechanism. The Security Protocol re-emphasized the government's responsibility for disarming the *Janjawiid*. Although these agreements seemed purposeful, the UK Department for International Development was less sure. As they saw it the Abuja talks were often 'liable to be thrown off course by events on the ground in Darfur, particularly when the parties to the conflict failed to live up to the commitments they have entered into' (International Development Committee 2005: 41). The rebel groups seemed not to be negotiating sufficiently seriously, with unclear leadership structures – some based in Eritrea – and uncertain and ill-defined demands. Equally, Khartoum was regarded as 'not an enthusiastic negotiator'. A group of 'concerned countries' was established, including Nigeria, Egypt, Libya, Chad and Gabon, to consider how the AU's involvement could be more effective.

Essentially, the difficulty with the AU presence was that its initial mandate was ceasefire monitoring. The revised mandate from October 2004 was extended to include some civilian protection but it did not extend to peace enforcement or disarmament. The mandate gave the AU mission the task of 'protecting civilians whom it encounters under imminent threat and in the immediate vicinity, within its resources and capability, it being understood that the protection of the civilian population is the responsibility of the government of Sudan' (ibid.: 43). This ambiguity needed to be clarified but the decisions about its mandate were for the AU's Peace and Security Council to make in consultation with the wider international community. The fundamental issue was whether the AU mission had sufficient troops. In March 2005 the total number of troops stood at only 1942, which was inadequate to meet the basic minimum of 6000, but it was not just a question of manpower. If AU troops were to be supported they needed logistical assistance and satellite intelligence, which the EU, UK and USA would have to provide. At no stage did Chris Mullen, then UK Foreign Office Minister for Africa, envisage any foreign troops being drafted in:

> The odds are that if any western force did intervene it would become bogged down and that some new cause for all the Jihadists in the world would emerge and we'd find ourselves very quickly being shot at by all sides, plus we would probably destabilize the whole of Sudan, which is the size of Western Europe and the last thing we want is a failed stated the size of Western Europe on our hands.
>
> (BBC TV 2004)

Clearly, although 'African solutions to African problems' was an attractive phrase, in reality the burden of the responsibility could be considerably onerous.

Oil, the UN and national interests

In 1999 the first shipment of crude oil was exported from Sudan. Three Asian oil companies were involved, from China, Malaysia and India, together with French–Belgian interests. By 2003, an estimated US$500 million had been accrued from oil and, although the reserves were not expected to be as large as those of Saudi Arabia or Iraq, they were, in fact, not known entirely (Human Rights Watch 2003). However, there was considerable speculation and some of it concerned western Sudan: 'Darfur is one of the richest yet underdeveloped regions of Sudan, with huge unexploited natural wealth, including crude oil reserves' (Jibril 2004b: 4). Further concerns were claims that 60 per cent of oil revenue was being spent on armaments and that Sudan's oil sales were funding the conflict in Darfur (cf. Human Rights Watch 2003; Prendergast 2004). Since the largest customer for these sales was China, which was also a permanent member of the UN Security Council, the supposed unity of the international community began to be challenged, especially when sanctions and an oil embargo were raised. The view developed that unless Sudan was credibly threatened with painful sanctions, such as an oil embargo, Khartoum would make no serious attempt to resolve the crisis in Darfur. But there was a problem:

> China, India, Malaysia and some European countries are dramatically expanding business ties with Sudan . . . Companies from those countries are investing billions of dollars and working closely with the Khartoum government with little concern about its role in recent mass killings in the Darfur region.
>
> (*Washington Post*, 24 August 2004, cited in http://platform.blogs.
> com/passionofthepresent)

As the focus of attention shifted back to the UN it became clear that China would not vote for an oil embargo on the grounds that it did not mix its business interests with politics. The former UN Security Council resolutions, nos. 1556 in July 2004 and 1564 in the following September, were both adopted under Chapter VII of the UN Charter, implying that the crisis in Darfur represented a threat to international peace and security. Given this, the UN Security Council could legitimately and legally adopt mandatory punitive measures against the Sudanese government in event of non-compliance, including economic sanctions and, if necessary, military action. Resolution 1564 expressed grave concern at the lack of progress with regard to security and the protection of civilians, and the disarmament of the *Janjawiid*, and demanded that Khartoum provide the Security Council with the names of its leaders and requested the establishment of an International Commission of Inquiry. The Security Council noted that it would consider measures such as actions to affect Sudan's petroleum sector, its government or individual members of the regime in the event of non-compliance.

Although these statements seemed purposeful there was division within the Security Council. China and Pakistan had abstained on the first resolution, whereas

Russia and Algeria ultimately supported it but felt Khartoum should be given more time. However, China, Russia, Algeria and Pakistan abstained on Resolution 1564. They all felt that sanctions were inappropriate even though 1564 only stated that it would 'envisage' sanctions after consultation with the AU. A subsequent resolution (1574) that made no mention of Khartoum's obligations under former resolutions was passed unanimously. It was clear that UN responses were sending out mixed messages that were, in part, the result of particular national interests. As the UK DfID report made clear:

> It is a scandal that interests in oil and arms exports can prevent the Security Council from acting firmly on behalf of the international community to protect the people of Darfur. It shames those countries which, fuelling the crisis in Sudan, are happy to turn a blind-eye to crimes no less serious and heinous than genocide. And it demonstrates the impotence of the international community to act to prevent such crimes and to fulfil its responsibility to protect.
>
> (International Development Committee 2005: 53)

These difficulties in the Security Council attracted considerable criticism from NGOs. The International Crisis Group roundly condemned the UN and pointed to five elements of failure within the international community: obfuscation, equivocal moral standards, posturing, lack of coherence within the Security Council and the reliance on humanitarian band aids (Prendergast 2004). These damning views accused the international community of adopting the line of least resistance in its collective response to Darfur by accepting delay, repeating meaningless rhetoric and calling for ceasefires rather than engaging in any action, with UN Security Council resolutions driven by countries simply responding to their own national interests rather than the crisis in Sudan (ibid.). Prendergast believed Darfur had found the international community wanting but, more especially, had revealed considerable weaknesses within the UN. Others were equally critical: 'While diplomats sit in New York and procrastinate, the people of Darfur are dying' (http:// news.bbc.co.uk/1/hi/world/africa/3643218.stm).

The next topic to divide the Security Council was whether to uphold the recommendation of the International Commission of Inquiry on Darfur that the crisis be referred to the International Criminal Court (ICC). Those responsible for atrocities should be brought to justice. Predictably, there were disagreements over an ICC referral and the Council struggled through its fifth week of negotiations. The UK's DfID was alarmed at the difficulties:

> If the UN Security Council fails to act on Darfur, it will once more find its position undermined, in two ways. First many will conclude that the workings of the UN Security Council do not promote the responsibility to protect. And, second, if frustrated Member States act successfully outside the authority of the Security Council, many will conclude that the UN is not necessary.
>
> (International Development Committee 2005: 58)

In the event, Darfur was referred to the ICC, which drew up a list of 51 people in Sudan who were suspected of committing war crimes in region. It seemed the Security Council was ultimately able to agree on this matter.

By June 2005, the British Secretary of State for International Development, Hilary Benn, having just returned from a visit to Sudan, was upbeat about the situation. He had visited camps and found that aerial bombing had ceased, indiscriminate civilian attacks had fallen and there were fewer clashes between government and rebel forces. He maintained that, in comparison with 2004, AU capacity had improved considerably and it was expected that 7500 troops would be deployed by the end of September 2005 (Benn 2005). Certainly there had been progress on the Comprehensive Peace Agreement (CPA); a treaty was signed between Khartoum and Sudan People's Liberation Movement and John Garang, the PLM's leader, assumed the role of First Vice President in July 2005.[1] Hilary Benn hoped that the new Government of National Unity in Khartoum 'would be able to resolve Darfur with the CPA providing a framework.' He also admitted that oil concessions had been made in Darfur and, although they could affect the international community who were involved in the oil business, ultimately, if peace occurred in Darfur, 'oil wealth would be a blessing for all people in Sudan.' Any political settlement in the region, however, was likely to 'take some time' (Benn 2005). Despite the UK Secretary of State's measured optimism, in July 2005 the UN 'Access to Justice for victims of sexual violence report', prepared at the initiative of the UN High Commissioner for Human Rights, found that 'Armed elements in Sudan's strife torn Darfur region, including law enforcement officers and the military continue to perpetrate rape and sexual violence, with the authorities seemingly unable or unwilling to hold them accountable' (www.arabicnews.com/ansub/Daily/ Day 050406/2005040618).

There can be little doubt that Darfur presented a profound challenge to members of the UN Security Council and revealed a real weakness at the centre of policy making within the organization. Economic and security concerns were compounded by national interests in oil production and concessions. As one analyst put it, 'oil companies are all keen for a piece of the action in the oil-rich areas in Darfur' (Waging Peace 2005). Cynics might suggest that the depopulation of the region was precisely necessary for a country estimated to earn US$1 million in oil revenue each day. Such forced population displacement could enable companies to engage in extraction work despite the entreaty of Alan Goulty, the UK's Special Envoy to Sudan: 'why should cattle, people and oil wells not be able to co-exist?' (Goulty 2003). It should be remembered, of course, that accusations of forced depopulation were not new charges against the Khartoum government. In 2001, the claim was made by a Chief Mirial in Ruweng County: 'The government drove the people out and took steps to ensure they did not return. It was clear the government and the oil company were now ready to begin oil exploration. They did not want any Southerners in the area' (deGuzman 2002: 12). This allegation prompted one analyst to conclude that specific strategies were being adopted which forged 'a pattern of depopulation in oil-rich areas – helicopter attacks on villages followed by murderous raids conducted by ground forces, looting, the torching of huts . . . the tactics used in Ruweng County certainly deterred the displaced from returning home.' The resulting vast empty regions supported the allegation that the 'government of Sudan is knowingly and deliberately depopulating the oil-rich areas of the South in order to secure the area for the oil business' (ibid.). Although no such direct connection was made in the case of Darfur, a Human Rights Report in 2004 accused the government of colluding with the militias in the region in a deliberate campaign to drive out the population through 'systematic rape and torture, to intimidate, humiliate and punish' (*The Times*, 21 July 2004, cited in http://platform.blogs.com/passionofthepresent). Clearly, whichever way the Darfur crisis is viewed, the associated issues of oil resources, reserves, concessions and production feature prominently.

At the heart of the Darfur conflict rest the distorted relationships between power, authority and rebellion. The generally accepted view of politics is that it is consensual, persuasive, participative and tolerant. Recourse to violence is a certain indication that appropriate political processes are absent and legitimate governance is unknown. Basic socio-economic indicators reveal uneven and unfair dispensations of benefits and the very real prospect of oil wealth has further exacerbated these divisions. Having said that, however, did the internationalization of the Darfur conflict demonstrate efficiency and effectiveness within the United Nations Security Council and among the wider global community? On one level, it was right that the international community was concerned with the humanitarian disaster that unfolded in Darfur but the prioritization of the Comprehensive Peace Agreement between Khartoum and the south led to divided loyalties and confused policies. The Sudanese government was not to be upset lest it backtrack on peace negotiations with the south, so the general argument went, but this gave Khartoum a permanent political and strategic advantage. From a pragmatic perspective, the resolution of the long-standing war between Khartoum and the south was an understandable priority but commentators cautioned: 'Western governments don't want to upset the peace process in the South by speaking out, thus, giving the ruling National Islamic Front a free hand. The NIF are very clever and consistently underestimated' (Lusk 2005).

However, a Darfur Peace Agreement was signed in 2006 with little impact and in 2007 it was announced that a hybrid African Union–United Nations Peacekeeping (UNAMID) force would be deployed. The UN Security Council resolution mandated 26,000 troops and police officers, but 'full deployment has been delayed and UNAMID is struggling with insufficient resources such as helicopters and heavy transport equipment' (Concordis International 2008). In February 2008 the UN Secretary General, Ban Ki-moon, appealed for more troops and vital equipment to support the 'critically under-strength UNAMID' force in order to stem the violence. But, he cautioned, 'UNAMID will only be as effective as the political process it is mandated to support' (UN News Service 2008). There are two aspects of which there can be little doubt: the ultimate solution to the Darfur crisis will rest not only within the international community and the deliberations of the United Nations/African Union, but also, more essentially, within the realm of politics and legitimacy. At some stage the state of Sudan will have to meet that challenge.[2]

9   Terrorism

Definitions of terrorism

Terrorism, historically, has been a concern for the international community. In 1937 the League of Nations introduced the Convention for the Prevention and Punishment of Terrorism, which, although never coming into force, did offer a definition of the act of terrorism: 'All criminal acts directed against a state and intended or calculated to create a state of terror in the minds of particular people' (UN Office on Drugs and Crime 2005). Table 9.1 outlines the definitions of terrorism adopted by various US agencies. Between 1963 and 28 September 2001 there had been 12 conventions and protocols signed in the United Nations, but there was no single universally accepted definition of terrorism (Mazzitelli interview 2004). The reason for this anomaly was that the term 'terrorism' was value laden within political spheres: 'one person's terrorist is another person's freedom fighter.' That much-used phrase was used to describe post-colonial or anti-apartheid liberation movements which resorted to violence as their last weapon against injustice.[1] In any case, violent and sporadic attacks against peoples for many differing reasons have been known throughout history, for example in the Roman Empire, during the French Revolution and within Russia in the nineteenth century.[2] Although

Table 9.1 Definitions of terrorism adopted by various US agencies

Agency	Definition
Department of Defense	The calculated use of unlawful violence to inculcate fear, intended to coerce or to intimidate governments or societies in the pursuit of goals that are generally political, religious, or ideological
FBI	The unlawful use of force or violence against persons or property to intimidate or coerce a government, the civilian population, or any segment thereof, in furtherance of political or social objectives
State Department	Premeditated, politically motivated violence perpetrated against non-combatant targets by sub-national groups or clandestine agents, usually intended to influence an audience

Source: www.milnet.com/state/2003/africaoverview.

currently terrorism of the Islamist variety is the focus of attention, in sub-Saharan Africa three indigenous groups were identified by the US State Department as 'terrorist' organisations: Al Itihad Al Islamiyya, an Islamist group in Somalia; the Lord's Resistance Army, a Christian group in Uganda; and the former military regime in Rwanda, the ex-FAR. Yet al-Qaeda cells and Hezbollah have been found to be active in a number of countries (Piombo 2007).

Radical groups

'How do you feel being surrounded by terrorists?' This question was asked of the author by a member of the Sudanese political/religious elite during lunch in Khartoum in 1997.[3] It was a good question, especially in light of the fact that al-Qaeda's leader, Osama bin Laden, had recently been resident in the country and still retained considerable business interests and networks. Sudan, at that time, was viewed by the West as largely a 'pariah' state with restricted diplomatic relations and combined military and economic pressures. Yet at a high level the country did have some contact with representatives of the US, who urged Hassan al Turabi, the National Islamic Front's leader, to move away from an aggressive Islamist agenda (Turabi interview 1997). What was interesting at that time was the Sudanese government's commitment from 1990 to support *jihad* (holy war) as an institutionalized part of the country's administration with regard to *zakat*. *Zakat* is the requirement to give alms as one of the Five Pillars of Islam (see Box 9.1). The Zakat Chamber in Sudan had been instituted to 'spread all over the areas of health, services and *jihad*' (Al Quusi interview 1997; *ElZakat Magazine* 1997: 5) (see Box 9.2).

Since the attacks of 11 September 2001, the international community has become alert to the political credo and global ambitions of radical Islamist groups around the world. But what of the activities of disparate Muslim groups operating in the Horn of Africa little more than a decade ago? As Alex de Waal asserts: for a 'few significant years, radical Islamists of all shades met in Sudan' (de Waal 2004: 43). Where was the world's attention at that time? What was the focus of African practitioners? Why was political Islam viewed as significant only in

---

Box 9.1 The Five Pillars of Islam

- Ritual prayer
- *Zakat* – Almsgiving
- Fasting
- *Al-Hajj* – Pilgrimage
- *Al-Jihad* – 'The Qur'an has permitted the use of weapons for protection of human life, self defence and in support of the oppressed.'

Source: Surty (1995).

Box 9.2 Sudan: the Zakat Chamber and *jihad* propagation

Since 1990, under the National Salvation Revolution government, the Zakat Chamber has extended support for the *Jihad* and *Mujahideen*, represented by the People's Armed Forces; the Popular Defence Forces; Nida Al-jihad Organisation; Al-Shaheed Organisation; Da'awa Islamia Organisation; International University of Africa; Holy Quran University and Omdurman Islamic University. The Zakat Chamber also extended support to charitable funds, for example, the Sharia Support Fund and the National Support Fund.

Source: Zakat Chamber (1997).

certain renowned and traditionally vocal regions? Well, the United States and France were quite aware of Islamist activities within Africa. Eighteen American soldiers were killed in Mogadishu, Somalia, during an attack in 1993 which was generally believed to have involved Islamic terrorists, and France had long been aware of radical Islam within its former colonial territories (Decalo interview 1995). Certainly, Islamic demands for a different global order had begun in 1989 with the Organisation of the Islamic Conference (OIC) calling for unity between Muslims in Africa and those living elsewhere (cited in Deegan 1996: 50). Dr Usman Bugaje, the Secretary General of the organization Islam in Africa, which operated in Nigeria, claimed Africa 'craved for Islam' as part of its quest for 'cultural freedom' and an 'alternative world view that could stand up to the challenge of the West' (Africa Events, May 1994, cited in Deegan 1996: 52). African leaders called upon the Islamic world to draw up a new global order: 'Islam is not merely a creed but a way of life. The Islamic community must become a recognized power in the international community' (Gambian President Dawda Jawara's address to the 1991 OIC Summit, cited in Deegan 1996: 115).

Today the political trajectory of many African states is uncertain and insecure. The threat of terrorism has highlighted global concerns about security and the vulnerability of 'weak or brittle' states and with extremist Islamist activity present in parts of Africa the need for stabilization and political reform has never been more pressing.[4] The OIC, however, was formed in 1971, and acted during the Cold War years as a counterbalance in Africa to the expanding interests of the Soviet Union. Islamic groups and organizations then could be seen as largely benign influences that could harness countries in religious traditionalism, thereby acting as a bulwark against encroaching communism. Autocratic African elites could also carefully balance the religious diversity of their populations with the support of external powers, particularly France, operating within its Franc Zone.

During the 1990s the Muslim population in Africa increased by an estimated 50 per cent (Deegan 1996: 117). Also, the majority of OIC members were from the African continent, with representatives from some states holding high office. Representatives of Senegal and Niger both held the office of OIC Secretary-General and a special Department for Africa Affairs existed within the organization's General Secretariat.[5] Perhaps it is not surprising, then, that links between the OIC and OAU (now the African Union) increased steadily, with some African states being members of both organizations (see Map 9.1). In fact, some commentators viewed the OIC and OAU as comparable given their dual emphasis on brotherhood and solidarity 'in a larger unity transcending ethnic and national differences' (Moinuddin 1987: 74; see also Brownlie 1983). Yet there were differences. Whereas the OAU Charter referred to a compact geographical area, the Charter of the OIC refers to the eligibility of every 'Muslim state', regardless of geographical location, to join the OIC. Eligibility exists when a state, anywhere in the world, expresses its desire and preparedness to adopt the OIC Charter (Moinuddin 1987).

According to the then Secretary-General of the OAU, Salim Ahmed Salim, the closeness between the two organizations was initially the result of their 'joint struggle for the freedom of peoples in South Africa and Palestine' (Salim 1995). During the 1990s, Salim urged 'Middle Eastern states within the OIC to help many African states in their struggle for economic development' (ibid.). Yet that help came with a set of conditions. Usually, in order to access funds from the Islamic Development Bank (IDB), a country had to be a member of the OIC and

Map 9.1 Member states of the Organisation of the Islamic Conference.

support the establishment of an Islamic state. One of the OIC's roles then, as now, was to 'promote the collective security of the Muslim community' (Deegan 1996: 118). But many saw the organization as having considerable radical potential. Moinuddin maintained that a change of principles enshrined in the OIC Charter could be accelerated and supported by a steady radicalization of Islamic orders at a national level. This would give an opportunity for radical elements in the Islamic world to pursue a militant course and 'translate it collectively through OIC action' (Moinuddin 1987: 110). Certainly, Sudan's Hassan al Turabi called for greater radicalism, claiming that the growth of Islamic revivalism demanded strong united action, nationally and internationally (Turabi interview 1997). Meanwhile, the Islamic Development Bank continued to hold the view that 'all its dealings would conform to *shari'a* law.'[6] However, the bank also had a 'Special Assistance Account' from which operations were financed to 'assist Muslim communities in non-member countries.' The priorities of Muslim communities were identified as vocational and administrative training, and educational programmes including Islamic education and scholarship programmes (Islamic Development Bank Annual Report 1992: 89).

Usman Bugaje of Islam in Africa asserted that 'Muslims within African states could create a variety of networks which can in time transform not only the economic but also the social political milieu' (Bugaje 1998: 28). In promoting such a comprehensive agenda, almost by stealth, Bugaje recognized that investment was 'not just economics' but had 'serious, if subtle, political undertones and implications.' It was therefore evident that: 'In these days of privatization and exploration of hitherto untapped economic resources of sub-Saharan Africa that Muslim capital could be crucial to the economic and political future of the region' (ibid.: 31). But how was this to be achieved? Islamic banking institutions would 'allow full rein to Muslim capital' (ibid.: 30). It was also claimed that Africa's plentiful resources in raw materials and minerals could be utilized to fund an Islamic *jihadist* agenda (confidential interview, Khartoum, Sudan, February 1997).

African states were attracted by the possibility of accessing greater resources through the IDB and its conduits of finance. In 1992, the bank's sectoral division of funding was as outlined in Figure 9.1 with more resources directed to social sectors than agriculture. Table 9.2 outlines the countries and projects supported by IDB financing. The Special Assistance Account funding concentrated on a range of socio-educational activities which aimed directly at the grass-roots level (see Table 9.3). Equally, funds for African states were available from Saudi Arabia in the form of Relief Efforts directed at sub-Saharan countries (Kingdom of Saudi Arabia 1986). Saudi Arabia reported: 'The [Saudi] Kingdom's role and efforts within the OIC has not been restricted to financial assistance, for its participation and efforts in the Committee for Solidarity with the Sahel Countries had a considerable impact – physically and morally.' In addition, the Kingdom encouraged other Islamic countries, including some of its sister Gulf countries, to take similar steps in support of the programme (ibid.).

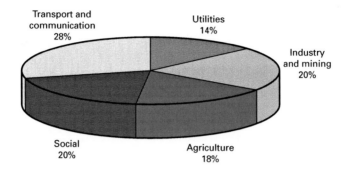

Figure 9.1 Islamic Development Bank projects 1993.

Table 9.2 Islamic Development Bank financing to least developed member countries (LDMCs) in 1992

Country	Project	US$ million
Benin	Rural health centres	6.01
Burkino Faso	Rural water points	5.19
Burkino Faso	Togo border road	1.57
Cameroon	Primary schools	9.08
Guinea	Extension hospital	7.25
Mali	Primary schools	5.81
Mali	Health centres	5.18
Mauritania	Irrigation project	7.00
Senegal	Extension university	9.32
Sudan	Irrigation development	9.50

Source: Islamic Development Bank Report (1993).

During the later years of the Cold War, Saudi development assistance for non-Arab African states totalled US$3500 million to 1986, with 34 non-Arab African states gaining the following assistance:

- Irrecoverable grants and donations valued at over $1000 million were extended to 34 African states for various social, human, economic and developmental purposes
- $1640 million in unconditional, concessionary development loans were granted to finance 140 development projects within 33 African nations.
- $725 million was granted in the form of concessional cash loans to support balance of payments and to help execute reform plans and economic adjustments throughout 11 African nations.

(ibid.)

Table 9.3 Special Assistance Account projects for Muslim communities in non-member states of the Islamic Development Bank, 1992

Country	Project	US$ million
Ethiopia	Construction of schools in Eritrea	0.49
Ghana	Institute of Islamic Studies, Nima	0.03
Côte d'Ivoire	Construction of vocational and training workshop	0.19
Côte d'Ivoire	Construction of Muslim students' building	0.14
Kenya	Construction of science laboratories	0.17
Kenya	Muslim secondary school, Garissa	0.26
Mauritius	Islamic cultural centre complex	0.49
Mauritius	Islamic education centre	0.24
Nigeria	Construction of Iqra primary school, Gongola	0.14
Nigeria	Construction and furnishing of school building	0.14
Nigeria	Construction of Magaji Rufai Islamiya school, Sokoto	0.16
Nigeria	Construction of Higher Institute for Arabic and Islamic studies	0.29
Tanzania	Construction of an Islamic college in Micheweni Pemba	0.55

Source: Islamic Development Bank Report (1993).

However, one recurring feature of African politics during the 1990s was tension between Islamic groups. In numerous countries, including member states of the OIC (see Map 9.1), clashes occurred. In Guinea, the government launched an 'offensive against Islamic fundamentalism' by sentencing Islamists for 'violence and inflammatory speeches'. The leader of the group, a young man from Mali, was trained in Algeria and went to Guinea with the intention of starting a *jihad*. Imams (Islamic religious leaders) came from Pakistan, Iran and Iraq with the intention of radicalizing Guinea's predominantly Muslim society. The country's Islamic League was alarmed: 'Fundamentalism is dangerous and we will fight it, but its concepts may strike a chord with thousands of young people with time on their hands' (Deegan 1996: 118). The government of Senegal deported two officials of non-governmental organizations (NGOs) from Sudan and Chad for alleged fundamentalist activities and later went on to close the local offices of five foreign Muslim charitable organizations on the grounds that they were acting as a cover for radical groups aiming to 'destabilise the country' (ibid.: 119). Demonstrations and confrontations between supporters of the Islamic Party of Kenya and members of the security services took place in Mombasa. Demonstrators in Ethiopia called on the government to give full authority to *shari'a* courts and to ban the Supreme Council of Islamic Affairs. The President of the Central African Republic, Ange-Feliz Patasse, accused the Muslim community of engaging in acts of violence and creating insecurity within the country. The Azaouad Arab Islamic Front claimed responsibility for the killings of civilians in Mali, and Islamic groups in Chad distributed leaflets calling on non-Muslim communities to 'convert to Islam without delay' or to leave the country. Meanwhile, Muslim student associations in Liberia warned the Muslim community 'to be mindful of people who may have a hidden agenda under the banner of Islam' (ibid.).

Ayatollah Khamenei of Iran asserted in 1993 that Muslims should pay attention: 'The Islamic struggle is like a traditional military battle. It is confrontation. You sit, think, show initiative and counter any move of the enemy' (ibid.: 120). Certainly, the government of Mauritania accused Iran along with Algeria, Sudan, Kuwait and Saudi Arabia of funding various Islamic organizations and cultural centres aimed at destabilizing the country. Sudan was engaged in 'the training of propagators for the Islamic cause' (Islamic African Centre 1996: 3, Article 3).[7] The Sudanese Islamic African Centre was committed to furthering Islam within Africa through 'the organization of training camps for students' together with the 'establishment of cooperative relations with all Islamic organizations and institutions in and outside Africa' (ibid.: 12, 'Objectives of the Department of Da'wah'). Within Sudan nine 'training camps' were established in 'very remote areas' and students were sent to Tanzania and elsewhere, 'where they engaged in very constructive work' (ibid.: 13).

These contradictory forces of Islamic expression within Africa reflected the fact that the religion was not a monolithic movement but contained many strands, such as Sufi, Mahdist and militant branches, all adding 'to the number of divergent social strategies' (Bayart 1993: 257; see also Soares 2007b). Yet, as competing agendas for African states, Islamic strategies were divisive and unsettling within the continent and served to undermine the security of many states. The combination of religious radicalism, power seeking, grandiose theory, the appropriation of financial dealings, and attempts to reorientate societies through the manipulation of non-governmental organizations has been formidable. Both Sudan and Somalia were central to a study which examined why varied paths and manifestations have been adopted by Islamists over decades. Why, the question was posed, did Islamists capture power in such a multi-ethnic, multi-religious country as Sudan? The answer seems straightforward: 'the structural weakness of the Sudanese middle class and the defeat of the left in the 1970s, combined with the polarization brought about by war, made it possible for Hassan al Turabi's genius to engineer an Islamist revolution' (de Waal and Salam 2004). Although Islam of a Mahdist strand had long been part of the country's history, ultimately it was Islamism in its *jihadist* mode that posed more of a threat to Muslims in Sudan, rather than their salvation.

Somalia, however, presents a different picture, a country steeped in Islam since the ninth century in which 99 per cent of the current population is Muslim. Its geo-political position was important, as close proximity to Arabia led to its membership in the Arab League in 1974. Consequently, new opportunities were available to young Somalians who could study in Saudi Arabia, where new Islamist trends were developing. The lapse into civil war in the early 1990s claimed numerous lives and opened a murky world of money transfers and Islamist claims and counter-claims. One leading Somali holding company, al Barakaat, was instrumental in negotiating large sums of remittance payments, estimated to be 'around US$300 million annually for the last decade.' By 7 November 2001, the US placed the company on a list of organizations funding terrorist activities. Roland Marchal makes clear that Islamists were not only interested in politics but also had their eyes firmly set on economic spheres. Any study of al Barakaat activities in Somalia would reveal 'the ambiguous role Islam (more than political Islam) has played in reshaping part of the business class throughout the civil war' (Marchal 2004: 140). In 1995, the Agricultural Bank of Sudan had what it referred to as 'Foreign Correspondent Banks', which included 'International Commercial Bank and Bank of Riaad [sic] in Jeddah, Saudi Arabia; American Express Bank in New York and London; Bank of Amman in London; Credit Lyonnais Bank in Geneva and the Netherlands; and [the] Dutch Bank in the Netherlands' (Rahim interview 1997).

Another shadowy area is that of the impact of Islamic NGOs in Africa. As part of an elaborate welfare network, alms (*zakat*) were dispensed for social and religious causes and the recipients have emerged as Islamic NGOs. The growth of Islamic NGOs, largely funded by Middle Eastern states, was significant during the 1990s but their aims were not simply education, health care and poverty alleviation. Many channelled funds to 'further the interests of particular Islamic groups' (Salih 2004: 180). Certainly, *zakat* funds in Sudan 'transcended borders', ultimately finding their way into 'Bosnia, Somalia and Tajikstan in support of our brothers' (Zakat Chamber 1995). Mohamed Salih cautions: 'Some Islamic NGOs in Africa may signify the emergence of highly centralized Muslim communities hostile to all values that are intrinsically African, including pluralism, tolerance and diversity of faith beyond the Islamic *umma*' (Salih 2004: 181). In Sudan, the Islamic African Relief Agency and the International Muslim Women Union operated to promote the country's regime (Elawad interview 1997; Albadawe and Satti interviews 1997). In fact, the Islamic African Relief Agency was included in a list of 25 Islamic charities and NGOs suspected of having links with terrorist financing networks and was investigated by the US Internal Revenue Service (http://fas.org/sgp/crs/terror/RL33020.pdf). Equally, the funding of the Islamic African Centre in Khartoum, which trained African Muslims, came from a number of countries, as outlined in Table 9.4. Students at the Centre came from Tanzania, Zanzibar, Kenya, Uganda, Chad, Niger, Nigeria and the Central African Republic

Table 9.4 Countries funding the Islamic African Centre, Khartoum

Country	% of amount of total funding
Saudi Arabia	25
Kuwait	15
United Arab Emirates	15
Qatar	15
Egypt	10
Morocco	10
Sudan	10

Source: Islamic African Centre (1996).

and were trained in using 'modern technological aids in the field of *Da'wah*', that is, the rigorous evangelization of Islamist views. In fact, the Centre had a Department of *Da'wah*, the aims of which are listed in Box 9.3 (Islamic African Centre 1996).

The Horn of Africa (Map 9.2) and especially Somalia is now a war-weary region struggling to come to terms with considerable social and security difficulties and still trying to deal with the impact of Islamist political gains of the 1990s (see Box 9.4). The area may now benefit from the gaze of the wider international community, which now seems more aware of the plight of people living in fear and poverty, but the United States had considered the Horn of Africa, including Kenya, Djibouti, Somalia and Sudan, to be a major source of terrorism before 11 September 2001. Box 9.5 outlines the formidable threats within the region.

African Union initiatives

One of the first Peace and Security actions of the AU Assembly was the decision to establish a Common African Defence and Security Policy, which was initiated by Colonel Muammar Qaddafi, the Libyan leader, in 2002 and instituted in 2004. This policy has to be viewed against the backdrop of increasing incidences of terror activity within the continent and the wider global security concerns aroused by the attacks on the United States on 11 September 2001 and subsequent terror attacks in Europe. Certainly, one analyst believed this policy was most 'important' in dealing with peace and security (Touray 2005: 635–56). African governments had for some time been concerned over the scope and seriousness of terrorism and the dangers it posed to the development, stability and security of states. The American embassies in Kenya and Tanzania were bombed in 1998 and more than 200 people died. In 2002 there was a combined attack on an Israeli-owned hotel in Mombasa, Kenya, together with an aircraft. In 1999 concern about terrorism

---

Box 9.3 Aims of the Sudan Islamic African Centre's Department of *Da'wah*

1 The training of workers to spread Islam and strengthen Islamic culture in the societies of Africa
2 The establishment of co-operative relations with all Islamic organisations and institutions in and outside Africa
3 The development of common strategies to be adopted by various bodies for the spread of Islam: the organisation of training camps for students in order to expose them to the work of *Da'wah* in the field. The idea of these camps is twofold: to help Muslim societies which need almost anything, while at the same time train our own students to implement some of the values which they learn here.

Source: Islamic African Centre (1996: 12–13).

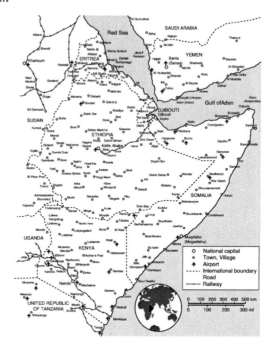

Map 9.2 The Horn of Africa.

was expressed within the OAU but it was not until after 11 September 2001 that the United Nations Security Council adopted Resolution 1373, an anti-terrorist measure that was binding on all UN member states. In October 2001, the African Summit also adopted the Dakar Declaration against Terrorism, in which African states unequivocally condemned all forms of terrorism in Africa and anywhere else in the world.

The AU Plan of Action for the Prevention and Combating of Terrorism in Africa was adopted by African leaders in 2002. The Plan laid down measures and strategies for combating terrorism in Africa and it assigned roles and responsibilities to member states, the AU Commission and the Peace and Security Council. The Plan called for all countries to:

- Enhance police and border control
- Enact legislative and judicial measures that discourage terrorist activities
- Operate the International Convention for the Suppression of the Financing of Terrorism (1999) which criminalises the act of financing terrorism
- Exchange information and intelligence on the activities of terrorist groups
- Co-ordinate at regional, continental and international levels against terrorism.

(African Union 2002a: 1)

Box 9.4 Somalia

In 1960 the British and Italian parts of Somalia become independent, merge and form the United Republic of Somalia, but border disputes with Kenya and Ethiopia continue. In 1969, Muhammad Siad Barre assumes power after a coup, declares the country to be a socialist state and nationalizes most of the economy. Somalia joins the Arab League but in the 1970s suffers a severe drought and widespread starvation. President Barre remains in power until 1991 when a power struggle occurs between the clan warlords Mohamed Farah Aideed and Ali Mahdi Mohamed, which results in the death and wounding of thousands of civilians. The UN and US try to restore order but in 1993 US Army Rangers are killed when Somali militias shoot down two US helicopters in Mogadishu and a battle ensues. The US mission ends in 1994 and UN peacekeepers leave in 1995, having failed to achieve their mission. Aideed dies and clan leaders elect Abdulkassim Salat Hassan as president. In 2001 the UN appeals for food aid for half a million people in the drought-hit southern part of the country. Political wrangling continues between rival groups and in 2006 scores of people are killed and injured during fierce fighting between rival militias in Mogadishu. It is the worst violence in almost a decade and militias loyal to the Union of Islamic Courts take control of Mogadishu and other parts of the south after defeating clan warlords. Somalia's long civil war and lack of central governing institutions have given terrorist organizations an opportunity to take advantage of the state's institutional collapse. The country was a refuge for the al-Qaeda group that bombed a Kenyan resort in 2002 and tried to bring down an Israeli aircraft. One prominent terrorist group was Al-Ittihad al-Islamiyyaa (AIAI) and a more recent violent, *jihadist* organization is believed to be led by Aden Hashi 'Ayro. Somalia is frequently referred to as a 'failed state' in that there has been a collapse in its governance, the rule of law and the ability to exert authority within its borders. This anarchical environment has provided conditions for terrorist groups to become active and virulent. In 2007 the UN Security Council authorized an African Union peacekeeping mission for Somalia but when it arrived further violence erupted between insurgents and government forces. The UN Special Envoy Ahmedou Ould-Abdallah described Somalia's humanitarian crisis as the worst in Africa. Nur Hassan Hussein, also known as Nur Adde, was sworn in as the new prime minister and asserted he would focus on a reconciliation process, security and gaining international confidence. The future of the country, however, is far less certain. With a divided nation, competing clan groups, internally displaced persons and the threat of terrorism and international reprisal it may take some considerable time before Somalia settles into normal governance.

Sources: EISA (2007a); International Crisis Group (2005).

Box 9.5 Terrorist groups within the Horn of Africa

- In May 2003, the Kenyan government admitted that a key member of the al-Qaeda terror network was plotting an attack on Western targets, confirming al-Qaeda's firm local presence.
- Djibouti's importance to terrorists derives from its transit capabilities and could increase its attractiveness to international terrorists.
- Somalia has played a role in Islamist terrorism.
- High-ranking officials in Sudan remain committed to the radical Islamist agenda.

Source: United States Institute of Peace (2004).

There are real and genuine concerns about the spread of al-Qaeda-related or -inspired terrorist activity in sub-Saharan Africa, especially in areas such as fundraising, recruiting and training. Various states across east, west and central Africa have been identified as vulnerable to such penetration. That is why the AU has established an African Centre for the Study and Research on Terrorism in Algiers, Algeria. The Centre, which is an institution of the AU Commission, aims to 'boost' its capacity in 'the prevention and combating of terrorism in Africa.' The Centre is designed to 'centralise information, studies and analyses on terrorism and terrorist groups' and to develop training programmes to deal with these threats. More specifically, viable and comprehensive strategies must be in place to combat terrorism: improved police and border control; legislative and judicial measures; suppression of the financing of terrorism; effective exchange of information; and coordination at regional, continental and international levels (African Union 2004). These plans are necessary but they also raise issues of capability. Certainly, these concerns have been discussed at high levels within the AU. How, for example, will African states be able to afford expensive 'airport border control equipment, appropriate computers for machine-readable passport control and expertise in border control intelligence'? Equally, with regard to the financing of terrorist activities, it is clear that 'money-laundering and the financing of terrorism are parts of a broader problem – that of financial abuse within Africa' (African Union 2003).

Terrorism and crime

Concerns about crime further complicate methods to deal with terrorism, as it is clear that terrorist activity is interlinked with other serious issues: human trafficking; narcotic dealing; financial irregularities; and criminal activity. For example, Africa 'is used as a transit point for cocaine from Latin America' (Mazzitelli interview 2004) The criss-crossing of criminal activity, smuggling and general lawlessness has long been a concern of the UN, especially when these activities obscure funding for terrorist organizations (ibid.). In fact, the United Nations Office on Drugs and Crime (UNODC) in its report on Crime and Development in Africa identified Sierra Leone 'as an excellent example of how what is ostensibly a civil war can substantially overlap with organised crime and interact with the interests of terrorists.' The rebel group the Revolutionary United Front (RUF) became

involved with organised crime and terrorism in a wide range of ways:

- The RUF bought guns from the Russian Mafia, as documented in the prosecution of gun trafficker, Leonid Minin
- Al-Qaeda affiliates bought huge amounts of conflict diamonds prior to September 11th bombings
- The Sierra Leone police report that members of the Armed Forces Ruling Council, the junta that had power in 1997–98, themselves pioneered the use of Sierra Leone as a transit point in the international drug trade.

(UNODC 2005: 20–21)

In fact, a 'crime–terror continuum' is seen to exist within Africa:

Instability is in the interest of terrorists because it diminishes the legitimacy of governments in the eyes of the mass populations – the very group terrorists seek to gain support from; and it is in the interest of criminal groups seeking to maximise criminal operations. This is especially true for groups engaged in wide-scale smuggling of licit or illicit commodities.

(ibid.: 18)

Certainly, it is true that diamonds from Sierra Leone smuggled through Liberia went directly via Hezbollah to fund their interests in Lebanon. In fact, Africa as a whole facilitates the organization's ability to 'raise, launder and transfer funds because of the large Shi'a and Lebanese expatriate communities that reside on the continent and the ineffectiveness of local law enforcement agencies' (Levitt 2004). The countries involved include Guinea, Sierra Leone, Liberia, Benin, Côte d'Ivoire, Senegal, the Democratic Republic of Congo and South Africa. Tanzania is a country which has also been identified as participating in the 'terrorist link of the trafficking of special stones' (Mazzitelli interview 2004). The African Union recognized that a 'propitious environment' existed in certain African states 'for criminal and contraband activities, in particular the looting of precious minerals and the illicit trafficking in and abuse of narcotic drugs' (African Union 2000). It also recognized that these issues must be pursued 'in tandem with efforts aimed at suppressing the financing of terrorism' (African Union 2003). Yet al-Qaeda-linked Sunni Islamist groups present a different threat from radical Shi'ite organizations tied to Lebanon and Hezbollah. It is estimated that around US$100 million is collected from Lebanese diasporas in Africa (Farah 2007). The benefits to Iran are considerable: access to mineral resources and a market for the export of ideology, religion and weapons. Sunni groups seek 'to build a network of like-minded *jihadist* groups to join the struggle to establish an Islamist *caliphate*, or land ruled by Muslims under strict Islamic *shari'a* law' (ibid.). In Somalia, for example, extreme radical organizations remain in place and continue to expand 'thanks to generous contributions from Islamic charities and the private sector' (International Crisis Group 2007c).

Terrorism has become a major threat to Africa itself. Transnational crime, however, is also a 'virulent phenomenon' that readily exploits weaknesses in the state and Africa is seen as 'particularly vulnerable to this incursion' (UNODC 2005). The notion of 'ungoverned space' has emerged as a way of describing certain parts of the continent. Essentially the term implies a 'physical or non-physical area where there is an absence of state capacity or political will to exercise control.' In those areas other organizations or agencies will assume the services and functions that the state should be providing (Piombo 2007). Certainly, Kano, northern Nigeria, which is under *shari'a* law, operates as a form of parallel state to the national government of the country,[8] whereas northeast Kenya, which borders Somalia, has been 'essentially cut off from the rest of the state' (Mair 2003). But it would be misleading to deduce that terrorist organizations prefer only weak and dysfunctional states. They may extract resources from conflict zones but they require environments where they can 'build long-term organizational and financial networks' (Piombo 2007: 2). The transnational nature of the threat and the ease with which radical groups can move within and between states makes it especially virulent and can also lead to the perception that sub-Saharan Africa is 'honeycombed' with terrorist organizations (confidential interview, Johannesburg, 2002). Certainly, there would appear to be 'mounting evidence' of a rising trend of terror-related activity in Africa, 'ranging from arrests of terrorist suspects and disruption of alleged terrorist operations in Kenya to recruitment activities by known al-Qaeda affiliates in Nigeria, to the abuse of South African travel documentation by foreigners on US and UK terrorist watch lists' (Shillinger 2006: 5).

Counter-terrorism strategies extend to military assistance, technological support and capacity building of states within Africa. In 2003, US President Bush announced a US$100 million East Africa Counterterrorism Initiative (EACI), which was designed to strengthen the capabilities of countries in the region. The Initiative included:

- Military training for border and coastal security
- Programmes to strengthen control of the movement of people and goods across borders
- Aviation security capacity-building
- Assistance for regional efforts against terrorist financing
- Police training
- Education programme to counter extremist influence.

(Wycoff 2004)

Also since 2003 the Terrorist Interdiction Programme computer system has been operational in certain airports in Kenya, Tanzania and Ethiopia in order that travellers may be appropriately identified. There is also a Trans-Sahara Counter-Terrorism Initiative. More broadly, responsibility for the continent in the US Department of Defense has for years been within three separate unified Commands: the European Command, with headquarters in Stuttgart, Germany; Central Command; and the Pacific Command. However, in 2006 the US announced it would create a separate Africa Command. The decision to form a separate Command was based on the need for focused and effective information about sub-Saharan Africa, a region that is larger than the United States, Europe, India and China combined, comprising 49 countries and a total population of 725 million (Farah 2007). Under the former divided Commands, intelligence was fragmented and disparate. However, as for various terrorist groups infiltrating, operating and co-operating within African states, there is little indication they are tiring of the continent. Africa itself must recognize that signing up to various anti-terror protocols is one thing; being determined to eliminate extremism and terror, root and branch, at the societal level, is another.

10 Conclusion

Although the preceding chapters have dealt with specific issues in contemporary Africa they are, in fact, deeply entwined with one another: development, politics, religion, society and conflict all impact on the nature of the continent. Now global security is a major international concern and it too is a critical factor within Africa. Of course, past years have represented an unsteady period for Africa, often buffeted by, and lacking the confidence and capacity to withstand, differing external pressures. Yet the continent now stands at a crossroads and with appropriate political will it may be able to accept the burden of responsibility for some of its political malpractice. Yet international communities must also recognize the discrepancies in trade practices which limit African development. The cry has gone out that struggling young democracies must not be allowed to fail but that implies that difficult decisions have to be made domestically, internationally and strategically. African states must no more be a virtual playground for terrorist organizations, destabilizing elements, corruption and autocratic governments.

The international community – including the West, China and Asia – is, in the American phrase, playing 'hardball' with the continent; the West in terms of security and combating terrorism; the East in the sphere of resource extraction and trade. Meanwhile, radical, Middle Eastern-funded, Islamist groups have settled comfortably in some African states, sure in the knowledge that Africa's 'triple heritage' will provide societal support. Both Islam and Christianity contribute to the cultural inheritance of Africa and have reflected modes and methods of political expression. However, and this is in many ways a fundamental and potentially treacherous point, the nature of Islam in Africa seems to be changing; an Islamist revival has taken place. That this change has taken place and carried African Muslims with it suggests the existence of a strong sense of affiliation and identification. In certain parts of Africa there has been, as J.-F. Bayart (1993: 92) pointed out, a form of drifting back to a pre-colonial period in terms of 'intra-continental and inter-continental interaction.' In other words, if European colonization attempted to banish or undermine Africa's Islamic heritage, these apparently repressed forces are now resurfacing. These tendencies support the *longue durée* approach to analysis of Africa, in that certain influences must form part of a nation's distinct historicity if they are to reappear at a later stage and in a different form.

Politics and democracy

A few years ago the then General Secretary of the Organisation of African Unity asserted that 'terror and violence within Africa goes beyond simply political and ethnic differences' (cited in Deegan 1996: 237), and this statement seems as relevant today as it was then. If conflict is endemic to Africa, what are its base causes? The ease with which outbursts of violence erupt together with the nature of their virulence indicates that systemic tensions are always bubbling under the surface of society. The answer to this issue often returns to the political deficiencies within the continent. More specifically, can foundations be laid for democratic change in countries emerging from prolonged civil upheavals?

Democracy, of course, requires certain minimal features: popular sovereignty, political competition, the provision of rights and freedoms, and equality before the law. For Joseph Schumpeter, democracies were distinguished from non-democracies 'by the way in which they acquire their rulers, not by the sorts of power which the rulers hold whilst they are rulers' (Schumpeter 1943: xxii). This is an interesting distinction and inevitably places considerable emphasis on the manner of elections and the nature of political parties. Equally, the political party has been regarded as a critical force in modernizing and constructing new political institutions (cf. Apter 1967; Huntington 1967). By ensuring that social cleavages are represented in the political arena they provide the basis for institutional cohesion. Parties and elections, then, are inextricably linked with the articulation of democracy. But, perversely, the nature of parties in Africa is seen to be one of the weaker links in the democratic chain. Consequently, some analysts have claimed that definitions of political parties are too 'rigid' and Eurocentric, whereas others have seen them as a 'Westernized' political instrument that simply conserves the power and authority of existing elites (cf. Randall 1988; Bayart 1993). There is no such 'government-and-opposition' Westminster-style form of governance in Africa and elections are often problematic, if not actually disputed, and traumatic occasions. So this essential aspect of democracy is flawed, but why? It is argued that the concept of legitimacy may not correspond to the same category as in Western civil society. Power in Africa is mainly instrumental and the 'big men' provide resources to their supporters which otherwise they would not enjoy (cf. Nugent 1995; Chabal and Daloz 1999). Under such assumptions there is no relevance in the party system for an opposition without the capacity to provide resources to its supporters. This is why elections become so contested; no party wants to lose. In Nigeria, the Yoruba have a phrase '*Kaka ki eku ma je sese, a fi se awa da nu*' (If you can't beat him, pull him down by all means), which essentially means: bring down a government at any cost.

It can be seen, therefore, that democracy is problematic even in states that are not emerging from conflict. However, for those who are, Marina Ottaway (1999: 135) maintains that an immediate shift towards multiparty pluralism and elections is 'not conceivable, especially in countries that still have not solved problems of power and authority.' In these circumstances, she argues, African leaders must restore security, rebuild the very capacity of the state to govern, revive devastated economies and endeavour to forge a common identity among the populace. However, others believe that demilitarization in African countries depends 'on the resolution of national conflict through inclusive multi-party negotiations and the introduction of democratic and effective governance' (Nathan 1998: 75). In a sense, the whole notion of post-conflict peace building has been predicated on the delivery of some form of democratic participation. But it is not only states emerging from conflict that battle for democracy; many relatively peaceful African states have still to resolve the combined issues of 'power and authority'. In those nations, it is suggested, political culture may be too firmly rooted in 'authoritarianism, elite rule and patronage' (Abbink 2006: 193). It is certainly true across Africa that political culture can be traditional, fragmentary or inconsistent (Deegan 1998). Existing patrimonial systems distort the political environment in that, although democracy might be regarded as good in itself, it may not be perceived as an actual material form of government. These ambivalences may have coloured the respondents' attitudes towards democracy in the Afrobarometer studies.

In a sense, the issue of politics and the extent to which democracy can succeed in the continent is one of today's most pressing concerns. For if democracy is unsustainable what forms of governance are left: the benign dictator; the president for life; the dominant party that never leaves office; the religious or political elite who appropriate rule; or something else? Whichever alternatives emerge, they do not look too good. The reason this sphere is so worrying is that it directly connects to the viability and success of development strategies. Equally, if the political environment is wrong all manner of difficulties emerge for wider society: for example, corruption, which seeps into society and undermines policy, administration, law and justice; the misuse of aid, which leaves people in poverty and neglect; and the recourse to violence, whereby differing groups compete with each other for power and resources with devastating consequences for populations affected by conflict.

Can the business community, international organizations and global players help the situation? In certain areas, yes they can: probity and transparency in commercial affairs and contracts, rapid intervention in countries that abuse their populations and a more direct engagement with the reality of life in many African states. But equally, Africans must assert their rights to legitimate government, civil society, freedom of speech and assembly, not by rioting and attacking each other but by articulating and promoting what is right and just. Perhaps that is one reason why liberal democracy is difficult to accommodate in Africa. Notions of consent; tolerance of others' opinions; public service rather than private egoism; working for the good of the nation and not personal gain; upholding the rule of law not on a whim but because it is right for the country – all seem in short supply. If Africans do not have these sentiments and seem not to want them, then no external authority can provide them. No policy will be able to impose them, neither the Millennium Development Goals nor Nepad. In 2008, a communiqué from the Nigerian Forum of State Independent Electoral Commissions called for an 'infusion' of the country's 'unique historical and socio-cultural experiences' into its political parties and electoral processes. Voter apathy had been caused by the 'lack of civic values, ineffective civic education, disregard of the rule of law and the absence of a democratic culture' (Ugwu 2008: 2). The extent to which Nigeria will be able to stem this tide of disaffection is open to debate.

Africa has the highest incidence of HIV/AIDS but UNAIDS has reported that now more people are receiving antiretroviral therapy. However, the incidence of deaths from curable diseases continues to be a major concern. Again these issues are connected to poverty, problems of development and governance weaknesses. The destabilization of societies following conflicts and wars exacerbates not only health issues but also those of human security. Displaced persons living in camps, afraid or unable to go home, often living in degradation, are vulnerable to disease and death. Recognizing that poverty, social marginalization and gender inequality create conditions that increase the incidence of disease has been a major emphasis of the UN. Yet HIV prevention programmes seem to be failing to reach those at greatest risk and the sexual behaviour of young men and women has not changed as rapidly as it could. Young women consistently have less knowledge of the disease and remain more susceptible. Fewer than one in ten children orphaned by AIDS are reached by basic support services and they also attend school less often than non-orphans. General school attendance, of course, can be generally low in many states (see Chapter 1 for data). These socio-economic problems are now viewed not simply as domestic problems of indigenous Africans but as pointers to future international security concerns (Box 10.1).

Terrorism and security

The West may try in its various ways to change the political environment of Africa, to forge development of one sort or another but the nature of international relations means that it will work to its own agenda and national interests. This is why the EU–Africa summit in Lisbon in 2007 began to stress 'shared interests' particularly with regard to current concerns about security and terrorism.

Box 10.1 Vital statistics

- 20,000 – the number of skilled workers Africa loses every year to developed countries
- $1 – the daily income of half of Africa's people
- 46 – average life expectancy of people in Africa
- 25% – the amount added to the average cost of government procurement because of corruption
- 70% – of Africa's food is produced by women
- 50% – of the continent's population is under the age of 17 years
- 42% – of Africa's population do not have access to safe water

Source: www.guardian.co.uk/hearafrica05/statistics/0,,1435604,00.

In fact the US National Security Adviser, Condoleezza Rice, made a similar point in 2001 as outlined in Box 10.2.

Table 10.1 outlines the incidences of terrorism in Africa and, of course, there should be 'shared interests' between the West and Africa. After all, the bombing incidents in Kenya and Tanzania contributed to more than 700 people killed in terrorism-related incidents and 6000 wounded (www.milnet.com/state/2000/africaoverview). However, at times Africans feel ambivalent about the West even with regard to terrorism and are more comfortable with other agendas. Reportedly around 1000 members of Osama bin Laden's al-Qaeda network were traced to Somalia, which received weapons transferred from Afghanistan (Hough 2002: 68). Equally, civil unrest and regional wars have been exacerbated by rebel movements and opposition groups using terrorism to further their political, social or economic objectives. It should also be acknowledged that a considerable number of African states are members of the Organisation of the Islamic Conference, and

---

Box 10.2 Statement on African Security and the Global War on Terror

One of the most important and tangible contributions that Africa can make right now is to make clear to the world that this war is one in which we are all united...We need African nations, particularly those with large Muslim populations, to speak out at every opportunity to make clear...that this is not a war of civilisations...Africa's history and geography give it a pivotal role in the war [against terror]...Africa is uniquely positioned to contribute, especially diplomatically through your nations' membership in African and Arab international organisations and fora, to the sense that this is not a war of civilisations. This is a war of civilisations against those who would be uncivilised in their approach toward us...Do not let the world forget that there were many African and many Muslim victims of al-Qaeda not only in Kenya and Tanzania but in the World Trade Centre.

Source: Rice (2001).

Table 10.1 Incidents of terrorism in Africa to 2000

Year	Number of incidents
1995	10
1996	11
1997	11
1998	21
1999	52
2000	55

Source: Hough (2002: 66).

the Islamic Development Bank and other Islamic NGOs have long pumped monies into grassroots projects as a means of attracting support. On occasions, states have viewed Islamic funds as a useful supply of resources without 'strings' and thereby failed to recognize they might be subject to an alternative political and development agenda (Deegan 1996).

In a way, Africa's current relationship with China is another example of a 'take the money and don't ask any questions' approach, which may be understandable in cash-strapped nations. But often there are future consequences to be considered. It is this lack of self-assertion when dealing with certain states, regions and organizations that is perturbing. The West may have its failings and its own concerns but Africa has no compunction in condemning its former colonial powers or criticizing the power of the United States and has been congratulated for doing so. Ali Mazrui's TV series, *The Africans*, aroused the comment of the eminent Palestinian, the late Edward Said: 'Here at last was an African, on prime time television in the West, daring to accuse the West of what it had done, thus reopening a file considered closed.' That file has not only opened but got 'bigger and bigger' (Bemath 2005). The question must be asked: will Africans open similar 'files' about their Arab heritage or Asian links?

The West is engaging in close security relationships with a range of African states. Kenya, for example, is considered strategically important in the 'Global War on Terror'; not surprisingly, as terrorist networks are claimed to be operational there. Under diplomatic and aid pressure the country instituted new counterterrorism measures yet civil society is fragmented and the political scene uncertain, as the violence following the 2007 elections indicated. Equally, in Tanzania, the procurement of radar systems from Britain led to accusations of fraud and the resignation of the former prime minister and his cabinet colleagues (EISA 2008d). Global security is now a preoccupying focus of the West and Africa is of major interest. In fact, in 2006 the US National Security Strategy affirmed that Africa was of growing geo-strategic importance and a 'high priority' of the administration of President Bush: 'Africa . . . is emerging on the world scene as a strategic player, and we need to deal with it as a continent' (US Department of Defense News Briefing with Principal Deputy Under Secretary Henry from the Pentagon, 23 April 2007, cited in McFate 2008: 113). In 2007, President Bush announced the establishment of a sixth territorial Unified Command, Africa Command or 'AFRICOM', which demonstrated the seriousness with which the continent was viewed. AFRICOM has been created 'to address at least six areas of concern contingent to US interests: counter-terrorism; securing natural resources; containing armed conflict and humanitarian crisis; retarding the spread of HIV/AIDS; reducing international crime; and responding to growing Chinese influence' (ibid.). For Sean McFate, a former adviser on US peace-building efforts in Africa, these moves are very significant: 'US security interests in Africa are considerable and Africa's position in the US's strategic spectrum has moved from peripheral to central. AFRICOM is more than a mere map change: it is a post-Cold War paradigm shift' (ibid.: 114). One of the important features of AFRICOM is that it intends to combine security with development as it views the two as inextricably linked and again it expects cooperation from African nations. Security is regarded as a necessary precondition to development and by looking after US interests it is hoped that AFRICOM will boost Africa's own interests. But the question arises again: are these interests 'one and the same?' (ibid.: 120).

A decade ago, some African nations lamented the demise of the former Soviet Union because the power they had exercised straddling the two superpowers, the USA and the USSR, had come to an end. The strategic, economic or political roles they played at that time had been conditioned by Cold War interests and they had become 'client states' of one or both of these powerful patrons; yet what of the global environment now? How does Africa perceive its role in the context of contemporary interests and concerns? How, for example, does it view China's economic ambitions, Islamist jihadist aims, the increasing role played by transnational crime syndicates or the emerging security agenda of the United States? In a sense, these are puzzling questions because there seems to be little certainty about Africa's position now or its likely attitudes in the future. This uncertainty arouses both suspicion and complacency in equal measure. On the one hand, suspicion emanates from the West in the shape of AFRICOM; on the other hand, complacency emerges from terrorist networks or drugs, crime and human trafficking organizations that seem to operate as though they have a licence to do as they please.

Chapter 1 discussed the issue of 'Africanness' and perhaps it is vital, more than ever, that the term be defined today. What does is stand for? How does it play in international circles? The time has come for the African Union, African governments, African civic organizations and African peoples to stand up for what really identifies and matters to the continent now. These views may seem rudimentary or unrealistic but, if Africa does not decide for itself in a globalized environment, there is no doubt others will. According to one of the laws of the scientist Isaac Newton, everything continues in a state of rest unless it is compelled to change by forces imposed upon it. It may be a law about motion but it could be applicable to life today. Significant changes are being forced on the international community: sustainable economics, terrorism, security, climate change, religion and politics. Africa, as part of that community, is not immune to such forces. What the future holds for the continent is difficult to predict but of one aspect there can be little doubt: Africa must begin to consider what its political, economic, social and international aspirations are, because there are no signs these problems will be either diminishing or disappearing any time soon.

Notes

1 Past and Present

1 Chapter 2 deals with religion more fully.
2 For historical analysis of this period see Nugent (2004); Davidson (1994); Mazrui and Tidy (1986).

2 Religion

1 See also the work of Graham Furniss, SOAS, University of London, available at www.soas.ac.uk/staff/staff30968.php.
2 Supporting material is also available at the Cultural Museum, Kano, Nigeria, as viewed in January 2005.
3 This statement was contained in the 1954 Election Manifesto of the Convention People's Party, entitled *Forward with the Common People*, cited in Deegan (1996: 18–19).
4 See Paul Nugent's excellent account of post-independence Africa (2004).
5 For a recent journalistic appraisal of the organization see Green (2007).
6 The author conducted the following interviews in Kano, Nigeria, 2005:
    1 The *Shari'a* Commission: Dr Sa'idu Ahmad Dukawa; Dr Muzzamuil Sani Hanga. The Commission implements *shari'a* law in Kano.
    2 Dr Auwalu Kawu: Co-ordinating Director, Information Resources and Network Centre.
    3 Dr Magashi: Organizer of YOSPIS, which concerns health at state level.
    4 Mohamed Auwal Umar: Senior Lecturer, Department of Sociology, Bayero University, Kano, who worked on World Health Organisation and USAID projects.
    5 A. Sanni Yakub: Chairman, Massalaka Community Development CBO.
    6 Al Haji Yusuf Umar: Chairman of Yakasai Zumuntu, the oldest CBO in Kano.
    7 Ibrahim Mu'azzam: Director, Centre for Democracy and Documentation, Kano.
    8 Dr Rasheed Olaniyi: Centre for Democracy and Documentation.
    9 Reverend Father Habila Musa: Priest at Our Lady of Fatima, Catholic Cathedral, Kano Centre.
    10 Reverend Bitrus Joshua Fraps: Baptist Church.
    11 Professor Abdalla Aulam: Centre for Hausa Cultural Studies, NGO, Kano.
7 In fact, the author had to meet members of the *Shari'a* Commission and request special permission to conduct interviews in Kano.
8 The cartoons of the Prophet in a Danish newspaper and the naming of a teddy bear Muhammad by a British school teacher in Sudan in 2007 aroused outcries and demonstrations against the perceived insults to the Prophet and Islam.

2 Analysis: Islam, law and society

1 Chapter 9 on terrorism considers the Islamist activism in Africa sponsored by Middle Eastern countries and groups.
2 For a more detailed discussion of Islam and women, see Chapter 5.
3 Interviews with female judges: Nagua Kamal Faud, Court of Appeal; Amira Yousif Ali, Supreme Court; Saniya El-Rasheed Mirghani, Head of Adminstration of Scientific Research, Supreme Court, Khartoum, 1997.

3 Development

1 For an excellent account of French and British aid policies see Cumming (2001).
2 Round table discussion at a meeting held at RIIA, Chatham House, London, UK, 17 July 2003.
3 britishhighcommission.gov.uk/servlet/FRONT?pagename=OpenMarket/xceterate/ShowPage&c=Page&cid=107171252562
4 For alternative interpretations of Nepad see Chabal (2002), de Waal (2002) and Maxwell and Christiansen (2002).
5 Summarized from the conference 'Reconciliation and Reconstruction in Africa: Beyond the Peace Agreements', Wilton Park, 26–30 July 2004.
6 See Chapter 8 below for a discussion of conflict diamonds.
7 See Chapter 8 Analysis on Darfur, Sudan.

4 Democracy

1 The present author worked on the 'Elections in Africa' project within the Africa Programme between 2003 and 2005 and was Co-Convenor of RIIA's Southern African Study Group between 1998 and 2002.
2 For extensive analysis of electoral behaviour see Elklit (2002, 2005); see also further details of Elklit's work at www.ps.au.dk/elklit.
3 For an excellent study of electoral systems in Africa see Lindberg (2006).
4 For more details regarding voter education and registration in South Africa, see Deegan (2001).
5 See recent works on parties in Africa: Carbone (2007); Bogaards (2007).

5 Gender

1 This subject is discussed more fully in Chapter 8.
2 See Chapter 7 for a discussion of refugees and human security.
3 See Chapter 7 for more details about HIV/AIDS.
4 For a discussion of women in South Africa see Deegan (1998, 2001).
5 Research conducted in Gabarone, Botswana, 2004.
6 Research conducted by the author at the Community Agency for Social Enquiry, Johannesburg, 2002.

7 Disease and human security

1 The author conducted a research trip to Kano, northern Nigeria, in January 2005.
2 The author witnessed such activities whilst researching in Africa.
3 Mkalipi interview 2002; research at National Electoral Commission, Gabarone, Botswana, which linked the notion of 'one vote; one partner'.

8 Conflict, Arms And Reconstruction

1 For an excellent review of current debates on violence see Leopold (2005).
2 Cf. www.unoorg/reform/panel.htm; www.un.org/secureworld; www.un.org/largerfreedom
3 For an interesting discussion of this topic see Wlodarczyk (2005: 679).
4 See Chapter 9 below for more details of crime and terrorism in Sierra Leone.

8 Analysis: Sudan: Darfur Crisis

1 In August 2005, John Garang was killed in a plane crash while travelling back from a meeting with President Museveni in Uganda. President Bashir asserted that 'Garang's death will only increase Sudan's determination for peace'. Despite riots and deaths following Garang's death, his successor, Sylva Kiir, assumed the role of First Vice President shortly afterwards.
2 For excellent analyses of the conflict see de Waal and Flint (2008); International Crisis Group (2007b).

9 Terrorism

1 For a consideration of the ANC's military wing in South Africa, see Deegan (2001).
2 The Sicari and Zealots in the Roman occupation of the Middle East; the Reign of Terror that took place during the French Revolution; the Narodya Volya in Russia, who described themselves as 'terrorists'.
3 The author researched in Sudan and interviewed Hassan al Turabi and other ministers in 1997.
4 The United Nations Panel of Experts in Liberia reported: 'The panel noted with concern that a number of non-governmental organizations were planning exit strategies and redeployment of their assets to the Middle East' (cited in UN Security Council Report S/2003/498, 24 April 2003: 13).
5 Dr Amadou Karim Gaye, Senegal, 1975–79; Dr Hamid Algabid, Niger, 1989–96 (Deegan 1996).
6 Author's correspondence with Dr Mukhtar A. Hamour, Department of Policies and Strategic Planning, Islamic Development Bank, Jeddah, Saudi Arabia, 21 January 1997.
7 The author conducted fieldwork at the Islamic African Centre, Khartoum, Sudan, in February 1997.
8 The author conducted research in Kano, Nigeria, in January 2005.

Bibliography

Interviews

Albadawe, Suad A. Secretary General (1997) International Muslim Women Union, Khartoum.

Ali, Amira Yousif (1997) Supreme Court, Khartoum.

Al Quusi, Dr Abdul Muneim M. (1997) The Trustee-General, El-Zakat Chamber, Khartoum, Sudan.

Aulam, Professor Abdalla (2005) Centre for Hausa Cultural Studies, Kano.

Community Agency for Social Enquiry (2002) Johannesburg.

Connolly, Father M. (1998) Holy Ghost Fathers, London.

Decalo, Professor Sam (1995) Port Elizabeth, South Africa.

Diescho, Professor J. (1995) Port Elizabeth, South Africa.

Elawad, Dr Abdalla Suliman (1997) Islamic African Relief Agency.

Farred, Glenn (2002) Programme Manager, South African National NGO Coalition, Johannesburg, South Africa.

Faud, Nagua Kamal (1997) Court of Appeal, Khartoum.

Former member of the UK forces (2005) London.

Fraps, Reverend Bitrus Joshua (2005) Kano.

Good, Dr Kenneth (2003) University of Botswana, Gabarone.

Haines, Professor R. (1996) Port Elizabeth.

Kawu, Auwal (2005) Kano.

Kodi, Muzong (2004) Transparency International Regional Director, Abuja, Nigeria, 25 November.

Masite, Sophie (1996) Mayor of Soweto, Johannesburg, South Africa.

Mazzitelli, Antonio (2004) Regional Representative for West and Central Africa, UN Office of Drugs and Crime, Abuja, Nigeria.

Mirghani, Saniya El-Rasheed (1997) Head of Administration of Scientific Research, Supreme Court, Khartoum.

Mkalipi, Monde (2002) Deputy Director Communications, National Youth Commission, Johannesburg.

Muazzam, Ibraham (2005) Director, Centre for Hausa Cultural Studies, Kano, Nigeria.

Musa, Father Habila (2005) Our Lady of Fatima, Catholic Cathedral, Kano.

Rahim, Mohamed Zain Abdel (1997) Deputy Managing Director, Agricultural Bank of Sudan, Gumhouria Avenue, Khartoum.

Representative of the South African Police (2000) Johannesburg.

Roric, The Right Reverend, Right Honourable Gabriel Jr (1997) Bishop of Rumbek Diocese.
Satti, Hasanat A., Assistant Secretary General (1997) International Muslim Women Union, Khartoum.
Seeletso, Tiro (2004) Secretary, Independent Electoral Commission, Gabarone.
Sithole, Johannes (2002) City of Tshwane Metropolitan Municipality, Pretoria.
Turabi, Dr Hasan (1997) former leader of the National Islamic Front and former Speaker of the National Assembly, Khartoum.
Umar, Al Haji Yusuf (2005) Chairman, Yakasai Zumuntu, Kano.
Walsh, Father J. (1998) London.
White, Dr Caroline (1996) Centre for Policy Studies, Johannesburg.

Works

Abbink, J. (2006) 'Discomfiture of Democracy? The 2005 Election Crisis in Ethiopia and its Aftermath', *African Affairs*, 105 (419) April: 173–99.
Abdalla, M. Z. and Suliman, K. M. (1995) 'The Potential Role of Federalism in Containing and Reversing Inter-retional Inequalities in Sudan', in Hassan M. Salih (ed.), *Federalism in the Sudan*, Khartoum: Khartoum University Press.
Abrahamson, Jennifer (2004) 'Where "Never Again" Whispers through the Harsh Desert Wind', *eAfrica*, 2 (November) (www.saiia.org.za/index.php?option=com_content&view=article&id=529:specialfeaturewhereneveragainwhispersthroughtheharshdesertwind&catid=74:eafrica).
Africa Insight (2002) Editorial, 32 (3) September: 2.
Africa Newsletter (2006) Africa Bureau, UNHCR (www.unhcr.org).
African Development Bank (2005) *African Development Report*, New York: African Development Bank.
African Red Cross and Red Crescent Societies (2007) 'Major Health Problems in Africa' (www.ifrc.org/WHAT/health/archi/fact/fhlthpub.htm).
African Union (2000) 'Bamako Declaration on an African Common Position on the Illicit Proliferation, Circulation and Trafficking of Small Arms and Light Weapons' (www.africa-union.org).
African Union (2002a) 'Plan of Action of the African Union High-Level Inter-Governmental Meeting on the Prevention and Combating of Terrorism in Africa.' Mtg/HLIG/Conv. Terror/Plan, Algiers, Algeria, 11–14 September.
African Union (2002b) 'The Protocol Relating to the Establishment of the Peace and Security Council of the African Union', Article 2(1) adopted by the 1st Ordinary Session of the Assembly of the African Union on 9th July 2002 in Durban (www.africa-union.org/root/au/organs/Protocol).
African Union (2003) Report of the meeting of experts to consider modalities for the implementation of the AU Plan of Action on the Prevention and Combating of Terrorism in Africa, Ethiopia (www.africa-union.org/Terrorism/terrorism2.htlm).
African Union (2004) 'Declaration of the Second High-Level Intergovernmental Meeting on the Prevention and Combating of Terrorism in Africa', mtg/HLIG/Conv.Terror/Decl. (11) Rev. 2 October (www.african-union.org).
Afrobarometer (2005) Citizens and the State in Africa, Part 5. Corruption and State Legitimacy,

Afrobarometer (2006) 'Citizens and the State in Africa: New Results from Afrobarometer Round 3', Working Paper No. 61.

Agoagye, Festus (2004) *The African Mission in Burundi: Lessons Learned from the First African Union Peacekeeping Operation*, Durban: African Center for the Constructive Resolution of Disputes (ACCORD), ELDIS.

Ahmad, Hazrat Mirza Tahir (1991) *Seventh Friday Sermon: The Crisis and the New World Order*, Surrey: Unwin Brothers.

Aidoo, T. A. (1983) 'Ghana: Social Class, the December Coup and Prospects for Socialism', *Contemporary Marxism*, 6: 142–59.

Al-Ashmawi, Muhammad Said (2007) 'Reforming Islam and Islamic Law', in J. J. Donoghue and J. Esposito (eds), *Islam in Transition*, Oxford: Oxford University Press.

Al-Farag, Muhammad Abdel Salam (2007) 'The Forgotten Duty', in J. J. Donoghue and J. Esposito (eds), *Islam in Transition*, Oxford: Oxford University Press.

al-Farsy, Fouad (1990) *Modernity and Tradition: The Saudi Equation*, London: Kegan Paul International.

All Party Parliamentary Group for Angola (2003) Report to the House of Commons, London, May.

Al-Mahdi, Sadiq (2006) Paper presented to World Congress on Middle Eastern Studies 2, Amman, Jordan, 13 June.

Amnesty International, IANSA and Oxfam International (2006) *The Call for Tough Arms Controls: Voices from the DRC's Control Arms Campaign*, London: Amnesty International, IANSA and Oxfam International.

Annan, Kofi (2002) *The Millennium Development Goals Report*, New York: United Nations (www.undp.org/mdg).

Appiah, Kwame A. (1992) *In my Father's House: Africa in the Philosophy Culture*, Oxford: Oxford University Press.

Apter, O. (1967) *The Politics of Modernisation*, Chicago: University of Chicago Press.

Arbache, Jorge Saba and Page, John (2007) 'More Growth or Fewer Collapses?', Policy Research Working Paper 4384, The World Bank, Africa Region, November.

Arkoun, M. (1994) *Rethinking Islam*, Boulder: Westview Press.

Awolowo, O. (1965) 'Nigerian National and Federal Union', in R. Emerson and M. Kilson (eds), *The Political Awakening for Africa*, Englewood Cliffs, NJ: Prentice-Hall.

Ayandele, E. A. (1966) 'The Missionary Factor in Northern Nigeria 1870–1918', *Journal of the Historical Society of Nigeria*, 3 (3): 140–53.

Ayubi, N. (1991) *Political Islam*, London: Routledge.

Baba, K. M. and Umaru, B. F. (2001) *Household Livelihood Strategies in Sokoto State of Nigeria: The Role of Informal Women's Savings Organisations*, Kano: CRD, Nigeria.

Bagader, A. (1994) 'Contemporary Islamic Movements in the Arab World', in Akbar S. Ahmed and H. Donnan (eds), *Islam, Globalisations and Postmodernity*, London: Routledge.

Baker, Bruce (2006) 'The African Post-conflict Policing Agenda in Sierra Leone', *Conflict, Security & Development*, 6 (1) April: 25–49.

Banani, Amin (1961) *The Modernisation of Iran 1921–41*, Stanford, CA: Stanford University Press.

Barber, J. (1999) *South Africa in the Twentieth Century*, Oxford: Blackwell.

Barrett, D., Kurian, G. and Johnson, T. (eds) (2001) *World Christian Encyclopedia: A Comparative Survey of Churches and Religions in the Modern World*, Oxford University Press, Oxford.

Batsell, Jake (2005) 'Aids, Politics and NGOs in Zimbabwe', in Amy S. Patterson (ed.), *The African State and the AIDS Crisis*, Aldershot: Ashgate.

Bayart, J.-F. (1993) *The State in Africa*, Harlow: Longman.

BBC TV (2004) 'The New Killing Fields', *Panorama*, 14 November (http://news.bbc.co.uk).

Begum, Sultana (ed.) (2004) *Sudan's Opportunity for Peace and Development? Visit to Sudan 27 June–4 July 2004*, London: Associate Parliamentary Group on Sudan.

Bellah, R. B. (1966) 'Religious Aspects of Modernization in Turkey and Japan', in J. L. Finkle and R. W. Gable (eds), *Political Development and Social Change*, New York: John Wiley & Sons.

Bemath, Abdul Samed (2005) *The Mazruiana Collection Revisited: Ali A. Mazrui Debating the African Condition, a Thematic Bibliography 1962–2003*, Pretoria: Africa Institute of South Africa

Benn, Rt Hon. Hilary (2005) Secretary of State for International Development. 'Update on the crisis in Darfur and the implementation of the Comprehensive Peace Agreement', paper presented at a meeting held at the House of Commons, 16 June.

Bhagwati, J. (1966) *The Economics of Underdeveloped Countries*, London: Weidenfeld & Nicolson.

Bhagwati, J. (1995) 'The New Thinking on Development', *Journal of Democracy*, 6 (4): 50–64.

Billington, R., Strawbridge, S., Greensides, L. and Fitzsimons, A. (1991) *Culture & Society*, Basingstoke: Macmillan/Palgrave.

Binder, L. (1988) *Islamic Liberalism*, Chicago: University of Chicago Press.

bin Talal, Prince Hassan (2006) Opening Address to the Conference 'Arab Civil Society, Functional Democracy, Global Governance and the Rise of Fundamentalism', Amman, Jordan, 13 June .

Blondel, Jean (1990) *Comparative Government*, Hemel Hempstead: Philip Allen.

Bogaards, Matthijs (2007) 'Ethnic Party Bans in Africa', in *4th ECPR General Conference*, Pisa.

Booysen, Susan (2002) 'In the Crossfire of Zimbabwe's War for Political Survival', *Africa Insight*, 32 (3) September: 3–10.

Bratton, M., Mattes, R. and Gyimah-Goadi, E. (2005) *Public Opinion, Democracy and Market Reform in Africa*, Cambridge: Cambridge University Press.

Brenner, L. (1993) *Muslim Identity and Social Change in Sub-Saharan Africa*, London: Hurst.

Brownlie, I. (1983) *Basic Documents in International Law*, Oxford: Oxford University Press.

Bugaje, Usman (1998) 'Trade, Debt and Development in Sub-Saharan Africa: A Muslim Initiative to the Rescue', *Dirasat Ifriqiyya*, 18 (January): 21–36.

Buhlungu, S., Daniel, J., Southall, R. and Lutchman, J. (eds) (2006) *State of the Nation: South Africa 2005–6*, Cape Town: HSRC Press.

Buijs, G. (1995) *Risk and Benefit as Functions of Savings and Loan Clubs: An Examination of Rotating Credit Associations for Poor Women in Rhini*, Port Elizabeth: African Studies Association of South Africa.

Bunting, Madeleine (2005) 'Spotlight Falls on Corruption of Africa', *The Guardian*, 5 March.

Bury, J. B. (1921) *Cambridge Medieval History Vol. 2: The Rise of the Saracens and the Foundation of the Western Empire*, Cambridge: Cambridge University Press.

Bush, R. (1983) 'The United States and South Africa in a Period of World Crisis', *Contemporary Marxism*, 6: 1–13.

Business Action for Africa (2006) 'Report on Corruption and Money Laundering', submitted to Africa All Party Parliamentary Group, House of Commons.

Business Day (2007) 'South Africa Debuts Tougher Laws on Rape', 14 December.

Callaway, Barbara and Creevey, Lucy (1994) *The Heritage of Islam*, Boulder, CO: Lynne Rienner.

Cammack, P., Pool, D. and Tordoff, W. (1991) *Third World Politics*, Basingstoke: Macmillan.

Carbone, Giovanni M. (2007) 'Political Parties and Party Systems in Africa: Themes and Research Perspectives', *World Political Science Review*, 3 (3): 1–15.

Césaire, Aimé (1956) 'Declaration at the First International Congress of Black Writers and Artists', *Culture et Colonisation, Presence Africaine*, (June–November): 10–15.

Chabal, Patrick (1992) *Power in Africa: An Essay on Political Interpretation*, Basingstoke: Macmillan.

Chabal, Patrick (2002) 'The Quest for Good Government and Development in Africa: Is NEPAD the Answer?', *International Affairs*, 78 (3) July: 447–62.

Chabal, P. and Daloz, J. P. (1999) *Africa Works: Disorder as Political Instrument*, Bloomington: Indiana University Press.

Chatterjee, Kingshuk (2006) 'Social Change and Identity in Muslim Societies: ISIM Workshop', *ISIM Review*, 17 (Spring): 10–11.

Chazan, N., Mortimer, R., Ravenhill, J. and Rothchild, D. (1988) *Politics and Society in Contemporary Africa*, Boulder, CO: Lynne Rienner.

Chebel, Malek (2006) '27 Propositions for Reforming Islam' (www.freemuslims.org/document.php?id=77).

Choueiri, Youssef M. (1990) *Islamic Fundamentalism*, London: Pinter Publishers.

Cicero (2000) *De Re Publica*, Loeb Classical Library, Cambridge, MA: Harvard University Press.

Cilliers, J. (2004) *Human Security in Africa: A Conceptual Framework for Review*, Johannesburg: African Human Security Initiative.

Clapham, C. (1985) *Third World Politics*, London: Croom Helm.

Clapham, Christopher (ed.) (1998) *African Guerrillas*, Oxford: James Currey.

Clover, Jenny (2002) *Refugees and Internally Displaced Peoples in Africa*, Institute of Strategic Studies, South Africa (www.iss.co.za).

Cohen, J. and Arato, A. (1995) *Civil Society and Political Theory*, Cambridge, MA: MIT Press.

Collier, P. and Dollar, D. (2004) 'Development Effectiveness: What Have We Learnt?', *Economic Journal*, 114: F244–F271.

Commission for Africa (2005) *Our Common Interest: Report of the Commission for Africa*, London: HMG.

Commonwealth Observer Mission to South Africa (1993) *Violence in South Africa*, London: Commonwealth Secretariat.

Concordis International (2008) Email newsletter, office@concordis-international.org, February.

Crone, Patricia (1998) 'The Rise of Islam', in Francis Robinson (ed.) *Islamic World*, Cambridge: Cambridge University Press.

Cruise O'Brien, Donal B. (1971) *The Mourides of Senegal*, Oxford: Clarendon Press.

Cumming, Gordon (2001) *Aid to Africa*, Burlington, VT: Ashgate.

Curtin, Philip, Feierman, Steven, Thompson, Leonard and Vansina, Jan (1995) *African History*, Harlow: Longman.

Dahl, R. (1989) *Democracy and its Critics*, New Haven, CT: Yale University Press.

Davidson, Basil (1994) *Modern Africa*, Harlow: Longman.

De Burgh, W. G. (1961) *The Legacy of the Ancient World*, London: Pelican.

Deegan, H. (1996) *Third Worlds: The Politics of the Middle East and Africa*, London: Routledge,

Deegan, H. (1998) *South Africa Reborn*, London: UCL Press.

Deegan, H. (2001) *The Politics of the New South Africa: Apartheid and After*, Harlow: Pearson.

Deegan, H. (2003) 'Elections in Africa: The Past 10 Years', RIIA Briefing Paper.

Degni-Segui, René (1996) Human Rights Commission's Special Rapporteur for Rwanda (www.un.org/womanwatch).

deGuzman, Diane (2002) 'A Report by Diane deGuzman edited by Egbert G. Ch. Wesselink', in Egbert G. Ch. Wesselink (ed.), *Depopulating Sudan's Oil Regions*, Brussels: European Coalition on Oil in Sudan.

Deutsch, K. (1953) *Nationalism and Social Communication*, New York: John Wiley.

de Waal, Alex (2002) 'What's New in the "New Partnership for Africa's Development?"<t>', *International Affairs*, 78 (3) July: 463–75.

de Waal, Alex (ed.) (2004) *Islamism and its Enemies in the Horn of Africa*, London: C. Hurst.

de Waal, Alex (ed.) (2005) 'Who are the Darfurians? Arab and African Identities, Violence and External Engagement', *African Affairs*, 104 (415) April: 181–205.

de Waal, Alex and Flint, Julie (2008) *Darfur: A New History of a Long War*, London: Zed Books.

de Waal, A. and Salam, A. H. Abdel (2004) 'Islamism, State Power and Jihad in Sudan', in A. de Waal (ed.), *Islamism and its Enemies in the Horn of Africa*, London: C. Hurst.

Diamond, L. (2004) 'Democratic Reform in Africa: The Quality of Progress', in E. Gymah-Boadi, *Democratic Reform in Africa*, Boulder, CO: Lynne Rienner.

Diamond, L., Linz, J. J. and Lipset, S. M. (1989) *Politics in Developing Countries: Comparing Experiences with Democracy*, Boulder, CO: Lynne Rienner.

Domichi, Ambassador Hideaki (2003) Director General of SubSaharan African Affairs, MOFA, Tokyo, Japan. Paper presented to the RIIA, UK, 17 July.

Donoghue, J. and Esposito, J. (eds) (2007) *Islam in Transition*, Oxford: Oxford University Press.

Dowden, Richard (1994) *The Tablet*, 18 June.

Dowden, Richard (2000) 'The Hopeless Continent', *The Economist*, 19 May.

Dowden, Richard (2007) *Analysis*, BBC Radio 4, December.

Drummond-Thomson, Jennifer (2005) 'The Curse of Tradition: The Gender Situation in Chad', *Inside AISA*, 4 (August/September): 4–5.

Dunleavy, P. and O'Leary, B. (1991) *Theories of the State*, Basingstoke: Macmillan.

Durkheim, E. (1982) *The Rules of Sociological Method*, London: Macmillan.

Eigen, Peter (2006) Chair of the International Advisory Group. 'Extractive Industries Transparency Initiative' (www.transparency.org).

EISA (2004) 'Principles for Election Management, Monitoring and Observation in the SADC Region', Electoral Handbook 13, EISA, Johannesburg.

EISA (2007a) *Regional Roundup*, 11 October.

EISA (2007b) 'African Leaders Confront Governance Challenges'. Report on UN

Conference on Good Governance, Burkina Faso, 24 October', *Regional Roundup*, 25 October.

EISA (2007c) 'Never Chanda, Mugabe Says No to Hostile Poll Observers', *Regional Roundup*, 5 December.

EISA (2008a) *Regional Roundup*, 7 April.

EISA (2008b) 'The Devastating Cost of Africa's Wars', *Johannesburg Reports*, 14 April.

EISA (2008c) 'Why was Kenya's Peer Review Missing in Action?', *Johannesburg Reports*, 15 and 16 April.

EISA (2008d) 'There is More to Democracy than Holding Elections', *Johannesburg Reports*, 25 April.

El-Affendi, Abdelwahab (2005) Presentation to a meeting, Centre for the Study of Islam and Democracy, University of Westminster, London, June.

El Talib, Hassan E. (2004) 'The Janjaweed', *Inside AISA*, 5 (Oct./Nov.): 3–4.

Elklit, Jorgen (2002) 'Lesotho 2002: Africa's First MMP Elections', *Journal of African Elections*, 1 (2) September: 1–10.

Elklit, Jorgen (2005) 'Minding the Polls', *Journal of Democracy*, 16 (4) October: 172–75.

ElZakat Magazine (1997) 'The Role of Zakat in the Economic Development and Social Justice', January.

Emerson, R. and Kilson, M. (eds) (1965) *The Political Awakening of Africa*, Englewood Cliffs, NJ: Prentice-Hall.

Esposito, J. L. (1994) *Islam*, Oxford: Oxford University Press.

EU–Africa Summit (2007) Lisbon (http://ec.europa.eu/development/icenter/repository/EAS2007_joint_strategy).

Falk Moore, S. (1994) *Anthropology and Africa: Changing Perspectives on a Changing Scene*, Charlottesville: University of Virginia Press.

Fanthorpe, Richard (2006) 'On the Limits of Liberal Peace: Chiefs and Democratic Decentralization in Post-war Sierra Leone', *African Affairs*, 105 (418) January: 27–49.

Farah, Douglas (2007) 'Terrorism in Africa', International Assessment and Strategy Centre, 16 January (www.strategycenter.net).

Fieldhouse, D. K. (1973) *Economics and Empire 1883–1914*, London: Weidenfeld & Nicolson.

Finer, S. (1962) *Man on Horseback*, London: Pall Mall Press.

Friedman, Steven (2004) 'Building Democracy after Apartheid', in E. Gyimah-Boadi (ed.), *Democratic Reform in Africa*, Boulder, CO: Lynne Rienner.

Fuller, A. H. (1969) 'The Peasant World of Time and Space', in A. Shiloh (ed.), *Peoples and Cultures of the Middle East*, New York: Random House.

Fyzee, Asaf A. A. (2007) 'The Reinterpretation of Islam', in J. Donoghue and J. Esposito (eds), *Islam in Transition*, Oxford: Oxford University Press.

Garnett, John (1991) 'The Role of Military Power', in R. Little and M. Smith (eds), *Perspectives on World Politics*, London: Routledge.

Garrett, Laurie (2007) 'The Challenge of Global Health', *Foreign Affairs*, Jan./Feb. (www.foreignaffairs.org/20070101faessay86103/laurie-garrett/the-challenge-of-global-health.html).

Geertz, C. (1967) 'The Integrative Revolution: Primordial Sentiments and Civic Politics in the New States', in C. Welch (ed.), *Political Modernisation*, Belmont, CA: Wadsworth Publishing.

Gellner, Ernest (1980) *Muslim Society*, Cambridge: Cambridge University Press.

Gibb, H. A. R. (1950) 'The Shari'a' (http://answering-islam.org.uk/Books/Gibb/sharia.htm).

Giles, Wenona and Hyndman, Jennifer (eds) (2004) *Sites of Violence, Gender and Conflict Zones*, Berkeley: University of California Press.

Giliomee, Herman and Simkins, Charles (1999) *The Awkward Embrace: One Party Domination and Democracy*, Johannesburg: Tafelberg Publishers.

Gordon, A. and Gordon, D. (eds) (2001) *Understanding Contemporary Africa*, Boulder, CO: Lynne Rienner.

Goulty, Alan (2003) UK Special Envoy to Sudan. 'Prospects for Peace in Sudan', paper presented to the House of Commons, 17 November.

Goytisolo, J. (1994) 'Islam in North Africa' (trans. Peter Bush), *El País*, 28 March.

Green, Matthew (2007) *The Wizard of the Nile*, London: Portobello.

Grinker, R. R. and Steiner, C. B. (1997) *Perspectives on Africa*, Oxford: Blackwell.

Grove, A. T. (1978) *Africa*, Oxford: Oxford University Press.

Gundy, Kenneth W. (2000) 'South Africa: Transition to Majority Rule, Transformation to Stable Democracy', in York Bradshaw and Stephen N. Ndegwa (eds), *The Uncertain Promise of Southern Africa*, Bloomington: Indiana University Press.

Guney-Ruebenacker, Havva G. (2006) 'Islamic Law: An Ever-Evolving Science under the Light of Divine Revelation and Human Reason' (www.averroes-foundation.org/articles/islamic_law_evolving.html).

Habermas, J. (1979) *Communication and the Evolution of Society*, London: Macmillan.

Haddad, Mohamed (2006) 'The Family as a Space of Social Integration in Islam', in Helmut Reifeld (ed.), *Marriage, Family and Society – A Dialogue with Islam*, Berlin: Konrad Adenauer Stiftung.

Hamzawy, Amr (2001) 'Changes in the Contemporary Islamist Discourse', *ISIM*, 8 (September): 7–8.

Haseeb, Khair el-Din (ed.) (1985) *The Arabs and Africa*, London: Croom Helm.

Hastings, Adrian (1994) *The Church in Africa: 1450–1950*, Oxford: Clarendon Press.

Hatem, M. (1993) 'Post Islamist and Post Nationalist Feminist Discourses', in J. Tucker (ed.), *Arab Women*, Bloomington: Indiana University Press.

Haynes, Jeffrey (2007) *An Introduction to International Relations and Religion*, Harlow: Pearson.

Held, David (1996) *Models of Democracy*, Cambridge: Polity Press.

Hemson, D. and O'Donovan, M. (2006) in S. Buhlungu, J. Daniel, R. Southall and J. Lutchman (eds) *State of the Nation: South Africa 2005–6*, Cape Town: HSRC Press.

Herodotus (2003) *The Histories*, trans. Aubrey de Selincourt, London: Penguin Books.

Hiltermann, Joost R. (1998) 'Stemming the Flow of Arms into Africa: How African NGOs Can Make a Difference', *African Journal of Political Science*, 3 (1): 119–28.

Horden, P. and Purcell, N. (2004) *The Corrupting Sea*, Oxford: Blackwell Publishing.

Hough, M. (2002) 'New York Terror: The Implications for Africa', *Africa Insight*, 32 (1): 65–70.

Hough, P. (2004) *Understanding Global Security*, London: Routledge.

Hountondji, Paulin J. (1995) 'Producing Knowledge in Africa', The Second Bashorun M. K. O. Abiola Distinguished Lecture, *African Studies Review*, 38 (3) December: 1–10.

Hourani, Albert (1970) *Arabic Thought in the Liberal Age: 1789–1939*, Oxford: Oxford University Press.

Hughes, A. (1992) *Marxism's Retreat from Africa*, London: Frank Cass.

Human Rights Watch (1994) 'Global Report on Women's Rights', *Human Rights Watch*, 6 (1) January.

Human Rights Watch (1998) *Sudan: Global Trade, Local Impact*, New York: Human Rights Watch, August.

Human Rights Watch (1999) 'Sierra Leone: Getting Away with Murder and Rape', 11 (3a), July.

Human Rights Watch (2003) 'Oil Interests in Sudan', paper presented to the Royal Institute of International Affairs, Chatham House, 25 November.

Huntington, S. (1967) 'Political Development and Political Decay', in C. Welch (ed.), *Political Modernisation*, Belmont CA: Wadsworth Publishing.

Hyden, Goran (2006) *African Politics in Comparative Perspective*, Cambridge: Cambridge University Press.

Independent Electoral Commission, Botswana (2002) *Voter Apathy Report*, Gaborone: Independent Electoral Commission.

Institute for Security Studies (2004) *Consolidating Peace and Security in Africa*, Pretoria: Institute for Security Studies.

International Crisis Group Africa (2001) 'Disarmament in the Congo: Jump-Starting DDRRR to Prevent Further War', Africa Report no. 38, 14 December.

International Crisis Group (2005) 'Somalia's Islamists', Africa Report no. 100, 12 December.

International Crisis Group (2007a) 'Crisis in Darfur', December (www.crisisgroup.org/home/index/gfm?id=306081-1).

International Crisis Group (2007b) 'Darfur's New Security Reality', Africa Report no.134, 26 November.

International Crisis Group (2007c) 'Somalia: The Tough Part is Ahead', Africa Briefing no. 45, 26 January.

International Crisis Group (2007d) 'Sierra Leone: The Election Opportunity', Africa Report no. 129, 12 July.

International Development Committee (2005) 'Darfur, Sudan: The Responsibility to Protect', *Fifth Report of Session 2004–2005*, House of Commons.

International Refugee Rights Initiative (2006) 'Expanding the responsibility to protect the displaced', *Refugee Rights News*, 3 (2) July: 1–2.

Islamic African Centre (1996) 'The Constitution of the Islamic African Centre of Khartoum', in *A Guide to the Islamic African Centre of Khartoum*, Khartoum: Islamic African Centre.

Islamic Development Bank (1992) *Annual Report 1992*, Jeddah: Islamic Development Bank

Islamic Development Bank (1993) *Annual Report 1993*, Jeddah: Islamic Development Bank

Jackson, Sherman (2007) 'Jihad and the Modern World', in J. J. Donoghue and J. Esposito (eds), *Islam in Transition*, Oxford: Oxford University Press.

Jibril, Abdelbagi (2004a) 'The Darfur Tragedy', *Inside AISA*, 5 (Oct./Nov.): 1–3.

Jibril, Abdelbagi (2004b) 'Carnage in the Darfur Region', *Inside AISA*, 2 (April/May): 4–5.

Johns Hopkins RC/RC Health Emergency Reference Manual (1999) (www.ifrc.org).

Joseph, R. (1987) *Democracy and Prebendal Politics in Nigeria: The Rise and Fall of the Second Republic*, Cambridge: Cambridge University Press.

Khadiagala, Gilbert (1996) Paper presented to the conference Regionalism and Leadership in African Security, Johannesburg, October.

Khan, Nighat Said (2000) 'The Women's Movement Revisited: Areas of Concern for the

Future', in Suki Ali, Kelly Coate and Wangui wa Goro (eds), *Global Feminist Politics*, Routledge, London.

Kiai, Maina (2008) 'There is More to Democracy than Holding Elections: Commenting on the Post Electoral Violence in Kenya', *EISA*, 15 April.

Kingdom of Saudi Arabia (1986) *Relief Efforts*, Riyadh: National Centre for Financial and Economic Information, Ministry of Finance and National Economy.

Khanam, Farida (2007) 'On Islam and Jihad' (www.alrisala.org/Articles/tolerance/jihad.htm).

Kokoke, A. and Mazrui, A. (1988) 'Uganda: The Dual Policy as the Plural Society', in Larry Diamond, Juan J. Linz and Seymour M. Lipset, *Democracy in Developing Countries: Africa, Volume 2*, Boulder, CO: Lynne Rienner Publishers..

Komolafe, Gbenga (2001) 'Informalisation and Occupational Development in Nigeria', Working Paper No. 3, Centre for Research and Documentation, Kano, Nigeria.

Kukah, M. H. (1993) *Religion, Politics and Power in Northern Nigeria*, London: Spectrum Books.

Kurzman, C. (1999) 'Liberal Islam: Prospects and Challenges', *MERIA Journal*, 3 (September).

Kututwa, Noel (2005) 'African Anti-corruption Commitments: A Review of Eight NEPAD Countries', The African Human Security Initiative Paper 7, January.

Lasswell, H. and Kaplan, M. (1950) *Power and Society*, New Haven, CT: Yale University Press.

Lentin, Ronit (2000) 'The Feminisation of Catastrophe', in Suki Ali, Kelly Coate and Wangui wa Goro (eds), *Global Feminist Politics*, London: Routledge.

Leopold, Mark (2005) 'Violence in Contemporary Africa: Reassessed', *African Affairs*, 104 (417) October: 685–95.

Lerner, D. (1958) *The Passing of Traditional Society*, Glencoe, IL: Free Press.

Levitt, Matthew (2004) 'Hizbullah's African Activities Remain Undisrupted', *Royal United Services Institute*, The Washington Institute for Near East Policy, 1 March (www.washingtoninstitute.org/print.phb?CID=4638template=CO6).

Lewis, Bernard (1966) *The Arabs in History*, New York: Harper & Row.

Lindberg, Staffan I. (2006) *Democracy and Elections in Africa*, Baltimore, MD: Johns Hopkins University Press.

Lipset, S. M. (1960) *Political Man*, London: Heinemann Education.

Lodge, Tom (1997) *Political Corruption in South Africa*, Broederstroom: African Studies Association of South Africa.

Loots, Elsabe (2006) 'Road Map for Africa's Recovery', *Africa Insight*, 36 (3–4) December: 2.

Luckham, R. (1991) 'Militarism: Force Class and International Conflict', in R. Little and M. Smith (ed.), *Perspectives on World Politics*, London: Routledge.

Lukes, S. (1988) *Emile Durkheim*, London: Penguin.

Lusk, Gillian (2005) 'Treaty Gives Sudan a Shot at Peace', *The Washington Times*, 25 January.

McFate, Sean (2008) 'US Africa Command: Next Step or Next Stumble?', *African Affairs*, 107 (426) January: 111–20.

Macpherson, C. B. (1973) *Democratic Theory – Essays in Retrieval*, Oxford: Oxford University Press.

Magasela, Wiseman (2006) 'Towards a Constitution-based Definition of Poverty in Post-apartheid South Africa', in S. Buhlungu, J. Daniel, R. Southall and J. Lutchman (eds), *State of the Nation: South Africa 2005–6*, Cape Town: HSRC Press.

Magubane, E. C. (1983) 'Imperialism and the Making of the South African Working Class', *Contemporary Marxism*, 6: 19–56.

Mair, Stefan (2003) 'Terrorism and Africa', *African Security Review*, 12 (1) (www.iss.co.za/Pubs/ASR/12no1/CMair).

Mandivenga, E. C. (1991) 'Resurgence of Islam: Implications for African Spirituality and Dialogue', *Religion in Malawi*, 3: 12–21.

Mans, Ulrich (2004) 'Briefing: Sudan: The New War in Darfur', *African Affairs*, 103 (April): 291–4.

Marchal, Roland (2004) 'Islamic Political Dynamics in the Somali Civil War, before and after September 11', in Alex de Waal (ed.) *Islamism and its Enemies in the Horn of Africa*, London: C. Hurst.

Mathekga, Ralf (2008) 'Institute for Justice and Reconciliation', *Business Day*, 23 January.

Matlosa, Khabele (2003) *Electoral System Reform, Democracy and Stability in the SADC Region: A Comparative Analysis*, Johannesburg: EISA.

Maxwell, Simon and Christiansen, Karin (2002) 'Negotiating as Simultaneous Equation: Building a New Partnership with Africa', *International Affairs*, 78 (3) July: 477–91.

Mazrui, Ali (1986) *The Africans: A Triple Heritage*, London: BBC Publications.

Mazrui, Ali A. and Tidy, Michael (1986) *Nationalism and New States in Africa*, London: Heinemann.

Mennen, T., Frye, E. and Messick, R. E. (2007) 'Enforcement of Anti-corruption Laws: The Need for Performance Monitoring', in *Global Corruption Report* (www.transparency.org/news_room/in_focus/2007/gcr_2007).

Mill, J. S. (n.d.) *Considerations of Representative Government*, London: H. Brown & Co.

Mistry, P. S. (2005) 'Reasons for Sub-Saharan Africa's Development Deficit that the Commission for Africa did not Consider', *African Affairs*, 104 (417) October: 665–78.

Mittelman, James H. and Pasha, Mustapha Kamal (1997) *Out from Underdevelopment Revisited*, Basingstoke: Macmillan.

Mkutu, Kennedy Agade (2007) 'Small Arms and Light Weapons among Pastoral Groups in the Kenya–Uganda Border Area', African Affairs, 106 (422) January: 47–70.

Moinuddin, H. (1987) *The Charter of the Islamic Conference*, Oxford: Clarendon Press.

Moyo, A. (2001) 'Religion in Africa', in A. Gordon and D. Gordon (eds) *Understanding Contemporary Africa*, Boulder, CO: Lynne Rienner.

Moyo, Gugulethu and Ashurst, Mark (eds) (2007) The Day after Mugabe, London: Africa Research Institute.

Mtimkulu, Bereng (2005) 'The African Union and Peace Support Operations', *Conflict Trends*, 4: 34–6. ACCORD, Durban.

Muhammaed, Yusuf Sarki (2002) 'Hero Worship', *Focus on Africa*, 13 (1) January–March: 51.

Musa, I. A. (1985) 'Islam and Africa', in Khair El-Din Haseeb (ed.), *The Arabs and Africa*, London: Croom Helm.

Mustapha, Dr Raufu (2007) Paper presented to the conference 'Nigerian Elections 2007', SOAS, University of London, 15 May.

Nathan, Laurie (1998) *Good Governance: Security and Disarmament*, Cape Town: Centre for Conflict Resolution.

Ndebele, Nothando (2007) 'Economy and Land', in G. Moyo and M. Ashurst (eds), *The Day after Mugabe*, London: Africa Research Institute.

Nepad (2005) Executive Summary. Available at www.nepad.org/2005/com4africa/06executivesum (accessed 3 January 2008).

Nepad Secretariat (2002) *Nepad at Work: Summary of Nepad Action Plans*, Pretoria: Nepad Secretariat.

Nepad Secretariat (2005) African Post-Conflict Reconstruction Policy Framework, Governance, Peace and Security Programme, June (www.nepad.org/2005/aprwforum/PCRPolicyFramework_en.pdf).

Nordstrom, Carolyn (1998) 'Girls behind the Front Lines', in Lois Ann Lorentzen and Jennifer Turpin (eds), *The Women and War Reader*, New York: New York University Press.

Nugent, Paul (1995) *Big Men, Small Boys*, London: Pinter.

Nugent, Paul (2004) *Africa since Independence*, Basingstoke: Palgrave.

Nwajiuba, Chinedum (2000) *Informal Credit in Liberalised Financial Market: A Study of Women Associations in Imo State*, Kano: CRD.

Nyanduga, Bahame Tom (2006) Special Rapporteur on Refugees, IDPs and Asylum Seekers, African Commission on Human and People's Rights (www.achpr.org; www.africancomtcoalition.org/content_files/files/SEMINARON INTERNATIONAL DISPLACE3MENTIN THE ECOWASREGION.doc).

Nzongola-Ntalaja, T. (1983) 'Class Struggle and National Liberation in Zaire', *Contemporary Marxism*, 6: 57–94.

Okuma, W. (1963) *Lumumba's Congo: Roots of Conflict*, New York: Ivan Obolensky.

Omari, C. K. (1984) 'Christian Muslim Relations in Tanzania: The Socio-Political Dimension', *Journal of the Institute of Muslim Minority Affairs*, 5 (2): 373–90.

Osborne, R. (2005) *Greece in the Making 1200–479BC*, Routledge: London.

Ostergard, Robert L. Jr. (2002) 'Politics in the Hot Zone: AIDS and National Security in Africa', *Third World Quarterly*, (April): 333–50.

Ottaway, Marina (1999) *Africa's New Leaders: Democracy or State Reconstruction*, Washington, DC: Carnegie Endowment for International Peace.

Ottaway, M. and Ottaway, D. (1986) *Afrocommunism*, New York: Holmes and Meier.

Ouma, S. O. A. (2005) 'Corruption in Public Policy and its Impact on Development: The Case of Uganda since 1979', *Public Administration and Development*, 11 (5): 35–52.

Oxfam (2007) 'Africa's Missing Billions', Oxfam Briefing Paper 107, Amnesty International, IANSA and Oxfam International (www.oxfam.org/en/policy/bp107_africas_missing_billions).

Parsons, T. (1968) *The Structure of Social Action*, New York: The Free Press.

Patterson, Amy S. (ed.) (2005) *The African State and the AIDS Crisis*, Aldershot: Ashgate.

Patterson, A. and Haven, B. (2005) 'Aids, Democracy and International Donors in Ghana', in Amy S. Patterson (ed.), *The African State and the AIDS Crisis*, Aldershot: Ashgate.

Pawson, Lara (2003) 'An Overview of democracy in São Tomé e Principe: Legislative Elections in 2002', special report for the Africa Programme, Chatham House, RIIA, January.

Pfaff, R. H. (1967) 'Disengagement from Traditionalism in Turkey and Iran', in C. Welch (ed.), *Political Modernisation*, Belmont, CA: Wadsworth.

Piombo, J. R. (2007) 'Terrorism and US Counter-Terrorism Programs in Africa: An Overview', *Strategic Insights*, 6 (1) January: 2.

Prendergast, John (2004) Special Adviser to the President of the International Crisis Group. 'The Darfur Deadline: Assessing International Response', paper presented at a meeting held at the House of Commons, 16 September.

Randall, V. (ed.) (1988) *Political Parties in the Third World*, London: Sage.

RDP News (1995a) June.

RDP News (1995b) October.

Reuters (2007) 'Sierra Leone's Civil War' (www.alertnet.org).

Rice, Condoleezza (2001) 'US Wants Africa to Support War', www.news.co.sa/, 30 October.

Riley, Major General Jonathon P. (2006) 'The UK in Sierra Leone: A Post-conflict Operation Success?', Heritage Lectures no. 958, Heritage Foundation, 15 June (www.heritage.org).

Robertson-Snape, Fiona (2006) 'Corruption, Collusion and Nepotism in Indonesia', *Third World Quarterly*, 20 (3): 589–602.

Robinson, Francis (1998) *Islamic World*, Cambridge: Cambridge University Press.

Roth, G. and Wittich, C. (eds) (1968) *Max Weber, Economy and Society*, vols. 1 and 2, New York: Bedminster Press.

Rustow, D. (1970) 'The Politics of the Near East', in G. Almond and J. Coleman (eds), *The Politics of Developing Areas*, Princeton, NJ: Princeton University Press.

Sabala, Kizito (2004) 'African Commitments to Combating the Spread of Small Arms and Light Weapons: A Review of Eight NEPAD Countries', AHSI Paper 4, August.

Said, Edward W. (1994) *The Politics of Dispossession*, London: Chatto & Windus.

Salih, M. A. Mohamed (2004) 'Islamic NGOs in Africa: The Promise and Peril of Islamic Voluntarism', in A. de Waal (ed.), *Islamism and its Enemies in the Horn of Africa*, London: C. Hurst.

Salih, M. A. Mohamed (2007) 'African Liberation Movement Governments and Democracy', *Democratization*, 14 (4) August: 669–85.

Salihu, Amina (ed.) (2003) *Community Empowerment Capacity Enhancement Needs Assessment*, Abuja: Kano State, CDD and World Bank Institute.

Salim, Ahmed (1985) 'Arab Communities in Africa', in Khair El-Din Haseeb (ed.), *The Arabs and Africa*, London: Croom Helm.

Salim, Salim Ahmed (1995) Paper presented to Royal Institute of International Affairs meeting, May.

Sandrey, R. (2006) 'The African Merchandise Trading Relationship with China', *Inside AISA*, 3 (December): 35–48.

SAPS (2001) 'Quarterly Report 1998', in H. Deegan, *The Politics of the New South Africa: Apartheid and After*, Harlow: Pearson.

Schumpeter, Joseph (1943) *Capitalism, Socialism and Democracy*, London: Unwin.

Shah, Anup (2003) 'Conflicts in Africa: Sierra Leone 2001' (www.globalissues.org).

Smillie, Ian, Gberie, Lansana and Hazleton, Ralph (2002) *The Heart of the Matter: Sierra Leone, Diamonds & Human Security*, Partnership Africa Canada (www.africaaction.org/docs).

Shillinger, Kurt (2006) 'African Soil is Fertile for Jihadists', *Business Day*, South Africa, 5 October.

Shils, E. (1975) 'Centre & Periphery', in *Essays in Macrosociology*, Chicago: University of Chicago Press.

Sibisi, J. (1996) 'Local Government in South Africa', *Democracy in Action*, 10, 5, 1 September: 11–15.

Smelser, N. J. (1966) 'Mechanisms of Change and Adjustment to Change', in J. Finkle and R. W. Gable (eds), *Political Development & Social Change*, New York: John Wiley & Sons.

Smelser, N. J. (1963) 'Mechanisms of Change and Adjustment to Change', in B. F. Hoselitz and W. E. Moore (eds), *Industrialisation and Society*, The Hague: UNESCO.

Soares, Benjamin F. (2007a) 'Rethinking Islam and Muslim Societies in Africa', *African Affairs*, 106 (423) April: 319–26.

Soares, B. (2007b) *Islam in Africa*, London: Palgrave.

Sonn, Tamara (1990) *Between Qur'an and Crown*, Boulder, CO: Westview.

South African Institute of Race Relations (2007) *South Africa Survey*, Johannesburg: South African Institute of Race Relations.

South African National NGO Coalition (2002) 'Africa and Nepad', *NGO Matters*, 7 (4): 15.

Spence, J. (ed.) (1999) *After Mandela*, London: RIIA.

Stern, Sir Nicholas (2005) 'Africa's Economic Prospects', paper presented at Wilton Park, May.

Stuart, Sir Moody (2003) Paper presented to Southern African Business Association meeting, London, 2 July.

Sule-Kano, Abdullahi (2004) 'Amajiri Phenomenon and the Crisis of Traditional Qur'anic School in Northern Nigeria', *CRD Newsletter*, January–March: 2–4.

Surty, Mohammed Ibrahim (1995) *Islam, the Qur'anic Overview*, Birmingham: Qur'anic Arabic Foundation.

Surty, Mohammed Ibraham (1996) *Muslims' Contribution to the Development of Hospitals*, Birmingham: Birmingham: Qur'anic Arabic Foundation

Surty, Mohammed Ibrahim (2000) *The Most Comprehensive Qur'anic Verse on Socio-Economic Ethics and its Relevance to Modern Life*, Birmingham: Qur'anic Arabic Foundation.

Sutton, F. (1963) 'Social Theory and Comparative Politics', in H. Eckstein and D. E. Apter (eds), *Comparative Politics: A Reader*, New York: The Free Press of Glencoe.

Tayob, Abdulkader (2006) 'Liberal Islam: Between Texts and its Modern Condition', *ISIM Review*, 18 (Autumn): 10–11.

Thomson, Alex (2000) *An Introduction to African Politics*, London: Routledge.

Throup, David (1998) *Economic and Social Origins of the Mau Mau*, London: James Currey.

Thucydides (1998) *History of the Peloponnesian War*, transl. Steven Lattimore, Indianapolis, IN: Hackett Publishing.

Tinsley, Becky (2005) 'Darfur – the Genocide Continues', *Waging Peace*. Info@ wagingpeace.info, June.

Touray, Omar A. (2005) 'The Common African Defence and Security Policy', *African Affairs*, 104 (417): 635–56.

Transparency International (2006) 'Global Corruption Barometer' (www.transparency. org).

Transparency International (2007) 'Global Corruption Report' (www.transparency.org).

Tripp, Aili Mari (2000) *Women and Politics in Uganda*, Oxford: James Currey.

Turabi, Hassan (1993) *Islamica*, 15 March.

Turshen, Meredith and Twagiramariya, Clotilde (1998) *What Women Do in Wartime*, New York: Zed Books.

Ugowe, C.O.O. (1995) *The Nigerian Legacy*, Ibadan: Hugo Books.

Ugwu, Emmanuel (2008) 'Electoral Commissions Seek Indigenous Political System', *EISA*, 12 May.

UNAIDS and World Health Organisation (2002) *AIDS Epidemic Update*, December 2002, Geneva: UNAIDS.

UNAIDS and World Health Organisation (2006) *Global Facts and Figures*, Geneva: UNAIDS.

UNCTAD (2007) *UNCTAD Handbook of Statistics 2006–7* (www.unctad.com/en/docs/ tdstat31).

UNFPA (2004) *The Cairo Consensus at Ten: Population, Reproductive Health and the Global Effort to End Poverty*, New York: United Nations Population Fund.

UNIFEM (2007) 'Capacity Development for Promoting Gender Equality in the Aid Effectiveness Agenda', Discussion Paper, September (www.unifem-easternafrica.org/genderequalityinaid).

UN News Service (2008) 'Sudan: Secretary-General Calls for More Resources for Darfur Peacekeeping Mission', 8 February (http://allafrica.com/stories/200802060232.html).

UN Office on Drugs and Crime (2005) *Crime and Development in Africa* (www.undoc.org/pdf/African_report.pdf).

UN Security Council (2003) Report on Liberia, S/2003/498, 24 April.

United States Institute of Peace (2004) 'Terrorism in the Horn of Africa', Special Report No. 113, January.

Upton, Maureen T. (2004) 'Global Public Health Trumps the Nation-State', *World Policy Journal* (Fall) (www.worldpolicy.org/journal/articles/wpj04-3/Upton.html).

Utomi, Professor Pat (2007) 'Nigerian Elections 2007', Step Back Lecture, Royal African Society, SOAS, 15 May.

Venter, Denis (2003) 'Democracy, Governance and Leadership: Towards an African Renewal', RAU Occasional Papers 1.

Waging Peace (2005) 'Dirty Money: Is Your Pension Propping Up Sudan's Dictators?' (www.wagingpeace.info/index.php).

Wagner, M. D. (1993) 'Trade and Commercial Attitudes in Burundi before the 19th Century', *International Journal of African Historical Studies*, 26 (1): 33–45.

Wai, D. (1985) 'African–Arab Relations in a Universe of Conflict', in Khair El-Din Haseeb (ed.), *The Arabs and Africa*, London: Croom Helm.

Wakili, Haruna (2001) *Pluralism and Religious Conflict in Nigeria: A Case Study of North Western Nigeria since 1970*, Kano: Centre for Research and Documentation.

Wallerstein, Immanuel (1983) 'The Integration of the National Liberation Movement in the Field of International Liberation', *Contemporary Marxism*, 6: 166–71.

Walsh, J. (1993) *The Growth of the Catholic Church in the Diocese of Jos 1907–78*, Ibadan: Ambassador Publications.

Walton, Michael (2005) 'Equity and Development', paper presented at Wilton Park, May.

Walubiri, Peter (2008) 'Uganda', *Regional Roundup*, 19 March, EISA, Johannesburg.

Weber, Max (1974) *The Protestant Ethic and the Spirit of Capitalism*, London: Unwin University Books.

Weiner, M. (1967) 'Political Integration and Political Development', in C. Welch (ed.), *Political Modernisation*, Belmont, CA: Wadsworth.

Welch, C. (ed.) (1967) *Political Modernisation*, Belmont, CA: Wadsworth.

Whiteside, Alan (2008) *HIV/AIDS: A Very Short Introduction*, Oxford: Oxford University Press.

Whiteside, Alan, de Waal, Alex and Gebre-Tensae, Tsadkan (2006) 'Aids, Security and the Military in Africa: A Sober Appraisal', *African Affairs*, 105 (419) April: 201–18.

Williamson, Roger (2005) *The Commission for Africa: Implementing the Findings*, Report on Wilton Park Conference SO5/9, 16–20 May.

Wlodarczyk, N. (2005) 'Aspects of Violence and the Logic of Conflict and Peace in Africa', *African Affairs*, 104 (417) October: 679–81.

Wolff, K. H. (ed.) (1960) *Essays on Sociology & Philosophy by Emile Durkheim*, Columbus, OH: Ohio State University Press.

Woodward, P. (1997) 'Sudan: Islamic Radicals in Power', in J. Esposito (ed.), *Political Islam*, Boulder, CO: Lynne Rienner.

World Bank (1993) *The IDA and the Tenth Replenishment B.02.4.93*, Washington, DC: World Bank.

World Bank (2006) *World Development Report 2006: Equity and Development* (http://web.worldbank.org/wbsite/external).

World Bank (2007) *Global Monitoring Report 2007* (www.worldbank.org).

Wycoff, Karl (2004) 'Fighting Terrorism in Africa', US Department of State (www.state.gov/s/ct/rls/rm/2004/31077).

Yinger, M. J. (1970) *The Scientific Study of Religion*, New York: Macmillan.

Youde, Jeremy (2005) 'Enter the Fourth Horseman: Health Security and International Relations Theory', *Whitehead Journal of Diplomacy and International Relations*, Winter/Spring (www.ciaonet.org/cowsepack/cp08/cp08g.html).

Young, C. (1980) *Ideology and Development*, New Haven, CT: Yale University Press.

Yousuf, H. S. (1986) *African Arab Relations*, Brattleboro, VT: Amana Books.

Zack-Williams, Tunde, Frost, Diane and Thompson, Alex (2002) *Africa in Crisis: New Challenges and Possibilities*, London: Pluto.

Zakat Chamber (1995) *ElZakat Report*, Khartoum: Zakat Chamber.

Zakat Chamber (1997) *Role of Zakat in Economic Development & Social Justice*, Khartoum: Zakat Chamber HQ.

Zebadia, A. (1985) 'Islam', in Khair el Din Haseeb (ed.), *The Arabs and Africa*, London: Croom Helm.

Index